The Prophet of the Andes

The Prophet
of the Andes

An Unlikely Journey to the Promised Land

Graciela Mochkofsky

Translated by Lisa Dillman

ALFRED A. KNOPF | NEW YORK | 2022

THIS IS A BORZOI BOOK
PUBLISHED BY ALFRED A. KNOPF

Published in the United States by Alfred A. Knopf, a division
of Penguin Random House LLC, New York, and distributed
in Canada by Penguin Random House Canada Limited, Toronto.

www.aaknopf.com

Knopf, Borzoi Books, and the colophon
are registered trademarks of Penguin Random House LLC.

All photographs are courtesy of the author unless noted otherwise.

Library of Congress Cataloging-in-Publication Data
Names: Mochkofsky, Graciela, 1969– author. | Dillman, Lisa, translator.
Title: The prophet of the Andes : an unlikely journey to the promised land /
Graciela Mochkofsky ; translated by Lisa Dillman.
Description: First edition. | New York : Alfred A. Knopf, 2022. |
Includes bibliographical references.
Identifiers: LCCN 2021043414 (print) | LCCN 2021043415 (ebook) |
ISBN 9781101875186 (hardcover) | ISBN 9781101875193 (ebook)
Subjects: LCSH: Villanueva, Segundo (Carpenter) | Jewish converts from
Christianity—Peru—Cajamarca (Department)—Biography. | Jewish converts from
Christianity—Israel—Biography. | Conversion—Judaism—History—20th century. |
Conversion—Judaism—History—21st century. | Cajamarca (Peru : Department)—
Religion. | Cajamarca (Peru : Department)—Ethnic relations.
Classification: LCC BM729.P7 M63 2022 (print) | LCC BM729.P7 (ebook) |
DDC 296.7/14092 [B]—dc23
LC record available at https://lccn.loc.gov/2021043414
LC ebook record available at https://lccn.loc.gov/2021043415

Jacket image: VisualCommunications/E+/Getty Images
Jacket design by Linda Huang

Manufactured in the United States of America

First Edition

To Gabriel and Ismael, in whom I place my faith

Thou hast shewed thy people hard things:
thou hast made us to drink the wine of astonishment.

—PSALMS 60:3

Author's Note

I'd been searching for something else, in early September 2003, when I came across an account by a rabbi named Myron Zuber. The title caught my attention: "Converting Inca Indians in Peru." It purported to tell the story of an Indigenous Peruvian, Segundo Villanueva, a "good Catholic" who, moved by a passage in the Bible, had renounced the ancestral faith to embrace what he saw as the one true religion: Judaism. After many years of suffering and persecution, Zuber recounted, Villanueva had amassed hundreds of followers who considered him a prophet. They all converted to Judaism and migrated to Israel.

The rabbi's tale was riddled with errors (to begin with, there are no "Inca Indians" in Peru, and Segundo was not Indigenous but mestizo), exaggerations, and, as I later learned, outright inventions, but no sooner had I finished reading it than I ran to the phone and called the number listed at the bottom along with an address on Blauvelt Road in Monsey, New York, where the rabbi was accepting donations for the community.

Although I introduced myself in English, the woman who answered the phone noticed my accent right away and, in a cheerful Spanish, told me Rabbi Zuber had died. She was his widow, Margalit, called Margarita back in Peru, one of the Jewish converts the account talked about. The others, including Villanueva and his family, now lived in Israel; if I wanted, she could give me their phone numbers.

And so it was that a couple of weeks later, on September 27, 2003, in the Jewish New Year 5764, I landed at Ben Gurion Airport with four kilos of yucca, which Naomi, Segundo Villanueva's daughter, had asked me to bring when I called from Buenos Aires. Yucca didn't grow well in her West Bank garden, the holidays were approaching, and she wanted to make a Peruvian dish.

Awaiting me in their settlement were also her two sisters, Raquel and Eva, and her daughter, Hadassa. When Naomi pulled the long brown tubers from the bag, there were exclamations of delight; they told me they were going to cook them for the night after Yom Kippur.

It was lunchtime. They had me go first in the line to wash hands. I turned on the tap and did so without thinking. Behind me I sensed contained laughter, shock. It took a minute for me to realize I'd misinterpreted as a matter of hygiene what was in fact a religious ritual.

"You're not religious?" they asked.

No, I explained. I'm the child of an Argentine Jewish father descended from Eastern Europeans and a Paraguayan Catholic mother whose grandparents were Basque, Guarani, and Danish. When they got married, my parents agreed that their children would be the ones to decide their own religious identity. My father was an atheist; my mother, observant. When my youngest brother was born, after a difficult childbirth, my mother announced that *I* had decided to be baptized Catholic with my newborn brother. The two of us look like her; my other two siblings, more like my father, stuck with his side, taking no religion; some time later, one of them decided to get baptized too. At my mother's insistence, I was sent to a Catholic school run by nuns.

At the time we lived in Salta, an Argentinian city in the Andes where, as in the Peru of the Villanuevas, most of the population is mestizo and vestiges of a racist, hierarchical social structure inherited from the Spanish remain. In catechism class, the nuns professed that my father wouldn't go to heaven; only those who'd been baptized could claim that right. For a long time, I was tortured by nightmares in which my father was burning in hell, and I implored him to convert to Catholicism. But over the years I gave up, not just on my attempt to convert him, but on Catholicism itself. Feeling separated from my father pained me, and it unsettled me that my paternal grandmother, when speaking about Jews, always employed a "we" that didn't include me. For years I struggled, feeling the need to reconcile my Catholic education with the pervasive assumption that with a last name so clearly Jewish—to Argentinian ears—I had to be Jewish myself.

The women smiled understandingly; after all, the clash between Catholicism and Judaism in Latin America was far more familiar to them than it was to me. I was middle class, from a country that, for most of the twentieth century, was home to the third-largest Jewish population in the world, after Israel and the United States. The Villanueva women, on the other hand, had been poor, mestizas, in a classist and deeply Catholic country where Jews made up less than .01 percent of the population. It had been a long, hard-fought battle to get to where they were. Even now, after everything they'd done to be seen as Jewish in the world, people tended to assume that they weren't.

They taught me how to wash my hands, pouring water from the pitcher over one hand first, then the other, and then over the first again. Over the following years, I learned as much as I could about rituals and the Jewish Bible. I took Hebrew classes so I could understand their language, a Spanish sprinkled with Hebrew words and expressions. I also learned about the many Christian credos they followed before finding Judaism and about Peruvian politics and religious history, as well as the economic and class divisions that informed their choices.

In the afternoon, the women introduced me to their mother, María Teresa, and took me for a walk through their settlement. During the first days I spent with them, they kept me apart from the men in the family. Segundo was not there, and I didn't get to see him until two years later. On that first trip, in Jerusalem I met his son Josué, who became a central source for this book. Although I had met the women first, they soon decided to step back. The men would tell the story.

Over the next fifteen years, the story of Segundo Villanueva and his community would take me, time and again, to the mountains and cities of Peru, to Colombia, to Israel, and to the West Bank settlements. It is a story that I often thought I'd understood and then realized I had misunderstood; a story that seemed to have one ending and then turned out to have another. A story that, nearly two decades later, I still find incredible.

Part One

The clouds hang heavy over the Peruvian Andes. Nothing moves, except the tenuous white tremble blanketing the mountain.

An hour goes by.

Then another.

Suddenly, from out of the clouds, comes a figure: half poncho, one-third hat. Beneath the red vicuña-wool poncho hang the hems of her skirts. Beneath them are thick black tights and the two muddy crusts that envelop her shoes. The woman's tall wide-brimmed hat makes her look smaller; her back is bowed under an invisible weight. Her eyes are hidden in a mass of wrinkles, and her mouth curves into something that might be a smile or a grimace. She walks slowly, so slowly, across the Andean foothills. As if she's been walking for hundreds of years. It seems impossible that she will ever arrive, that there is any place at which to arrive at this altitude.

But when the sun finally casts its warmth, the clouds lift and one can see Rodacocha, a smattering of adobe shacks, pastures, and potato fields impossible to find on any map, having no church, no school, no police station or health clinic. A single dirt road, which until recently was simply rutted cart tracks, runs through the middle of it. Cajamarca, the closest city, is a six-hour walk if you know the shortcuts, three if you've got a horse.

Gaggles of geese and hens peck the ground in mechanical fervor. The hatted woman stops by a pile of fetid slop, which pigs the size of rams defend from the ferocious assault of some dogs. She lets out a shout that reveals toothless gums, and the dogs take off toward a long sky-blue hut as her husband emerges from within.

A hundred paces away, across the road, some adobe ruins are threatening to collapse definitively. The roof and two of the four walls already have, leaving the structure's mud and straw entrails on view. Two rotted wooden shutters hang from the back window like broken bones. The blackened dirt floor is overrun by weeds.

That shack, the man says, is where his cousin Segundo Villanueva was raised. The one who went off in search of another faith and never returned. And up there is where his father had his potato field; that's the trail he used to ride on his horse; there's the hill where his mother got the tragic news. Everything was as it is now, just as it is now, except for the trees.[1]

As it is now: with no horizon. Wherever you look, mountain and more mountain. It's as though the only possible escape were up in the sky—when it's not clouded over. How was it— how *is* it, the visitor wonders—even possible to envision a different life from within these confines?

Actually, this is not in fact where it all began. It began almost five hundred years earlier, down the mountain, in the valley that was, for a brief moment in history, the heart of the Incan Empire, the Tahuantinsuyo, or center of the world. The fertile plains are where the Inca Atahualpa ruled over nine million subjects, across two and a half million square kilometers. He'd just vanquished his most formidable rival, his brother Huascar, who had ruled from Cuzco, in a brutal war. Victory was intoxicating: he was the personification of a god, Son of the Sun, Powerful Lord of the Four Parts of the World. He was to be carried in a litter. Forever more. Should his feet ever touch the earth, catastrophe would follow.

And thus they never touched it. He held himself above all things human. Was that the reason why, when his sentries warned him that a group of strangers was approaching—166 men with sixty-two horses—he attached no importance to the matter? Or perhaps it was because his warriors numbered in the thousands. Or maybe he assumed nobody would do anything but surrender at the sight of Cajamarca, his fortified city in the foothills, with houses two hundred strides long surrounded by low walls and covered with wood and straw, two thousand subjects living in them, colorful fabric filling great storehouses, and great stone steps that led, beseechingly, up to it from the valley.[2]

Did they not sense their own insignificance, those 166 men with their sixty-two horses, on beholding it? No, they did not. They were intent on conquering, spurred on by implacable ambition. Or by complacency. Or by desperation. For thirty years, their leader, the Spaniard Francisco Pizarro, had sought glory and fortune in the new continent known as the Indies. Hernán Cortés had found both in the North, on defeating the Aztecs. Dreaming of equal success, Pizarro had claimed for himself the lands of the South, which the Spaniards referred to as Birú and believed to abound in gold and silver.

Others had failed to conquer. It seemed likely that Pizarro would fail as well. He'd crossed sterile coasts and infested mangroves; he'd known hunger, infection, and terrible pain. Many of his men had deserted; others had died. The most tenacious had marched on with him in the scorching sun, survived a bubonic plague, fought hostile tribes, gasped for air in the never-ending rocky mountains and on frozen savannas. And here they were: a band of survivors still convinced of their victory. Or maybe exhaustion, avarice, and the need to conquer were all they had left.

Shrewdly, they requested permission to stay in the area, and the Inca—condescending, scornful—conceded it. They settled on his land and studied the city. The central square was walled. There was only one way in or out. If they could only corral all the "Indians" inside it . . .

On the afternoon of November 15, 1532, at Pizarro's request to confer, the Inca Atahualpa entered the square on a gold-and-silver palanquin, escorted by eight thousand warriors. Hidden in the structures enclosing the plaza, Pizarro's men were so terrified they wet themselves.

Not their commander. Pizarro had a plan.

But it couldn't be executed straightaway. According to his mercenary contract with the Spanish Crown, he was required to explain himself before killing. A punctilious document, which he had carried with him from the other side of the ocean, instructed him what to say: that the conquest was being carried out in the name of God and the conquered could save themselves if they submitted to Him.[3]

Pizarro didn't know how to read, but he'd brought from Spain, for this very purpose, six men of the church who did. Of the six, only one, Vicente de Valverde, was still at his side: the others had died, deserted, or simply remained behind.

Valverde took a few steps toward the Inca, who, bedecked in his crown and wearing an emerald necklace, looked on him scornfully from atop his palanquin. The priest was clad in what was left of his Dominican black habit; in his hand he clutched a book. That book, he explained to the Inca with the help of an interpreter, contained the truth of God: the God and the religion he'd come to reveal and to which he commanded submission.

A new god! As though in response, the Sun, omnipotent god whose temple had been erected in that very plaza, began to set magnificently in the west.

The Inca signaled to the priest to pass him the small rectangular object he held. He took it, examined it, turned it over, perplexed. Valverde reached out a hand to show him how to open the book. Miffed at the man's familiarity, the Inca rebuffed him, striking Valverde's arm. He opened the book and examined it closely, apparently fascinated. Then he closed it and flung it to the ground.

The book, so sacred to Valverde that before opening it he would kiss it, landed five feet away; the interpreter rushed to retrieve it and return it to him. Holding it in his clenched hand, Valverde ran to Pizarro, shouting what some witnesses claimed were words of vengeance and others said were exclamations of fear.

As far as Pizarro was concerned, formalities had been complied with; he gave the prearranged signal to his men. The explosions coming from incredible, hitherto-unseen weapons and the charge of horses frightened the Inca's warriors who, hurling their arms to the ground, attempted to flee through the plaza's one narrow exit. Hundreds died in the crush; the rest were killed by harquebuses and muskets or skewered by the implacable swords of Spain. The last rays of the Sun died out as the massacre ended.

Imprisoned, the Inca offered to buy his freedom with two rooms full of silver and another of gold. The Spaniards agreed, and the Inca honored his part of the deal. But the Spaniards did not honor theirs. They kept the gold and silver, and allowed only for the Inca to choose his form of death: at the stake, or by garotte. And they added a condition: if he did not want to be burned, he had to accept the *true* God—the God of his captors. To die burned at the stake was unthinkable for the Inca: consumed by flames, he would not be brought back in the next world. So to ensure the salvation of his body, he was forced to accept that of his soul.

Valverde himself baptized Atahualpa. Once the ritual was over, he was strangled to death in the Cajamarca plaza, before his horrified people. The Spaniards displayed his body in a church that Pizarro ordered built on the ruins of the temple to the Sun.

His subjects were now orphaned, with no Inca and no faith. There had been a cluster of villages where, until that time, multiple coexisting gods were worshipped without problem: Inti, god of the Sun; Pachamama, goddess of nature; Pachacamac, god of earthquakes; the Apus, gods of the hills; Catequil, the oracle god; Huari, god of war; Urcuchillay, god of animals; Supay, god of the underworld. Some had their own temples and shrines; others were venerated on vessels, in tombs, the mummies of ancestors, trees, plants, and mountains.

The Spaniards' theology, however, would brook no competition.[4] Hernando Pizarro, Francisco's brother, took a group of soldiers and stormed the temple to Pachacamac, an important place of pilgrimage predating the Incas themselves. He broke the Pachacamac idol and humiliated the priests. Sepulchres, *huacas* (revered objects), and temples were likewise destroyed throughout the conquered territory.

The victors and their priests spoke of a God whose son had died to save all men, including the vanquished. But they had to accept Him as their only God or suffer the consequences.

Preexisting religions were reviled as idolatry. A new force, the Inquisition, came from Spain to eradicate them via torture and the stake. It cemented the idea of infinite suffering, known as hell, that the Spanish priests had brought to the Andes. The new churches were filled with terrifying images in which idol worshippers burned in eternal fire for disobeying this new God.

They were also filled with figures and statuettes of the Son of God, his mother, the Virgin Mary, and countless saints that resembled *huacas,* the objects representing their now-forbidden gods. The priests soon discovered that the venerable figures of their saints were being used in secret as *huacas* so that people could keep worshipping their old gods.

That was all the vanquished had left. Two attempted insurrections were put down by force, and disease, oppression, and sorrow finished off the rest. More than 80 percent of the Inca Empire's population disappeared in the forty years after Pizarro's arrival; nine million were reduced to little more than one million, their births and deaths authenticated by church sacraments and marked by a calendar including Christmas, Easter, Sunday Mass, and saints' days. From this—the plunder of some, the subjugation of others, and a religion that theoretically united them—was born Peru.

Decades after Pizarro, in the final days of the sixteenth century, Cristóbal Fernández Nieto de Villanueva would come to Cajamarca from Spain. Like other Europeans, he surely came in search of the fortunes he envisioned as boundless and at his disposal. What he found instead was that the conquistadors and their descendants were killing one another over the spoils, which the Spanish Crown would in the end forcibly seize with the help of their armies. Adventurers like Villanueva abounded in both cities and countryside, where they found no fortune whatsoever and exploited the vanquished in order to survive.

The Spaniards' plunder had obliterated everything, even the land. Rumi Tiana, the hill against which the city was set, was renamed Santa Apolonia; the Inca's buildings were now mere ruins; the storehouses full of fabric—the pride of Tahuantinsuyo—had also been destroyed, as had the shrines.

Out of the avarice and misery, a new order was emerging. Villanueva witnessed Cajamarca reborn as a colonial city of tile-roofed houses with patios, churches on every street, and an economy based on agriculture and mining. New landowners claimed the prosperous parts of the valley, while the Inca people, and later their descendants, were reduced to servitude, de facto if not de jure. Villanueva, too, managed to lay claim to fertile land in the valley; he too was served by those who had once been in charge.[5]

But masters and servants were destined to mix. And Villanueva witnessed this as well: the birth of a new people, born of the union between Spanish men and Andean women. His own descendants would come of this intermingling: the spaces reserved for the wives of his son Juan and grandson Cristóbal would remain blank on his family tree, for in early Peruvian history only the Spanish and the Inca nobility had names.

Without the social status of their European ancestor, however, the Villanueva mestizos were sent off to the mountains, to settlements like Encañada and Sorochuco, to unknown territories like Rodacocha, and even higher up the mountain, to the remote Milpoc, where the air was so thin it was difficult to breathe and the earth neither possessed nor produced the riches that it did in the valley. The higher up the land, the less it was worth: the only things that grew in the pastures of Rodacocha were barley, potatoes, and yucca.

But there the Villanuevas, unlike the majority of their neighbors, were still their own masters, with an illusion of privilege that was preserved and transmitted from generation to generation, down an increasingly impoverished lineage.

And so it was that:

Cristóbal fathered Juan, who fathered Cristóbal.

Cristóbal fathered Miguel, who fathered Juan.

Juan fathered Andrés, who fathered Juan.

Juan fathered Bartolomé.

Bartolomé fathered Segundo Aquiles.

Segundo Aquiles fathered Álvaro,[6] who fathered Segundo.

When he was old enough, Álvaro received an indeterminate percentage of high fields on which potatoes and yellow grassland grew, and the Rodacocha shack in which his grandfather Bartolomé had lived and died—a thick mud and adobe rectangle with rammed-earth floor, wood beams, and thatch roof that received very little light through its narrow door and small back window but stayed cool when the sun was scorching and warm when frost fell. It also stank of wood smoke, food, and the crowded-together bodies of Álvaro, his wife, Abigail Correa, and their five children.

The neighbors would see Álvaro return from Cajamarca with slippers for Abigail and fresh fruits for the children, and whisper. He spoiled them so! Didn't even make them work. His firstborn, Segundo Eloy, was such a smart, curious boy that his father decided to give him the education his ancestors had never had. Álvaro hired a teacher from Cajamarca by the surname of Camacho who would walk six hours to Rodacocha to teach Segundo to read and write. When he reached the age for third grade, Segundo was sent to his grandmother's house in Cajamarca to attend school.

Álvaro tended the farms of Rodacocha, the potato fields and

pastures of Milpoc, high up the mountain, and employed a ranch hand there to care for his cattle. Around noon on Thursday, November 9, 1944, Álvaro left on horseback for the city of Celendín, crossing the mountain headed east to buy some bulls. He carried with him four hundred soles, some cold meat, four ponchos, a wool blanket, and two calves he was planning to leave in Milpoc, where he'd spend the night awaiting his neighbor Herminio Lozano, who was to accompany him to Celendín.

On Saturday, close to 11:00 a.m., the residents of Milpoc heard two shots fired. They were not alarmed; there were always hunters around there. The following day, a hand from a nearby farm found Álvaro close to the shack on his pasture in Milpoc, sitting on the ground, his torso slumped forward and a wound to his chest. Seventy paces away, dogs fought over what remained of Herminio Lozano, shot to death and with his face disfigured by knife wounds. In his mouth, the medical examiner found a five-centavo silver coin.[7]

Abigail was there for the autopsy. When she saw the bullet from the Winchester .44 removed from her husband's chest, she knew that the weapon had been his own and the murderer could be none other than Filadelfio Chávez, a neighbor whom Álvaro had lent it to two months earlier. Though they'd been friends, they were on bad terms. Álvaro had reproached Filadelfio, saying that the man's animals had ruined his potato field, and Filadelfio, rather than apologize, had threatened to kill him.

Four years later, the prosecutor working the case accused Filadelfio of the double homicide. According to his investigation, Filadelfio, who in his youth had stood out in the army for his marksmanship, had been drinking sugarcane liquor in the shack with Álvaro and Herminio the night before he killed them. Another local, Belisario Villar, had moved the corpses and mutilated Lozano's face so that he wouldn't be recognized. He was charged as an accomplice. Someone else, the prosecutor said, had placed the "coin of magic" in Herminio's mouth in order, as per local belief, to guide the police to the killers. Filadelfio's hand, Virgilio Chávez Carranza, was identified as a second accomplice: he'd stolen the money with which Álvaro planned to buy the cattle.

Despite the prosecutor's accusation, the judge freed the accused and closed the case.

Abigail denounced corruption: she told her children that the judge had asked her for money to sentence the guilty, but she'd had nothing to give him. The injustice filled Segundo with rage. He was seventeen when he lost his father, twenty-one when the murderer was set free.

"He killed with a bullet, and I will kill him with my own hands, because he's left us without our daily bread," he swore to his mother and sisters.[8]

Segundo's sisters threw themselves at him to stop him.

Shouting and weeping, his mother begged him: Don't do it. But what else could he do?

They'd lost their father; they'd lost most of their land, having been compelled to sell it; they'd lost Rodacocha. They'd had to move in with his grandmother in the city, and now Abigail was selling meat in the market and straw hats in the square.

Segundo had gone to Lima to become an officer in the civil guard. It had been his father's dream to see him in those tall black boots, one hand on the hilt of his Spanish foil, perhaps chasing bandits like in 1920s Cajamarca. He'd come to the exam well prepared. In his notebook, Segundo had written,

"The fundamentals of discipline: absolute obedience to laws, regulations, and superiors."[9]

But neither obedience nor preparation had saved him from the impediment he'd had since birth: Segundo stuttered.

That involuntary defect disqualified him. His father's last wish had been thwarted.

Segundo admired the physical strength he'd inherited from his father. Even the forensic pathologists who performed his father's autopsy had noticed his "athletic" build. When he was still a boy, his father had chased a puma to a river, grabbed it by the tail, and thrown it into the water, where he'd strangled it with his own hands. Segundo too was capable of such feats: capable of felling a tree with a machete, capable of snapping thick branches with his bare hands, capable of knocking his cousins down and beating them at wrestling. Capable, if so required, of killing a man.

What else could he do?

There was one thing left: his father's trunk, a trunk that had been in the family for generations.

In March 1905, knowing he didn't have long to live, Segundo's great-grandfather Bartolomé, who was illiterate, had called a justice of the peace to dictate his will. He had started by listing the dogmas of his faith, the *sovereign mystery* of the Trinity, Father, Son, and Holy Spirit. He had then proceeded to list a dozen plots, farms, and meadows of indeterminate size and worth; four mares; one brush; three large tables and three small tables; eighteen chairs; and one large trunk. Bartolomé's trunk went to Segundo Aquiles, and after his death, to Álvaro. It was now Segundo's inheritance.

Many years later, Segundo would tell his children the two simple facts: that his father had been killed; and that he had opened the trunk. Looking back, it seems impossible for it to have been any other way, impossible for him not to have been led by an invisible hand to that old chest—impossible that he would have chosen to kill instead.

But then, at age twenty-one, when all he could think about was revenge, what was he looking for by riffling through the family inheritance? Hidden treasure? A message? Some ulterior desire, a new dream? Perhaps a souvenir? Or his destiny?

What he found was the Bible.[10]

What was a Bible doing in his father's trunk? There were no Bibles, or should be no Bibles, in a Catholic house. Especially not the house of a *cholo* from the hills. A Bible in one's home was not illegal, but it was an act of arrogance; it was heresy, a sign of audacity or insanity. Missionaries and colporteurs had been stoned, sometimes killed, by the neighbors when they tried to sell Bibles in these Catholic towns. When Álvaro was a boy, owning a Bible was an anathema. Perhaps that's why he had never mentioned it or shown it to his family; perhaps that's why it was hidden at the bottom of his trunk.

Like his siblings, Segundo had been baptized in Cajamarca Cathedral. His mother took the children to Mass whenever they went to the city. They sat on the long wooden penitents' benches on one side of the lengthy nave flanked by walls covered in images of saints. There Segundo, like all Catholics, *listened* to the Bible that the priest read from, standing at the magnificent gold-leaf altar. He listened but did not understand, for the priest read in Latin, a language neither Segundo nor almost anyone else in all of Cajamarca knew. The Bible was for priests; they alone were permitted to read it and understand it. To the faithful of Peru, who'd had religion imposed on them four centuries earlier, the Bible had always been inaccessible.

And yet now here one was—in Spanish and within reach. In his strong hands, it was a small, delicate book with pages soft as silk and a mysterious black cover that seemed to contain a treasure:[11] his father's final, secret bequest. Ignoring bloody centuries of obedience, Segundo opened the book and began to read.

The first thing he found was a table of contents that listed two parts:[12] the Old Testament, with thirty-nine books, and the New Testament, with twenty-seven. A total of 793 pages. Then the beginning: Genesis. God created the world from nothing and filled it with all the things that Segundo still saw around him now: the day and the night; the heavens and the seas; the grass, trees, and fruits; the sun, the moon, and the stars; the reptiles and the fowl; large animals and cattle; and finally man, "in God's image," to have dominion over all things. Creation took six days. On the seventh day, God relaxed. And "God blessed the seventh day, and sanctified it: because that in it he had rested from all his work."

From the first man, Adam, and the first woman, Eve, Segundo read on, came generations who spread across the earth. But rather than thank their Creator, humans disobeyed, unleashing wrath and punishment. Far from learning their lesson, men filled the world with evil and violence, and "repented the LORD that he had made man on earth." To right his error, God sent a flood to destroy the earth and humanity, except for Noah, who had been faithful. With his descendants was "the whole earth overspread," and God promised not to destroy it again. Later, God chose one of those descendants, Abraham, to whom he offered a covenant: "between me and you and thy seed after thee in their generations for an everlasting covenant." God would give him "all the land in Canaan for an everlasting possession" and would make of him and his descendants a great nation with a great name; he would be *their* God and protect them for all time. In exchange, he demanded the obedience that he had yet to receive.

In order to test Abraham, God commanded him to sacrifice his son Isaac. When Abraham, knife in hand, prepared to obey, God stopped him: he had proven his faithfulness. In place of human sacrifice, God commanded him to circumcise himself as well as all the men of his house as an expression of the everlasting covenant between them.

Genesis went on to recount the story of this family through one chosen son in each generation: after Abraham, Isaac; after Isaac, Jacob; after Jacob, Joseph. This story gave an account of deeds, men, and women that Segundo had never heard spoken of at church. Although it was common in Peru for children to be baptized with biblical names like Juan (John), Pedro (Peter), and Pablo (Paul), there were many other peculiar names, such as Pildash, Jidlaph, Nahor, Milcah, Gaham, Thahash, and Maachah.

Despite the plethora of strange and wondrous events that occurred there, the land of Canaan sounded familiar to Segundo. It was the world of his father, of Rodacocha, of Milpoc, full of donkeys and goats, roast lamb, udders and milk, crops harvested or ruined. The people there concocted the same petty schemes, found themselves in the same absurd predicaments.

In Genesis, bloodlines and relations were wildly entangled. It was not only Adam and Eve's children, or Noah's descendants who, having no other option, coupled and raised offspring: Abraham married his half sister Sarah; Nahor, his niece Milcah. Cousins married as well: Isaac and Rebekah; Esau and Mahalath; Jacob and Leah and Rachel. And Reuben lay with Bilhah, his father's concubine, and Judah with his daughter-in-law Tamar, and Amram with his aunt Jochebed. Wasn't Rodacocha like that, too? His grandmother Evarista, at forty-seven, had formed a union with Juan Correa, the twenty-one-year-old brother of Segundo's mother, Abigail. Filadelfio's mother was cousin to Álvaro, Segundo's father, but had also had a child with Abigail's father. Abigail's mother, in turn, was Filadelfio's aunt. And that was just his immediate family.

Their disputes were similar as well. In Milpoc, Álvaro had accused his friend Filadelfio of allowing his animals to destroy Álvaro's potato field; in retaliation, Filadelfio had set fire (at least according to Abigail) to Álvaro's shack. Juan Correa had reported Álvaro, his brother-in-law, for having stolen eight of his cows; Correa himself, however, had been imprisoned several times for cattle theft. And Filadelfio had killed Segundo's father.

In Genesis, Jacob deceived his own brother and father in order to receive Esau's birthright and had to flee to distant lands, from which he returned, after certain misfortunes, fearing vengeance. But after Jacob passed another test, God gave him a new name, Israel, and his brother, rather than make him pay for his scheming, embraced and welcomed him. Joseph, the son of Jacob who was detested by his ten siblings, was thrown into a well and then sold to people who took him to Egypt. But with the help of God he managed to become the Pharaoh's highest-ranking officer, and when his brothers came to Egypt in search of bread because of famine, Joseph forgave them and the family was reunited.

Though the people of the Book were as envious, suspicious, resentful, and greedy as those he'd known throughout his childhood and adolescence, the favor of God, to whom they paid tribute and showed obedience, distinguished them and ultimately brought them redemption and salvation. They were like any other men, but with Him in their lives they were special.

Segundo was overcome with awe-inspiring emotion. God was speaking to him. Through the Book, He was showing him the way to live. By the time he finished Genesis, Segundo's world had been created anew, or perhaps it had simply been revealed to him for the first time.

Like the men of the Book, he too must be different. But how? The answers he needed were certainly to be found in the Book.

At the end of Genesis, Abraham's descendants were reunited in Egypt. When he died, Jacob—(Israel)—said that of each of his twelve sons would be born a tribe. And his son Joseph, on his deathbed, announced that they and all of their descendants, the twelve tribes, would return to Canaan, the land promised by God.

Four hundred years later, in the second book, Exodus, the descendants, called the children of Israel, or Israelites, were enslaved by a new king of Egypt who ordered them to kill all of their sons. One of them, Moses, was saved by his mother and raised by one of the Pharaoh's daughters. God then sought him out, to lead the people of Israel back to the land of Abraham, a "land of milk and honey" to which Israel was called to return. Through Moses, God punished Egypt with a series of plagues and calamities. Then, through Moses, He led the people through the desert and back to Canaan.

Their journey took up all of Exodus and the following three books, Leviticus, Numbers, and Deuteronomy. When the Israelites were beset by hunger and thirst, God miraculously provided them with freshwater, quails, and bread. But this time he also laid down stricter rules about the way men needed to behave in order to earn his favor, rules that stipulated exactly what to and not to do. From the top of a mountain called Sinai, he dictated to Moses the Ten Commandments that Segundo already knew from the priests. But it also indicated the way to repent or repair other transgressions. Everything from when to free slaves to how to repay debts or damages and how to treat foreigners. It also provided specific instructions on exactly how to worship: they were to build a temple called a tabernacle, with specific measurements and characteristics, in which priests who dressed a certain way were to sacrifice animals to Him in a certain way and on certain days. All of the priests were to come from the tribe of Levi, to which Moses belonged, beginning with his brother Aaron. Leviticus went into detail about rules for purity and cleanliness, both physical and spiritual: not only one's body but also one's sins had to be cleansed.

Infractions were severely punished, often with one's life. Time and again, Moses had to beg God to forgive the people of Israel; in each case, even mediating clemency, there was a high price to pay. And thus God condemned the people to wander the desert for forty years; He opened the earth and sent plague when the people rebelled against Moses; and finally, He kept Moses, Aaron, and the rest of their generation, with only two exceptions, from entering the promised land, apparently as punishment for not having obeyed His instructions to the letter.

Segundo grappled with the complexity of those rules, which in many cases were of another era. How was he to make sense of them and practice them *now*? Were they still valid? There was so much to read in order to make sense of God's will. But what he did understand, what he grasped immediately and with the shocking force of revelation, was that the priests lied.

Again and again, God told the Israelites to "not make unto thee any graven image," and to destroy the idols they had worshipped in the past. When the Israelites disobeyed and worshipped an idol of gold, God threatened to destroy them all. It was only the pleas of Moses that stopped Him. In exchange, Moses himself called for exemplary punishment, the sacrifice of three thousand men. The prohibition was quite clear. And yet Cajamarca was overflowing with idols. For what, if not idols, were the images of saints, the statues of the Virgin and the Lord of Miracles used in processions? Since the time of the

Spaniards, the fact that a small squadron of men conquered powerful Cajamarca had been attributed to San Miguel, San Pablo, San Gabriel, the Apostle Santiago (James), and the Virgin rather than the shrewdness, determination, and impiety of Pizarro or the arrogance and vulnerability of the Inca. The churches of San Francisco, Belén, Recoleta, and Santa Catalina were illuminated by candles lit to the saints, before whom the poor knelt to ask for good fortune, for work, for health, for protection from the blows of fate. On the saints' days of San Pedro and San Pablo, a procession of carriages transported the images of men and women venerated as miraculous for their devotion and suffering in the name of faith. And on the night before, the faithful got drunk and lit fireworks, as they did during Carnival. And it was the Catholic Church itself that had imposed this pagan worship.

In the Bible, God very clearly ordered His faithful to keep the Sabbath, the seventh day, on which He had rested from His creation, holy. They should neither bake nor work on the Sabbath—"not you, God specified, nor your son or daughter, not your servant, not your cattle, not the stranger in your midst." So strict was the rule that when a man was found to have gathered firewood on Saturday, the Sabbath, God ordered his brothers to stone him to death. And yet the priests claimed that Sunday was the holy day. Nobody worked on Sunday, the shops were closed, and the faithful went to Mass. How, when, had this lie been imposed? And how many other things might they have invented? A false version had supplanted that arduous but very clear message from God, and Segundo seemed to be the only one who knew it.

In the Bible, people of God were not called Vatican or Catholic but Israel. Israel: the name moved him, as if it were some secret invocation. But where was Israel now? Where, in all of Cajamarca, in all of Peru, could he find it? Israel had been wiped from the face of the earth. How, when, by whom?

In the following books—Joseph, Judges, First and Second Samuel, First and Second Kings—God helped the Israelites take Canaan, their promised land, through fire and bloodshed, and then lived there for generations. Their leaders were first judges and then kings who governed the federation of the twelve tribes in two kingdoms, those of Israel and Judah. They defended themselves constantly from enemy attacks, until they were brought together by a great king named David, to whom God promised, "I will appoint a place for my people Israel, and will plant them, that they may dwell in a place of their own, and move no more; neither shall the children of wickedness afflict them any more, as beforetime."

Two other books, First and Second Chronicles, summarized all that Segundo had read until that moment, from the creation of Adam to the fall of the Kingdom of Judah at the hands of his enemies and the destruction of the Temple of Jerusalem. Then the children of Israel were expelled from his land and enslaved in other lands, this time in Babylonia. The following two books, Ezra and Nehemiah, recounted the liberation of the people by a king named Cyrus, who ruled from then on over the ancient land of Canaan and allowed them to return to Jerusalem, where the walls and temple where God was worshipped were rebuilt. As though to teach people exactly how to adore Him, the following books, Job, Psalms, Proverbs, Ecclesiastes, and Song of Songs, were dedicated to praise.

But had the people of Israel not triumphed? The following sixteen books explained why they had not. In each of them, the prophets—Isaiah, Jeremiah, Ezekiel, Daniel, Hosea, Joel,

Amos, Obadiah, Jonah, Micah, Nahum, Habakkuk, Zephaniah, Haggai, Zechariah, and Malachi—told in various ways, through dreams and visions sent by God, of Jerusalem and its temple falling into the hands of enemies because the people, or their kings, had sinned again. They would lose their land, be sent into exile in Babylonia. But God would not forget His pact, His promise: they would return, led by one of His envoys, a new king, to start a new, definitive period of peace and happiness, in which the God of Israel would be recognized as the one God throughout all the nations of earth.

The visions, images, and words of the prophets weren't always easy to understand: wheels infused with a living spirit; men with four faces and four wings, seraphim with six; storms and winds and clouds and thunder; rams with horns that grew until the animal butted west, north, and south without anyone who could stop it; the fly in the rivers of Egypt, the bee of Assyria . . . Still, Segundo felt that the Bible was talking to him personally. In Zechariah, there were images of horns, colored horses, a lampstand of gold, a stone with seven eyes—symbols there were hard to comprehend even for Zechariah himself, who asked the angel of God to show him the meaning.

God, referred to as Jehovah, ordered His people to escape their exile in Babylonia and return to Jerusalem; Zerubbabel would lead them and lay the first stone for the foundation of the new temple. "This is the word of the Lord unto Zerubbabel, saying, Not by might, nor by power, but by my spirit."

Reading this phrase, alongside so many portentous affirmations—just one more sentence in a long litany of annunciations and visions—Segundo understood, he finally accepted, that he needed to renounce his vengeance: his father had been murdered, yes, but now Segundo answered to another Father, and this one was offering him guidance, a new life, a new purpose, and the strength—not *his* strength, but *His*—to pursue it and achieve it. *Not by might, nor by power, but by my spirit.*[13]

The first part of the Bible, the Old Testament, ended with a promise: God's chosen would bring eternal peace and prosperity.

The second part told the story of His emissary. The New Testament was familiar to Segundo: the life and passion of Christ, born of the union between a virgin and the Holy Spirit. Jesus preached love, performed miracles, gathered disciples, was betrayed, condemned, and crucified.

But having now read the first part of the Bible, Segundo discovered inconsistencies in the second. The tone was notably different; the content contradicted things previously said and at times defied common sense. Jesus was simultaneously the Son of Man, the Son of God, and the son of a union between a virgin and a spirit. His life was told four times in a row, in the Gospels of Matthew, Mark, Luke, and John, and in each of them there were suggestive differences. In Matthew, it said that Jesus descended directly from Abraham and David and that there were forty-two generations between Abraham and Joseph, husband of Mary, mother of Jesus Christ. But the Bible immediately established that Joseph was not the father of Christ, and when Joseph prepared to leave his pregnant wife for another, an angel of God appeared before him in dreams to reveal the true conception of the child who would "save his people from their sins." In Luke, the generations were tallied at sixty-four, and the angel appeared to Mary, not to Joseph. Mark made no mention of how Jesus had been conceived nor of his genealogy. And Matthew's emphasis on reading the actions of Jesus in light of the prophecies revealed in the Old Testament was not found in any of the other three.

More discrepancies were peppered throughout the tales of

Christ's youth, in the details of his miracles, his actions, the date of the Last Supper, even the moment of his resurrection: Was it three women who found Jesus's tomb empty, as Mark stated? Or two, as Matthew claimed? Was it several, as Luke declared? Or just one, as per John? Did they bring oil and spices to anoint his body, as Mark and Luke said, or was his body already in linen clothes with the spices before being placed in the sepulchre, as John said?

Jesus died on the cross, but then he was resurrected, and then he rose into the heavens, which was the scene that opened the following book, Acts of the Apostles, in which the followers of the resurrected Jesus brought the news of the coming of the Messiah prophesied in the Old Testament to the other children of Israel—now also called Jews, since they were descendants of the Kingdom of Judea—and then to the Gentiles, first in Jerusalem, and later in the rest of the world.

Acts ended with the story of Saul, a Jew who persecuted and killed Jews who followed Jesus Christ for violating the law of Moses by worshipping a false idol—this supposed Messiah called Jesus. But then Jesus himself appeared before him on the road, and Saul, who at this point was called Paul, became his most fervent promoter.

The following fourteen books of the New Testament were Paul's epistles to the early Christian communities. In them he sought to answer the same questions plaguing Segundo. Jesus, said Paul, was the Messiah from the prophets' visions and the consummation of God's promises to Israel, the descendant of Abraham, Moses, and David. And yet his coming was news that concerned not simply the children of Israel—the Jews— but also the Gentiles, who were now included.

How was this to be understood? Circumcision was no longer

obligatory; obeying the law was no longer necessary. Believing in God was enough. Jesus, said Saul, or Paul, had changed everything. But how? It was supposed to be that Jesus had come to ensure adherence to the law God had decreed in the first part of the Book, the law that Moses had declared *eternal,* but with his arrival, Paul repeated in his epistles, the law had expired and there was no obligation to follow it. So what did that mean for the entire Old Testament, which had moved Segundo so, had revealed to him so much about the world, about God, about himself?

The New Testament was supplemented with four additional, briefer letters from other apostles and one final book, Revelation, full of strange and dramatic images, seals, candlesticks, fiery flames, angels of death, and colored horses, which Segundo had already encountered from the prophets of the Old Testament. A decisive battle between good and evil culminated in the Second Coming of the Messiah, a definitive coming in which there was "a new heaven and a new earth . . . the holy city, new Jerusalem, coming down from God out of heaven."

And that was the end: a new prophecy, a new condemnation, a new hope, a new challenge. But how to undertake it, how to understand it? Throughout the Book, one commandment had been unwavering: be faithful to God. And yet generations of men had failed. He could not fail. But how was he to fulfill a command that was also an enigma? The Book left so many questions, too many; it said so much, too much, but also left so much, too much, unsaid; it was extraordinary how much he now knew and how much he had yet to discover. In the many years to come, years he would dedicate to reading and understanding the Book, Segundo would ask himself the same terrible questions over and over again.

What was His will?

What did He want of man?

What did He want of *him*?

How ought he to live?

How was he to prove his obedience?

How ought he to worship?

How could he be a man of God?

The Bible was an encrypted message from God: impossible to obey without first deciphering.

First, however, he had to solve the riddle of his own life. His stutter being irreversible, he would never become a civil guard. He was abandoning his father's wishes, his plan for him; even his church. While he figured out what to do, to be, he stayed in Lima, working as an apprentice at a carpenter's workshop. Through a cousin, he met María Teresa Aguilar, the cousin's cousin and two years older than him, also from Cajamarca. They got married and were soon expecting a child.

When Segundo returned to Cajamarca, in 1950, at the age of twenty-three, he was a new man: he had a carpenter's license, a wife, and a baby daughter, new dreams and new truths.

The city had changed very little; it has hardly changed today: there is still the magnificent plaza where the Inca was strangled, and the rooms he filled, to no avail, with gold and silver to pay his ransom; the baroque Spanish cathedral on one side of the square and, directly across from it, on the other side, the "Indian" church; the majority of houses in the center look as if they have been standing there since colonial times. During business hours, the narrow, paved streets are now thronged with motorcycles and minibuses full of tourists, but after lunch the long siesta hour begins, a time when the hill of Santa Apolonia, with its enormous Catholic cross, reigns over the silent valley as it did five hundred years ago.

Segundo harbored his secret discovery and was eager to reveal it. His wife, too, had a secret but was eager to keep hers hidden—at least from her husband. María Teresa had an oval face and full lips, wavy black hair and narrow eyes, and a broad smile that made people feel at ease with her. She had a sweet voice and had been taught to follow her husband but also to fear the Catholic God and the punishment that disobedience bore with it. Ever since she was a child, she would wake up at dawn to get to the cathedral in time for the first Mass and was often found sitting in the benches alone, praying.

When their first daughter was about to be born in Lima, Segundo was in Cajamarca helping his mother harvest potatoes in the small field she'd managed to hold on to in Rodacocha. Knowing that María Teresa might give birth in his absence, he'd left two explicit instructions: first, if it was a girl—as indeed it was—María Teresa should name her Raquel, after the shepherdess Jacob had fallen in love with in Genesis, for she was "beautiful and well favored"; second, under no circumstances should the child be baptized.

But María Teresa wavered. The Catholic Church taught that the soul of a babe who died without baptism was doomed to remain in limbo for all eternity. What if Raquel got sick? What if she died? Or survived? Children who were not baptized grew horns, the sign of the devil, from their foreheads. Could she take that risk simply to obey her husband? She baptized Raquel in secret. When he returned to Lima, Segundo was unaware of the betrayal but sensed her hesitation. Until that point, he had taught his newfound truth only to his younger brother Álvaro, or Alvarito, as his sisters called him, eight years his junior. Luckily, Álvaro had never attended the Catholic Church, which made things far easier. Segundo had told him about the Sabbath, about forbidden and authorized foods, and about morality, and in particular had instilled in him the need to study the Bible in order to find the truth. Nothing was more important: he should dedicate all of his energy to the task, all of his free time. In his teens, Álvaro considered rebelling against this burden: he wanted to play soccer with his friends. But Segundo was adamant. "You're wasting your time with those things," he said (or at least this was how Álvaro recalled it years later, when he was no longer a mere follower but the more outgoing of the two explorers, moving from city to city, town to town, revelation to revelation). "That won't get you into heaven," Segundo warned him. He must study.

Segundo later convinced his cousins Demetrio, Vitaldo, and Manuel Guerra the same way, during wrestling bouts. They were his very first followers. But María Teresa didn't see him as a second father, a brother, a comrade, or a leader. She believed in the church in which she'd been raised and knew how to dig in her heels. How could he make her see? If he couldn't even convince his wife, how could he convince others?

Was she a Catholic? he asked. Roman Catholic and Apostolic, María Teresa replied. And did she believe in the Catholic Bible? She did. Then get out your Bible, he challenged her. He told her to open to the book of Habakkuk, guided her to the verses he wanted, and asked her to read aloud: "What profiteth the graven image that the maker thereof hath graven it; the molten image, and a teacher of lies, that the maker of his work trusteth therein, to make dumb idols? Woe unto him that saith to the wood, Awake; to the dumb stone, Arise, it shall teach!"

Your Bible is talking about you, Segundo told María Teresa. You, who adore the idols in your church, false idols, but God is One, and accepts no idols.

It was written in the Bible and yet contradicted the church's teaching, which venerated the Virgin and saints. How could she reconcile such a contradiction? María Teresa could find no answer. Her husband's logic was indisputable, and she never doubted him again. They would not baptize their following children: Jocabeth, named for the daughter of Levi in Numbers; Noemí, Ruth's mother-in-law in the book of Ruth; Eva, the first woman in Genesis; Josué, Moses's successor; and Oseas the prophet.

His early successes within the family did not satisfy Segundo. He wanted to spread to everyone the truth: God had addressed not him specifically but all men. He had to reveal His message. But deciphering it was too much work for one man alone. He needed to discuss it, to confer with others.

When Segundo was able to hire employees in his carpenter's workshop in Cajamarca, he quickly recruited them. Soon he had assembled a small circle of believers. They met two nights a week at his mother Abigail's home, where Segundo, María Teresa, and their children had lived since their return from Lima. It was a spacious house on Calle San Salvador, three blocks from the main square, the Plaza de Armas, built in traditional Cajamarca style. The adobe home had a flat front wall with two heavy wooden doors on the ground floor; over each one, on the second floor, were two windows with wooden shutters, like eyes on a face, topped with a sloped tile roof. Inside, a long corridor led to rooms off to the left, including the main living room, and then ended at a broad patio full of trees and plants.

In that living room, groups of men sat to discuss the Bible (the women could hear, but they did not participate in the discussion): employees and customers, friends and relatives, people Segundo had met at other discussion groups, and even young men who'd just come down from the mountains to make a living in Cajamarca, people Segundo met on the street and offered lodging and a job in his workshop.

That was how he recruited a man eleven years his junior, José Salirrosas Leyva, born in San Marcos, sixty-seven kilometers from the city. José had been abandoned by his mother when he was five months old. Raised first by his paternal grandmother in the countryside, at the age of four he went to live with another woman he called Auntie, though they were not related. At the age of six he was sent to work. From that time on, he'd been alone. He worked in a house, keeping the owners' son company and entertaining him. José had taught himself to read using newspapers, and his first book was a Bible, which he bought for twenty soles, having saved most of the thirty soles he earned per month. He was deeply moved by the story of Egypt: a people freed from bondage by God. At the age of seventeen, he entered the army, and at twenty he arrived in Cajamarca. Segundo met him on the street selling bread and, after speaking to him about the Bible, offered him lodging in his home and took the young man into his group.

Wiry and comparatively tall, Segundo had a long face and pointy chin, a long round-tipped nose, wide forehead, full lips, black hair, and copper skin. His eyes, framed by brows that peaked like mountains, glinted almost fiercely. He rarely smiled. Quiet, though firm and severe, he remained calm until something—an act of disobedience against God or a lie, for instance—riled him. Like Moses, who was "slow of speech, and of a slow tongue," Segundo lacked a way with words. When he was inspired and tried to expand on an idea too quickly, or when his emotions got the best of him, his jaw seized up mid-sentence, and he had to fight to recover. But people were moved by his rigor and vehemence, the intensity of his glimmering eyes, his endless curiosity, and his questioning of Scripture. He encouraged debates that sometimes turned into fights. He would accept no half-truths or ambiguity. When he was convinced, he was like an arrow shot straight on target, never wavering. But he didn't impose himself; Segundo always left open the possibility of a new discussion.

He didn't ask people to take his word: the truth was written, it was right there, in the Book. This was his technique, the same one he'd used with María Teresa: repeat a Catholic affirmation that he condemned as false—for example, that it was a mortal sin not to attend Mass on Sunday—and challenge people to find it in the Bible. Show me where it says that, brother, do me the favor. Then he'd open the Book to Exodus 20:8–11, or Leviticus 23:3, or Deuteronomy 5:12–15, and make his interlocutor read for himself the passages in which God ordered that Saturday, *sábado,* the Sabbath, be respected and kept holy.

Who could refute that?

His followers were moved by the conviction and sincerity they sensed in him. Segundo had one face, not two like the Catholic priests. Thanks to him they saw that they'd been lied to, saw that there were other laws, other instructions to follow—another message altogether, one that was addressed to them.

But, again, who could decipher the message?

What was His will?

What did God want of Man?

What did He want of *them*?

And how could they obey God's instructions *exactly*?

In Leviticus, for instance, God stipulated the proper way to carry out a sacrifice or make an offering in order to wash one's sins and maintain purity. A good part of Leviticus was, in fact, a manual detailing which offering to make for a given offense: parts of lambs, bulls, or birds, the blood of one animal or another, unleavened bread, a certain food, or the entrails of cooked animals, and what to do with them, how to present them.

How were they to proceed? Were they seriously supposed to bring a lamb without blemish to an altar and offer it to the priest if someone violated a commandment? And which priest? Which altar? Leviticus forbade the eating of camel because it was an impure animal. That was easy: there were no camels in Cajamarca. Leviticus named the birds that were not to be consumed: the owl, the vulture, the raven, the nighthawk. How about the turkey, the chicken? Deuteronomy provided an additional list of beasts that were clean for consumption, including the deer, the ox, the gazelle. There were no deer, oxen, or gazelles in Cajamarca. But what about the Peruvian guinea pigs known as *cuy*? Was *cuy* okay? How could they know for sure?

And it wasn't just food. Deuteronomy 16:1–2 ordered to observe the month of Abib and "keep the passover." What month was Abib? Where was the almanac to explain it, since the Bible included no almanac? And what happened if they did it wrong? What would that make them?

They could see how much was wrong with what they'd learned from the Catholics. They could contest Sunday, baptism, saints, the Virgin, Mass, and priests. But what about what was right? How should they worship God, show Him their love, their obedience, fidelity, and faith, if not in the way the priests had taught them?

They needed a guide to the Book, someone more knowledgeable, a pastor who understood and could lead the rituals.

They needed a church: the *true* church of the Book.

But where were they to find it?

As if on cue, previously unknown churches began to spring up all over, churches with their own temples and their own names, their own leaders, their own rituals. It took Segundo a very long time to comprehend where they'd come from, to learn about their rebellion, similar to his own—which had given rise to the churches' existence four hundred years earlier—and about how they came to Cajamarca.

At the same time the Catholic Church was imposing the Bible on the Inca in the walled square, others were arguing over and questioning it. Their rebellion was sparked by the same questions Segundo would ask himself centuries later: What was God's true will? How was one to show Him faith? What was the road to salvation? Which practices and conduct should be followed in order to earn the Father's approval? How was one to be an authentic believer?

But these were all moot points if they couldn't answer another, prior question: Who could interpret His message? The answer to this would determine what the true church of God really was, what the true religion was, and not be a mere human institution plagued with human bias, ambition, weakness, and folly.

The Catholic Church, controlled from Rome by the supreme pontiff, had imposed a single answer: *it* was the true religion. Only the Catholic Church spoke for God on earth, only the pope could interpret Scripture and convey its meaning. This was established in the Book: Jesus had told his apostle Peter that he would be the rock on which he'd build his church, the one whose faith would be unfailing. Popes were his legitimate successors; therefore, they could never be wrong.

But there were circumstances, Segundo would learn in encyclopedias and history books. In the fifteenth century, Christianity found itself divided; multiple monarchies tried to control it; priests and bishops served local kings and princes before they did the far-off pontiff in Rome. In an attempt to regain its unity and autonomy, the church became as vertical and as ruthless as the kingdoms. Soon the church was as wayward, as consumed by intrigues of wealth and power, as they were. Saving souls became big business: in the fifteenth century, the church began selling "indulgences," a sort of safe passage that opened the gates of heaven to anyone who could afford to buy them. When Martin Luther, a professor of theology, rose up against the corruption of indulgences, he found grounds for his critique in the New Testament. It was written that Jesus had redeemed the sins of all humanity; therefore, it did not fall to people to exhibit works and merits, because Christ himself *was* the work and the merit. Having faith in Jesus as Christ was the only thing that was required. It was all in the Bible: there was no greater authority. Thus, the Book must be translated into the languages of every people. Any person of faith could find divine truth by reading it: the Book contained everything, and in it nothing was mistaken. Understanding the Bible was difficult, true, but all that was needed was discussion among the faithful.[14]

The Catholic Church rejected these ideas: only the church could speak for God. They excommunicated Luther, waged wars on the heresy now called the Protestant Reformation, decreed that only their version of the Bible, in Latin, was correct. But they could not prevent the loss of northern Europe, a supreme loss from which they feared they might never recover. The church resolved not to lose Spanish America, which they'd taken in the conquest. And so, as a guardian of the faith, they sent the Inquisition, a tribunal formed to punish heresies, to fight the introduction of Bibles translated into Spanish or Native languages to the Americas, for those would put the Book within anyone's reach.

They were so successful in their mission that when Peru finally declared independence from Spain in the nineteenth century, the country remained faithful to Rome. In fact, until 1836, twelve years after independence, professing belief in any religion other than Catholicism was still a crime punishable by prison in Peru. Lima's liberal elite attempted to call the steadfast Catholic hegemony into question, but received only precarious authorization to allow Protestant churches to enter the country if they submitted to strict regulation: they could allow only foreigners to enter their temples; they had to abstain from pros-elytizing any Peruvians; their windows and doors were required to remain shut during services. And although formally they could not be stopped from introducing translated versions of the Bible, they spread the idea that all translations were false.

Nothing changed until, in 1888, an Italian named Francisco Penzotti arrived in Callao, the port city adjacent to Lima. He'd been sent by the American Bible Society, a continental associa-tion of Protestant churches. The Arequipa authorities arrested him for selling Bibles door to door. He was freed only after the president of Peru himself intervened, fearful of an inter-national scandal. Penzotti again began traveling from town to town, Bible in hand. Sometimes he was stoned by frightened mobs. And yet he managed to sell more than seven thousand Bibles in one year.

Then the Catholic Church ordered the closure of Protestant meetinghouses. After being harassed, Penzotti sent his two old-est daughters to Chile to keep them safe. In 1891, at the church's urging, he was jailed once more, this time under horrific con-ditions. Knowing that he was ill, the Peruvian government, through the Italian consulate, offered him a quiet exit from the country. Penzotti rejected the offer.

His case was then taken up by Lima's frustrated liberal elite, still seeking to defy the church's power. Two thousand people marched in the streets, demanding freedom of worship. Eminent community members visited Penzotti in prison and, in a supreme act of defiance, sat to read the Bible with him in Spanish. One of the visitors took a photo of Penzotti in his cell, surrounded by other prisoners. Published by *The New York Herald,* the photo caused precisely the international scandal that the government had feared. The Peruvian Supreme Court of Justice absolved Penzotti. He'd spent eight months in prison. An overjoyed public walked him home.

Other missionaries, mainly North American and occasionally European, followed his example: they arrived as Bible sellers and offered to discuss the Book's content. Once in a while, they amassed a few followers. But as soon as they left Peru due to illness, persecution, or simply to go on other missions, their congregations dissolved, disappearing along with them.[15]

It seemed nothing could move the Catholic empire entrenched in Latin America. In 1910, when twelve hundred delegates from Protestant churches met in Edinburgh at the World Missionary Conference[16] to discuss evangelizing the world and dividing up its territory, the general consensus was that they should concentrate on places like Africa and China, full of unbelievers, and abandon any attempt to penetrate the territory dominated by Rome.

A few churches, though, defied this consensus and remained in Latin America, challenging the Catholics' hostility. Among them was the Seventh-Day Adventist Church, which an Aymara man named Manuel Zúñiga Camacho joined. Manuel had been born in 1871 in Platería, an Indigenous town on the shores of Lake Titicaca, where the peasants lived in constant battle with the rich landowners trying to steal their land. In the army he met Eduardo Forga, the son of a prosperous family in Arequipa who'd become evangelical and preached to the Indigenous. Forga gave Manuel his first Bible and taught him to read it; he also instilled in him the idea that education was the weapon that would save his people.

Manuel opened a school in Platería and later led an Aymara delegation to meet with the Peruvian president in Lima, to ask him to build other schools along the shores of the lake and put an end to the landholders' plunder. Alarmed, the bishop of Puno dispatched priests to Platería to persuade the peasants not to send their children to the rebel's school. The priests cited scenes from Exodus: if their children devoted themselves to heresy, the wrath of God would rain famines and plague down upon them. But the Aymara didn't trust the bishop or any other member of the Catholic Church who was an ally of the landholders. The bishop openly accused Manuel of inciting a rebellion and forced him to close the school.

Manuel decided that only the presence of foreign missionaries could protect them. He still corresponded with Forga, who, having converted to Adventism, now observed the Sabbath on Saturday. Under his influence, in 1908 Manuel began to do the same and persuaded the tiny Adventist mission in Lima to send the American-born Ferdinand Stahl and his Swedish wife, Ana, to Platería.

Feeling protected, Manuel reopened his school in 1909; within a few months he had more than sixty pupils. Ferdinand was a nurse and Ana a teacher; they opened a health clinic. As an Adventist minister, Ferdinand neither spoke of salvation nor emphasized dogma. Instead, his sole message was this: Jesus loved them, and they should believe in him. He read them the Bible, taught hygiene, persuaded them to get vaccinated against smallpox. Eight hundred Aymara attended his services each Saturday. Ferdinand began to ordain some of them as ministers.

In 1913, they built a second school, larger than the first, as well as a clinic and an administrative center for the mission. More alarmed than ever, the bishop of Puno stormed into Platería on March 3, along with the governor, two justices of the peace, a priest, and two hundred residents from another town enlisted as shock troops. The Stahls, at the time, were not in Platería, having gone to purchase supplies. Manuel, too, was absent. The invaders destroyed the school's materials, poured out medicines, and made off with their electrical equipment. Then they forced the Aymara to kiss the bishop's ring. Five Adventists refused and were tied with ropes in front of everyone. At that moment, Manuel arrived. The bishop told him he had orders from the president of the republic to put an end to the heresy. Manuel replied that if that were the case, the president would have sent the prefect, not the bishop. He reproached the priests for corrupting the Aymara people, encouraging their drinking during religious holidays; the Adventists, on the other hand, offered them the Gospel and education.

The bishop ordered him tied as well, but not one of the two hundred there present dared to do it. The priest who accompanied the bishop then got down off his horse and whipped Manuel; the justices of the peace enthusiastically joined in. Manuel's son, eleven years old, begged the bishop to order them to stop before they killed him. The bishop had Manuel tied, and took him and the other five rebels to jail, together with two more they found along the way.

The judge in Puno freed them a week later and referred the case to the Supreme Court of Lima since a bishop was involved. Five months later, the court absolved the Aymara, echoing the public's indignation against the church, which recalled the bishop from Puno until things calmed down. Too late: a senator from Puno introduced a bill to eliminate from article 4 of the constitution the phrase asserting that the Peruvian state "does not allow the public exercise of any other [religion]." It was approved on October 20, 1915. From then on, article 4 said only that "the Nation professes the Roman Catholic and Apostolic religion: it is protected by the State."

In response, the Diocese of Puno wrote a letter denouncing a supposed revolt incited by Stahl. A commission convened by the president investigated accusations and ended up praising the Adventist mission: the Aymara of Platería had better living conditions than other Indigenous peoples. Four years later there were forty-six Adventist schools in Peru, forty-five of which were run by Aymara who'd been educated in Platería.

While the Adventists were fighting for, and winning, their place in Peru,[17] the churches that had complied with the Edinburgh accord had set off, as per their resolution, for the distant lands of China. But when the 1949 Communist Revolution rejected all religions and gods, thousands of pastors were expelled from the country. With no mission or purpose, they once again took out their world maps, and this time they did decide to conquer Latin America. A decade later, a quarter of the world's almost twenty-one thousand Protestant missionaries were ranging the continent with their Bibles.

They arrived not as a single unified church but as dozens. Luther had based his church on the freedom to read and discuss the Bible, which contained the divine truth, single and infallible. But interpretations varied country to country, city to city, scholar to scholar, believer to believer, and a different interpretation was all it took to found a new church. Each dissenting reader accused the authorities of their particular church of having committed the same sin as the popes: imposing an incorrect interpretation. Each one scoured the Book for the grounds on which to base their criticism, the truth that had been disregarded by the new priests. They always found it, and with this new truth there began a new church. As a fierce defender of the Catholic Church, the theologian Johann Eck had warned his enemy Luther, "Martin, there is no one of the heresies which have torn the bosom of the Church which has not its origin from the various interpretations of the Scripture. The Bible itself is the arsenal whence each innovator has drawn his deceptive arguments."[18]

Deceptive or not, in the four hundred years between Luther and Segundo, those arguments had spawned dozens and dozens of new, opposing Protestant sects, from which infinite local churches sprang up all over the world.

At least seven of them were preaching their seven different truths in Segundo's Cajamarca.[19] First, there were missionaries from the Free Church of Scotland. They arose out of a series of discrepancies and rifts that began with the Reformation itself, when John Calvin had distanced himself from Martin Luther over, among other things, his emphasis on the doctrine of predestination. When King Henry VIII of England broke with the Catholic Church for his own reasons, that gave birth to the Anglican church, which adopted Calvinist precepts. The Anglican doctrine was taken up by the Church of Scotland and blended with Celtic traditions to form what was called the Presbyterian doctrine. But in the nineteenth century, some of the faithful were of the opinion that the state and landholders had too much power over the church and created the Free Church of Scotland, which gave greater emphasis to the Gospels and the communal nature of faith. They survived only until 1900, when the church joined the United Presbyterian Church of Scotland. A fraction of them, however, rejected this union and stuck with the name Free Church of Scotland.

The Methodists, on the other hand, had broken with the Anglican church because they believed that men and women were not predestined to be saved or condemned but could achieve salvation through faith, that the Holy Spirit would send them the deep conviction that they had been saved, and that their good deeds would "perfect" them as Christians. In other words, faith alone was not enough; there had to be deeds.

Then there were the Pentecostals, who believed that, as in Acts of the Apostles, every time the church held services, the Holy Spirit descended upon the faithful and transformed them, causing them to speak in tongues. This baptism with the Holy Ghost was the key to salvation.

The Assemblies of God shared the basic beliefs of the Pentecostals, from whom their movement stemmed, and shared their belief in the possibility of miracle cures by divine intervention, but were a separate organization.

The Nazarenes believed not only in the grace that God bestowed upon all men and the forgiveness of sin by the sacrifice of Jesus but also, like the Methodists, in the doctrine of Christian perfection and in performing good deeds, especially among the poor.

The Peruvian Evangelists, founded on the idea of bringing the salvation of the Gospel to every corner of the nation, had tried unsuccessfully to form a church that elided the differences between the various Protestant denominations.

Which to adhere to, Segundo wondered, when they all claimed to be the authentic church of God? Which, of all these, was the true religion?

How to decide?

There was only one way. Through the Bible.

Segundo wanted to know, wanted to learn. But he also wanted to explain, to reveal what he'd learned, perhaps teach. That was why he visited every church or religious group he could find, every one that opened its doors to him. But the moment he began asking troublesome questions, those doors were closed in his face. And although he wanted to discuss the Bible with as many scholars as he could find, in his view most of their churches were in the wrong. For him, as for Luther, the Bible allowed for only one truth, and all readings were aimed at finding it. Accordingly, of the seven new churches he'd found in Cajamarca, only one could be right. But Pentecostals and Assemblyists, Methodists and Nazarenes, Scottish Presbyterians and Peruvian Evangelists all had one error in common: they claimed that Sunday was sacred, something that was never mentioned in the Bible. Only one of the churches in Cajamarca, the seventh, truly understood that Saturday was the day God had commanded be kept holy. They understood it so well, in fact, that they proclaimed that the salvation of humanity depended upon it.

The Seventh-Day Adventist Church[20] had emerged in the United States during the Second Great Awakening, an early nineteenth-century religious revival that stimulated a series of reform movements that brought forth new prophets and new churches. One of these reforms was led by William Miller, a Baptist who had once discredited all religion, only to return to it even more fervently. Miller deduced from his reading of the book of Daniel that the Second Coming of the Messiah was imminent; by his calculations, it would occur on a very specific day: October 22, 1844. Hopeful, his followers prepared for the end of times. On that wondrous day, however, rather than the Advent, what occurred was what came to be known as the Great Disappointment. There was no sense contending that there had been errors in computation, postponing, offering a later date; the calculation had been false.

Among the disappointed was Ellen White.[21] Then sixteen years old, she spent the night crying and awoke at dawn, disconsolate. Fifty thousand others felt the same way; many abandoned the movement. Not her. She kept praying for an explanation.

And she prayed.

And prayed.

In fact, she was praying at the family altar of friends in Portland, Oregon, when, as she later recounted, a light enveloped her and swept her up to heaven. As she was flying, she looked down in search of the Adventist people, but saw no one anywhere. "Look a bit higher," a celestial voice suggested. And then she saw it, not on earth, but in heaven, moving toward a city in the distance: a light. An angel explained to her that it was "the midnight cry," as in Matthew 25:6. The light shone upon the Adventists' feet so they would not trip; at the front of the procession was Jesus.

This revelation alone would have been enough to deem her a prophet, but she was to have many more. Through them, she understood that the Great Disappointment had not been the result of erroneous calculation; it was not that she, and fifty thousand others, had believed in vain. No. It was that the Messiah had not returned because the people were not keeping the Sabbath.

The prophetess wrote of her trips to heaven and encounters with angels and God—more than two thousand during the course of her life—in forty books and more than five thousand articles. These texts became the basis for the Seventh-Day Adventist Church, which, founded in 1863, spread all over the world and grew to tens of millions of followers.

Jesus had spoken to her in English, because Ellen White was American, but her books were translated into Spanish, and Segundo read the copies sold by Adventists in Peru.[22] According to them, on October 22, 1844, Daniel's prophecy *had* been fulfilled, but not in the sense Miller had understood it. The sanctuary had been cleansed, indeed, but in heaven, not on earth. In heaven was a sanctuary, the true tabernacle. There, Christ ministered from above. In 1844, after the twenty-three hundred days of atonement predicted by Daniel, the second stage of atonement had begun: Christ was conducting an investigative judgment, a study of the heavenly records of each soul since the beginning of times; the result of this investigation would determine the souls' fate. During the Judgment, according to a passage in Revelation, the righteous would be separated from the sinners. Those who were saved would wake from the dream of death and live eternally, while those condemned would be totally destroyed. Thus the Adventists believed, like other Christians, not only in the eternity of the soul but also in an eternity for the whole person, provided the person was a true believer. Body, mind, and spirit were indivisible, and therefore not only the spirit had to be preserved; food and caring for one's health were also essential. This explains their militant abstention from drinking and smoking, and their frequent vegetarianism, as well as their emphasis on building hospitals and schools.

The Adventist Church would play an essential role during the Second Coming, the Adventists believed. It was the "remnant." The term could be found in many books of the Bible and referred to those who, in times of widespread apostasy, had been selected as the keepers of the commandments of God and the faith of Christ. The Adventist Church's unique role was to proclaim God's final message to the world at the time of the Judgment and the second Advent of Christ.

Although the Adventists concentrated more on the end of the Bible than the beginning, more on the eschatology of Revelation than the deeds and instructions of God found in the first five books, the Pentateuch, which Segundo especially loved, the Adventists, he believed, had the virtue of adherence to the letter of Scripture. They saw the Bible as a road map to God.

When the Adventists came to Peruvian cities, competing with the droves of Protestant missionaries who'd been displaced from China, they thought they would have more luck attracting the faithful by speaking of social and practical issues leading to a better life.[23] Hadn't that been the experience of Manuel Zúñiga in Platería? They held talks on abstention and offered five-day plans to quit smoking. That was how they grew, mainly in Indigenous and rural communities and among impoverished urban workers with whom their message resonated the most.

In Cajamarca, under the dual leadership of the local colporteurs Manuel León and Luis Montoya, some twenty people gathered to study the Bible and pray at a member's home on Avenida Alameda de los Incas. Segundo and his followers often showed up at these meetings to listen, but also to question and throw into doubt the pastors' sermons, to ask whether perhaps this or that passage might not have a different interpretation. Just like other groups before them to whom Segundo presented questions they found inappropriate or irrelevant, the Adventists resented it. They were not interested in questioning their dogma. Segundo found that although he'd finally chosen a church, the one of the true Sabbath, that church had not chosen him.[24]

Would he have to remain alone? Would his group be forced to grapple with the enigmas of the Bible on their own? At that moment of unease, what Segundo had experienced so many times before happened again: what he sought, he found. He didn't have to keep searching for a church, because the church came to him.

It was called the Seventh-Day Adventist *Reform* Movement, and though it shared with the Adventists almost all of the same beliefs and rites, it was in fact a rival church. It had emerged of a disagreement during World War I, when Adventist leaders in Germany authorized the faithful to enlist in the military and to fight on the Sabbath. This approval violated the Adventist tradition, begun in the American Civil War, of refusing conscription and presenting conscientious objection; more dramatically, it also violated two of the Ten Commandments: not to kill, and to respect the Sabbath. Once the war was over, the German Adventist leaders asked forgiveness for their error, but the rebels did not forgive them, and in 1925 they created their own church. Only 2 percent of the world's Adventists went with them, but the group was concerned about dogma, not numbers.[25]

The Reformers struggled to understand how the Adventists' betrayal could have occurred. The answer inevitably lay in the Book, and there, inevitably, they found it. It was right there in Revelation 18:1–4, where it was written that an angel came down from heaven, crying, "Babylon is fallen." They saw that they had been wrong when they identified the Adventist

Church as the remnant. It was now clear to them that it was indeed the opposite: sinful Babylon, fallen from grace. They, the Reformers, were the real remnant. They were more literal in their interpretation of Scripture, strictly vegetarian, not merely as a way of caring for the body, but as an external sign of faith.

Early on, the Reformers had sent out missionaries to the Americas.[26] One of them, Eugenio Laicovschi, a pastor from Bessarabia, arrived in Peru in 1933. He was following up on a letter from a Peruvian who had read about them in a magazine and wanted to know more. But Laicovschi encountered many obstacles; he fell gravely ill with malaria, and when he recovered, he faced fierce opposition both from the Catholic Church and from the Adventist missionaries. He found, with dismay, that his potential church members were so poor that they couldn't help with his expenses or travel costs, as was the case in other missions. It took many years for the Reformers to penetrate Peru. So when they heard of Segundo and his group, the local Reform pastors came forward readily, with genuine interest, to discuss the Bible with them.

That opening, as well as their observance of the Sabbath on Saturday, strict dietary restrictions, dogmatic zeal, and social conservatism—women wore long skirts, no makeup or jewelry, and used no perfume—appealed to Segundo and his group. For a time, they attended without joining, but soon they wanted more. It wasn't enough to understand the Bible and have someone to discuss it with: they needed a guide if they wanted to live according to God's will, and a community with whom to share and celebrate it, a place to carry out rites, and true pastors to lead them. They wanted to attend Sabbath school, the guided Bible study group that gathered every Saturday morning. They wanted to participate in the Lord's Supper, a communion service held four times a year, in which the Reformers ate unleavened bread, drank grape juice, and washed each other's feet.

So they decided to join the church formally. This required that, like John the Baptist and like Jesus himself, they receive a new baptism. Like their Adventist progenitors, the Reformers practiced adult baptism, seeing it as a conscious acceptance of God, and opposed the baptizing of children required by the Catholic Church. To receive it, Segundo, his brother Álvaro, and the rest of the group were submerged not in the waters of the Jordan in Canaan, as in the Bible, but in the modest yet available San Lucas in Cajamarca.

There was another reason to convert as well. As full members of the Adventist Reform Movement, they would receive a periodical, the *Sabbath Bible Lessons,* every three months. Published by the movement's General Conference steering committee in the United States, each volume had 30, 60, sometimes 120 pages, sans illustrations; the content was organized in the form of questions and answers.[27] Each issue dealt with a specific book from the Bible, or with basic concepts of Adventism, such as health and caring for the body, and began with a brief preface explaining the meaning of the lesson to follow.

The book of Isaiah, in fact, took up five entire issues spanning 1957 and 1958. In them, they learned that his prophecies spoke both of the "period assigned to humanity" in which they lived and of a history more familiar to Segundo: that of the Israelites' captivity in Assyria and Babylonia, the prospect of their liberation and return to their land, and the promise of a new king, or Messiah, who would lead them to a time of peace and prosperity. In the *Sabbath Bible Lessons* the Bible was interpreted in the light of the imminent coming, that is, in the light of its final book: the plan of redemption was outlined in Revelation, and without the knowledge contained in it, the entire Christian experience would be null.

This was invaluable material. For the first time, Segundo had other texts, other experts beyond those he could find in Cajamarca, to help him crack the message of the Bible. This discovery led him to look for more such texts. He bought an encyclopedia and began to read about Mesopotamian antiquity and the peoples at war with biblical Israel.

They seem to have found their church, the true religion—a new identity, even. There was a particularly obscure passage in Revelation that Segundo, his brother Álvaro, and some others spent a long time discussing one day. It referred to a central tenet of the Reform church, the belief that at the end of times a group of 144,000 descendants of the tribes of Israel would herald the Second Coming of Christ. This number referred to a special group of "living saints" and, according to the Reform church, should be taken literally; every Reformer should strive to become one of them. The 144,000, Segundo read in Revelation 14:1, "had his Father's name written in their foreheads." What did that mean? They concluded that perhaps they needed to take new names. Álvaro chose Aarón (Aaron), who had been Moses's brother and was chosen by God to be the first priest. Segundo recalled the passage from Zechariah—"Not by might, nor by power, but by my spirit"—and chose the name Zorobabel (Zerubbabel) for himself. They didn't abandon their birth names, but privately added these new names as a sign of their commitment.

Four times a year, they met to share the Lord's Supper, a reminder of Jesus's last supper, eating unleavened bread and drinking grape juice after washing their feet. They no longer celebrated Christmas or Easter. They learned that keeping the Sabbath as God intended it to be kept meant not working, playing sports, or going to the cinema and that the Sabbath began on Friday at sundown and ended a day later, when the sun went down once more. In those twenty-four hours they were to rest, study and discuss the Bible, teach it to the children, do charitable works, and eat.

While Cajamarcans continued feeding themselves the way they always had—eating any creature that darted through the mountains, basting it, roasting it, or stewing it as had their grandmothers before them, and their grandmothers' grandmothers before them—the Villanuevas renounced *cuy*, rabbit, pork, and, as demanded by the Reformers, all other meat.

Each rule, each change, implied sacrifice. The men were forced to leave their jobs because God forbade them to receive their wages on the Sabbath, and Saturday was usually payday in Peru. The neighbors, still Catholic for the most part, whispered and pointed. In order to be observant, Segundo resolved, they would have to keep separate; so he moved his family to a house that bordered a field and yet was only a few minutes from the Plaza de Armas, allowing him to keep his carpenter's workshop but also to slip in and out unnoticed. It sat on a four-thousand-square-foot lot on Calle Leoncio Prado and had thick white-washed adobe walls supported by heavy wood beams, keeping the rooms cool; though the doors were single leaf, they were so heavy that a child could not open them alone, and so low that anyone over five feet ten would have to stoop to enter (Segundo was five feet five). The packed-dirt floors were twelve inches below street level, so those crossing the threshold sort of fell inside. The only two rooms lacked windows. But in the large grounds out back, Segundo used partitions and sheeting to build two additional rooms and a wood-fire stove. There was no bathroom, but the San Lucas River was only a block away; in fact, in March and April, when it rained, the house often flooded in the swell.[28]

María Teresa turned the patio into her own Garden of Eden: a wonder of herbs, plants, fruit trees, and flowers, with rosebushes of every color born of her very own grafts, a large fig tree with black fruits, and artichoke plants. Segundo made poultices to treat burns, bites, allergies, and chilblains. When the weather was nice, he would sit out under the peach tree, children seated all around him, and tell them the story of Joseph, Jacob's favorite son, who was sold by his brothers to the Egyptians.

In 1958, Víctor Chico joined the household. He was a boy of ten who'd lost his father four years earlier. His father had been at work building a mountain road; one day, they dynamited the mountain, and a large rock flew out and crushed him. His mother had joined the Adventist Reform Movement in Cajamarca and met Segundo through the church. Soon, Víctor became one of Segundo's disciples and ate and slept at the house so often that he was like one of the family.

In time, Segundo built a second floor, which he enclosed with partitions, and built a staircase of thick unhewn wood connecting it to the patio. He was after more space not for what were now the nine members of the household but for his Bible study group. For, although he had formally and sincerely accepted the Adventist interpretation, accepted baptism, and obediently adopted the church and its religion, he had not renounced his search for a deeper understanding of the Bible.

Through the Reform Movement, he'd met other "readers of the Bible," as he referred to them: men and women devoted to deciphering God's message. It was there that he met Víctor Castillo, a man twelve years his junior, born in Asunción, a rural area south of Cajamarca. Víctor's parents were nominally Catholic but not truly practicing. As a boy, Castillo had moved to Trujillo, a large industrial city on the Pacific some 180 miles southwest of Cajamarca. At seventeen, one day he'd been walking down the street and a voice caught his attention. He'd followed the sound inside a small rented establishment. The preacher there noted his interest and, when the service was over, invited him to join his church—the Adventist Reform Movement. Soon, Castillo began working as a colporteur. He traveled to the north of Peru selling Bibles, as well as magazines and books on natural medicine. Castillo understood that few people were interested in biblical literature, but nearly everyone was concerned about their health or that of someone close. He used health as a foot in the door. "You've got to whet their appetite," he said. Castillo was charismatic, likable, a good talker. Sometimes he brought a loudspeaker with him, and whenever he saw the opportunity, he'd stand on a corner or in a plaza and preach to anyone who would listen.

While passing through Cajamarca, Castillo attended a meeting with Segundo's group. Later, he visited him at home. Then he came back to meet with the group again. Finally, Castillo joined them. He ended up organizing a handful of followers in Trujillo with whom he could discuss what they read and attempt to understand each passage. He was the first and most enthusiastic reader of the Bibles he sold up and down the coast of Peru.

On the second floor of Segundo's house in Cajamarca, the study group, which had up to twenty-five people, always began with an Adventist hymn, which those gathered sang with all their heart, accompanied by a guitar:

Holy, holy, holy! Lord God Almighty!
Early in the morning our song shall rise to Thee;
Holy, holy, holy, merciful and mighty!
God in three Persons, blessed Trinity!

Then they would sing a psalm, and Segundo would read a Bible passage, which could be from the Old or the New Testament. One day, for example, it might be Genesis 17:10–11, in which God mandated the Israelites to circumcise their children "in the flesh" in order to keep their covenant with Him. What did this passage mean? he would ask. It clearly mandated *physical* circumcision, and the same command could be found in Leviticus, Jeremiah, and at least two dozen passages from the Bible. But an even larger number of verses suggested that circumcision was not a physical but a *spiritual* pact. Deuteronomy 30:6, for example, clearly referred to the circumcision "of the heart." And again, in Romans 2:29 Paul wrote that "true circumcision is of the heart, spiritual not literal." Which one was God's will? The discussion would go on, each man quoting from a different passage, until Segundo would settle the question by quoting Paul, for example from his first letter to the Corinthians: "Circumcision is nothing, and uncircumcision is nothing, but the keeping of the commandments of God." That was the end of the debate, and they all accepted it: circumcision occurred in the heart, in the spirit, not in the physical body.

Segundo would then invite them to pray, each according to what he carried inside. They together would recite another psalm and conclude the session by reciting, "In Jesus's name: Amen."

The most advanced, like Segundo and Castillo, persisted, continuing to study further on their own. After a long workday, they spent the night, each at his home, studying the Bible until they fell asleep. Saturdays they spent all morning and all afternoon studying (together, when Castillo visited Cajamarca) and then shared findings and questions.

They brought the most impenetrable questions to the Reform leaders and felt exasperated when they could provide no answers or when they refused to engage in the discussion. Segundo had his doubts about some of Ellen White's visions. According to her, Jesus had gone from the "first apartment," the holy place in the heavenly sanctuary, to "the holy of holies, the second apartment of the sanctuary," from which he performed his ministrations. That is, following her claim, Jesus was a priest. But to be a priest, one had to descend from the tribe of Levy, like Moses, like Aaron, and Jesus belonged to the tribe of Judah; it made no sense for him to be a priest.

Segundo and Castillo also noted that it was unclear what had happened to the name Israel. It appeared in the Bible for the first time as Jacob's new name and then became the name for all those who descended from him: Israel was the people of God. There was no change to this name throughout the entire book. So why had the name been abandoned? Where, in what place, page, verse of the Bible was this change mentioned? And if there had been no name change, then wasn't the name given by God more valuable than the ones attributed to churches organized so much later? Catholic, Protestant, Baptist, Methodist, Adventist . . .

The Reform pastors grew annoyed by their questions, which deviated from Adventist doctrine. Politely but firmly, they avoided giving an answer. There was no time for explanations; everything in the service was preplanned; they'd talk about it some other time.

Segundo, his brother Álvaro, and Castillo concluded that

the pastors had not studied the prophets in depth and that they simply had no answers to important questions. During one of the movement's general assemblies in Lima, Álvaro and Castillo stood, in the name of the group, and asked a question they'd been obsessed with for some time. At least twenty-one times the Bible instructed to keep the day of the new moon; it was in Isaiah, in Ezra, in Kings, in Chronicles . . . Why did the Reformers not keep it?

They had no answer.

And why did they cook on Saturday, if it was written that they must not do so? The Reform leaders offered no answer either. They said they would get back to them "right away" but never did. Nor did they want to answer where in the Bible was the Trinity of God the Father, Son, and Holy Spirit explained. It had never made sense to Segundo. In the Pentateuch, God was one and only one, and so it was written. Why three, then? And why uphold the Catholic doctrine against divorce? If there was infidelity, there should be divorce. But the pastors neither accepted it nor explained it.

In 1962, one of Peru's leaders in the Adventist Reform Movement, José del Carmen León, suddenly announced that from that moment on Segundo and his group were forbidden to meet with the other leader, Mariano Linares, or any of his followers, whom he said no longer belonged to the faith. Shortly thereafter, Linares met with them and made the same demand: that they no longer meet with León and his followers. The true movement was the one he himself was leading.

But why? Segundo wanted to know. They had been part of one and the same church. What were the differences now? Neither León nor Linares had a straight answer to these questions.

It turned out, Castillo discovered, that it was not simply a question of León against Linares, nor was Peru the only thing at stake: this was a worldwide confrontation. About a decade earlier, before Segundo and his group had joined the Reformers, at one of the movement's general assemblies, the movement had fractured when they elected their new leader.[29] A Brazilian named Carlos Kozel, a pioneer in Reformer evangelization in Peru in the early 1930s, was favored by a majority of delegates there. But his rival, the Romanian Dumitru Nicolici, demanded they also accept absentee ballots from those delegates who backed him but had been unable to travel to the assembly because they lived in Communist countries. Indeed, if those absent had also voted, Nicolici would have been elected president; because this was not allowed, Kozel had won. Nicolici had rejected the election result and taken off with his followers. For years afterward, both sides disputed the church's money and its followers, on the streets and in the courts. Having started in Europe, the fight took a decade to reach Cajamarca. Now Linares and León too were choosing a faction, one aligning with Nicolici, the other with Kozel; and, like them, they were fighting over the money—which Víctor Chico concluded was at the center of the local split—and the faithful.

Segundo, Castillo, and their group of readers found no doctrinal differences whatsoever between the two groups, nothing in the Book that allowed them or encouraged them to back one side or the other. So they announced they would wait for them to reconcile their differences and finally be able to concentrate on what mattered: deciphering and abiding divine will.

In response, the two leaders closed the doors of their respective churches to them and spread the word that they should not be welcomed. Castillo, who had spent his entire religious life in the Reform Movement and earned his living selling Bibles for them, did not want to leave the group. He cried the day he was told to pick between one of the leaders, or the street. But he wouldn't choose. His salvation mattered more, he told them, and he left with Segundo and the others.

And thus, once again, almost a decade after choosing the Adventists, they were without a church. Soon, they would also be without their beloved publication, because only members of the church received it. They were alone.

With no publication and no leader, where could they get answers? Not from the Catholic Church, which lied. Not from Protestant pastors, who refused to respond to them. And did they even need them, anyway? The Assemblyists, as they now called the members of their reading groups in Cajamarca and Trujillo, appealed to Segundo to form their own organization and carry on. Men like him were actually the ones who would find the answers.

At age thirty-five, Segundo had discovered newfound strength, new maturity, within himself. The Assemblyists were right. After all, didn't he know more than the leaders who in theory should have been the ones teaching them?

And so in 1962 he founded his own church.

He named it Israel of God. The name was derived from the Book. The Pentateuch taught that "Israel" was the word referring to God's chosen people, the descendants of Abraham, Isaiah, and Jacob, as they'd never tired of telling the Reform leaders. But they also accepted what they'd learned from them: that both in the prophets and in Revelation, "Israel" referred no longer to those descended from Abraham but to all the faithful, the remnant, the core that had never strayed from the path or fallen into temptation and heresy, as others had. It was written so in Isaiah 10:22: "For though thy people Israel be as the sand of the sea, yet a remnant of them shall return." And in Jeremiah 31:7: "O LORD, save thy people, the remnant of Israel." That remnant included the blood descendants of Israel but also the Gentiles, who, according to Paul's letters, had been included in the plan of salvation thanks to the sacrifice Jesus made. They would carry the good news of the Messiah throughout the world, converting pagans and announcing the Second Coming.

Once the name was chosen, it was time to delineate the structure. But how did one go about building a church? The instructions had to be in the Book, but where? The Catholics based their church on the New Testament; the Adventists, on Revelation. Both had turned out to be a deceit.

Perhaps the magnitude of the task would have been too much had they not discovered, through their constant inquiries, that others like them had also seen the need to find the truth for themselves after attempting to learn from teachers in foreign churches and had fallen into the same dilemma.

One of them stood out: José Alfredo Loje, the leader of a small group headquartered in Lima. Not for his personal history or his origins, which were similar to those of anyone else. He'd been an Adventist until he was expelled, first from the Industrial Institute of Miraflores, run by the church, where he'd been accused of sexual misconduct, and some time later from the Adventist School of Chepén, where he'd been given a second chance with a teaching post but had again committed the same offense. He had then begun to visit churches and Adventist groups, introducing himself as a missionary. In response, the church had sent out a communiqué to all Adventist institutions, denouncing him. Loje was undaunted; he formed his own church, which, in essence, followed the very same Adventist doctrine he'd been taught.

In the 1940s, he had heard about a new church in Chile, one that had also branched off from the Adventists and practiced rituals no one else in Peru (nor almost anywhere else on the continent) was familiar with, and he had traveled to visit it. It was called the Evangelical Church of the New Covenant, but people referred to it as the "church of the *cabañistas*" (tenters), because once a year they set up tents on their land to celebrate the Feast of Tabernacles, commemorating the Israelites' passage through the Sinai Desert. It was one of two unique, small groups, each with a few hundred followers sprinkled throughout the country, which had split over political views, one accusing the other of harboring Communist sympathies, illegal in Chile.[30]

The *cabañistas* were attempting to establish coherence between the readings of the Old and New Testaments, between Abraham, Moses, David, and the prophets, on the one hand, and Jesus and Paul, on the other. Thus, they believed that Israel was the *spiritual* people of God and therefore they, too, the *cabañistas,* formed part of it. Their way of worshipping God, their religious rites, were those laid out in the Pentateuch; all they had to do was understand the connection to the Advent of Jesus and its meaning as stated by Paul in his letters.

Loje had used those ideas to refound his church, now under the name Israelite Evangelical Association of the New Covenant. He kept the Saturday Sabbath but used a different calendar, one taken from the Old Testament.[31]

Álvaro had heard that they kept the feast days described in Leviticus 23, which no one else in Peru kept, and had visited them at their meetinghouse in Lima. On his return, Álvaro brought Segundo a copy of the calendar Loje used as his guide. This was the answer they'd been fruitlessly searching for with the Reformers: on it, the new moon was marked as the first day of the month. Intrigued, Segundo too traveled to the capital to meet Loje and hear him present his doctrine.

Loje had condensed it into a fifty-page pamphlet he called *The Treatise on the Seven Words of Knowledge.* The document detailed the proper way to celebrate the feast days described in Leviticus 23: the Sabbath, which he referred to as Shabbat, the seventh day of each week; Passover, or Pesach, in the month of

Nisan, for seven consecutive days; First Fruits, or Omer, also in the month of Nisan; Pentecost, or Shavuot, seven weeks after Passover, in the month of Sivan; Trumpets, or Rosh Hashanah, which was the feast of New Year, in the month of Tishrei; Atonement, or Yom Kippur; and finally, also in Tishrei, was Cabañas, that is, the Feast of Tabernacles, or Sukkot, which lasted seven days.

Loje seemed to discover a harmonious way to unite the Pentateuch's very specific references to the history of the people of Israel, the passion of Christ as described in the Gospels, and the prophecy of his return in Revelation. Specifically, this meant that Passover, with the washing of feet, celebrated the people of Israel's liberation from Egypt but *also* the ritual of Christ's death and resurrection; First Fruits, the following Saturday, was a feast of the first harvest (Leviticus 23:10–11) and *also* of the resurrection of Christ (Matthew 27:51–53); Pentecost commemorated, yes, God's giving of the law to Moses but *also* included an entire day of prayer and song in praise of the Holy Spirit who had descended over the apostles like "an early rain"; Tabernacles, it was true, celebrated the people of Israel's journey through the desert, but was *also* part of a wider celebration of man's journey on earth. New Year, or the Feast of Trumpets, was celebrated as the day of Jesus's birth on the lunar calendar, since the Gregorian one was a human, rather than divine, construction.

Just before undertaking His creation of the heavens and the earth, Loje taught, God had met "in counsel" with His son, Jesus Christ, to consider His next work. It was then that He decided to create the feast days, "as a testimony to Jesus and so that all creatures could enjoy all the divine privileges by participating in the glorification of the Son of God." In other words, God knew from the very beginning everything that was to occur, including His own son's sacrifice. And by sending the rites to Moses, as explained in the Old Testament, He was not only referring to all that occurred in that moment but anticipating what would be recorded in the New Testament. The entire Bible could be read through this new lens: by thinking that God had anticipated every event that was to occur before He'd even begun His creation of the world, of man and his travails. The feasts, rituals of worship, the series of tasks given specifically to Israel, were the key ever offered to the faithful to unlock the history explained in the Book. There were seven feasts, as were the days of creation, the perfect number of God. Laws had been imposed on man to *help him in his spiritual growth.* Obeying them was vital if one wanted to obtain salvation.

In *The Treatise on the Seven Words of Knowledge,* Segundo thought he had found the coherence he'd lacked to unite the parts of the Bible—the beginning, the end, and everything in between. Perhaps this was the instruction manual he required. Whenever he could, Segundo traveled twenty-four hours by bus to meet with Loje and his Israelites of the New Covenant, and then returned to Cajamarca on an equally exhausting journey to convey all that he'd learned. He studied Loje's writings carefully and embraced his interpretation: they, too, would from now on follow the lunar calendar; they, too, would restructure their lives and their worship.

Segundo had refused, however, to join Loje's church. It was true that his interpretation and doctrine seemed to be correct. But how could he follow a leader who on Saturdays cooked with fire and made his employees work? Who continued to believe in and preach the Trinity, referring to the Father, the Son, and the Holy Ghost not as one God but as *gods.* And who, much to Segundo's horror, had a miniskirted secretary sitting beside him. Segundo had already learned that God's message could never err, but what could—and very often did—was the man transmitting it.

Segundo had no intention of being a prophet or messiah. The meetings of Israel of God on the second floor of his home were assemblies of brothers. Anyone was at liberty to suggest that an interpretation of a passage, word, or book of the Bible struck him as mistaken and offer another in its place. All the man had to do was to find three Bible passages upholding his assertion.

Segundo believed not in simply exerting power but in the fundamental importance of knowledge and teaching. From the Protestants, therefore, came the idea of governing through a council of elders, or wise folk. Segundo and Castillo were among them, of course, but so too were Álvaro, Demetrio Guerra, and José Aguilar.

Guerra, the cousin with whom Segundo had practiced wrestling and who had been one of his early followers, was keen and impassioned and had stood firmly beside Segundo over the years. Aguilar, who was the same age as Segundo and equally studious when it came to the Bible, had joined them in Trujillo. He came from Loje's church and had a predilection for the prophetic books, in which he found keys to much of what was going on at the time and would occur in the future. He was learned in history and philosophy and always reading. Aguilar went around with a briefcase in which he carried a small chalkboard that he pulled out whenever he came across someone he could discuss things with. "We can study the Bible to discover the truth," he would always begin. He traveled the Andes by foot, through villages and farms, in search of pastors, friends, and anyone interested. He was kind and joyful, easily likable, and straightforward and had a ready smile and neat mustache. People appreciated the fact that he was as well spoken as Castillo but easier to be around; people felt comfortable with him. When not traveling through the mountains, he preached at a small rented locale in El Alambre, a poor neighborhood in Trujillo where he lived with his wife and children.

But while Segundo preferred discussion and Bible study, the assembly clamored for clear leadership. Someone had to tell them what to do. If there were five on the council, who should they turn to? The two most central members were Segundo and Castillo. They still lived far apart, one in Cajamarca and the other 180 miles away in Trujillo, and though they were one and the same church, each had his own local followers. One of the two, or someone else, the Assemblyists maintained, should make the decisions for all. For example, someone needed to tell them where to meet for feast days. And what each family had to bring for each occasion. And there were so many other practical matters that required final, concrete decisions.

So it was resolved that they'd leave it to luck, as did the apostles after the death and resurrection of Christ. It was written in Acts 1:21–26 that the apostle Peter saw it necessary to choose one among them to replace Judas Iscariot, who had been their treasurer before he betrayed Jesus and hanged himself. Two candidates, Barsabbas and Matthias, were proposed. The apostles cast lots to choose between them; Matthias was elected. So, once a year, all those present at the Israel of God assemblies wrote the names of the candidates for leadership on small scraps of paper, folded them up, and tossed them into a bag. Then a child was asked to pull one out. Whoever was chosen would lead the church that year. Segundo and Castillo, of course, were always among the candidates.

As far as doctrine, the new church combined Adventist rites

and worship with Loje's Israelite feast days and Segundo's strict tone. On the Sabbath, rest and Bible study were mandatory. The Reformers, like Loje, had believed that heating food, turning on lights, and listening to the radio on the Sabbath were acceptable; that was no longer permitted. One Friday evening at Segundo's house, the food was still half-cooked on the stove. "Hurry, sisters," he told the women cooking, "the sun will soon be gone." The cooks both revered and feared Segundo, but the food was not ready and they kept cooking. "It matters more to obey and serve God than to listen to men," he thundered, quoting from Acts 5:29, and dumped a bucket of water on the fire.

The group went back to eating meat after concluding that the Reformers' vegetarianism was a deceit. Leviticus 11, Víctor Castillo observed, listed the clean and unclean animals, and the clean ones, he said, "shall ye eat." So why not eat them? It was true that Paul, as the Reformers maintained, had said, "Wherefore, if meat make my brother to offend, I will eat no flesh while the world standeth, lest I make my brother to offend." But to Castillo it was clear that Paul was not seeking to implicate others in this affirmation; eating meat was not forbidden, they resolved.

As they'd learned from Loje, at Passover they prayed, ate unleavened bread, and rested for seven days. During the Feast of Weeks, or Pentecost, they prayed, ate leavened bread, gave thanks to God for the fruits of the earth, and did no work for eight days. During Tabernacles they slept in tents for a whole week. And on fast days, nobody ate, whether adult or child. Like the Reformers, the men wore dark colors and the women dressed in long skirts and wore no makeup. The children were forbidden to play with anyone who did not belong to the community.

They didn't register Israel of God with the Peruvian authorities, since they deemed human permission unnecessary; they answered only to God. But their lives were becoming increasingly difficult. They could ignore Catholic society, but Catholic society was not ignoring them. Keeping the Sabbath was difficult for those whose employers required them to work on Saturday. When they got to school on Mondays, the children were rapped on their hands with rulers for having missed Saturday morning classes. Catechism was a mandatory subject in public schools; the children in Israel of God recited their lessons by heart while telling themselves, as their parents had taught them, that the words coming out of their mouths were nothing but lies.

Some faltered and worked on the Sabbath or sent their children to class.

It went on like this for five long years. Segundo longed to move. He dreamed of living someplace where they were free to serve God without interference, someplace where the children would grow up pure and uncorrupted. And everyone wanted to escape poverty, to find some way to subsist that would allow them to be independent.

"And I heard another voice from heaven, saying, Come out of her, my people, that ye be not partakers of her sins, and that ye receive not of her plagues."

But where to go?

They took inspiration from another group that had stemmed from Loje's church. The church had gone into decline for lack of followers and finally ended up folding, but before it did, it helped produce a new prophet. Ezequiel Ataucusi Gamonal[32] had been an Adventist, like Loje, and like him had also been expelled, although not for moral infractions but for showing up one fine day dressed head to toe in a garnet-red tunic, offering his tale of ascension to the heavens, a tale reminiscent of that of Ellen White.

The way he told it, Ezequiel, a cobbler and carpenter from the southern city of Arequipa, had had a series of visions since the age of twelve but hadn't understood what they were until an Adventist missionary gave him his first Bible, in which he read Isaiah and realized that it was God speaking to him. One day he was taken to the First Heaven, where there was a city made of white metal, then the Second Heaven, which was a dark desert, and the Third Heaven, where God, Jesus, and the Holy Spirit sat awaiting him at a table. God wrote the Ten Commandments on a chalkboard and ordered Ezequiel to copy them down on a card. Jesus ordered him to take them to the entire world.

Ezequiel was drawn, as Segundo had been, by Loje's observance of the feast days of the Pentateuch and joined his church. But he soon found it limited in ambitions and decidedly too small. He too created a new church, which he called the Evangelical Association of the Israelite Mission of the New Universal Covenant. He seems to have set his sights if not literally on the whole world, then at least on all those who had come down from the mountains in search of a better life on new roads built by the government in the 1950s. They lived, first in clusters of dozens and later in hundreds of thousands, in miserable slums in Peru's larger cities. In just twenty years, Lima had more than tripled its population, and more than one-third of it lived in *pueblos jóvenes,* so-called young towns: overcrowded shanty-towns full of shacks made of tin, drums, cardboard and wood scraps, rugs, and boxes.[33] Only a privileged few had homes with adobe walls, and an exclusive minority enjoyed houses made of brick. These adventurers had created in their wretched suburbs a cultural mélange some referred to as "chicha culture," a fusion of their Andean past and urban present that contained uncertainty as well as a thirst for hope, which preachers like Ezequiel aspired to quench with their divine messages.

Ezequiel offered them something Loje and others had failed to create: a syncretic "chicha" *religion* that brought together the God in the Bible and their own ancestors. In the books of Job and Isaiah, he found proof that Peruvians were the chosen people. According to him, the Inca had wrought the wrath of God by hurling the Bible to the ground during his fateful encounter with the conquistadors in Cajamarca's central square. God had sided with the Spaniards and thus Atahualpa had lost his empire and his life. The Catholic Church was evil on earth. But the Incas' descendants would migrate one last time to the Land Without Evil, Paititi, the sacred city the Incas dreamed of that over time had blended with ideas of El Dorado imagined by the Spanish. There, in that land located in the Amazon jungle, Atahualpa's head and body would be joined again, and the Second Coming would take place.

With this in mind, in 1964 Ezequiel founded a colony on the edge of the Amazon closest to Lima. He called it Alto Paucartambo Piñaplás Canaan of Palestine. They celebrated the Full Moon, Passover as the Lord's Supper, Pentecost, Azymes (the feast of unleavened bread), and the Sabbath. They used the river to baptize in the Holy Spirit and circumcised their hearts but not their foreskins. The faithful called Ataucusi Father Israel.

Early on, Segundo visited Ezequiel in Lima and listened to his ideas with genuine curiosity, just as he listened to anyone interested in the Bible. There was some common ground, of course, in the observance of the Sabbath, the Full Moon, and the Old Testament feasts, but just as with Loje, he found little to admire in him as a leader or preacher.

His brother Álvaro continued paying visits to Loje, and during one of those visits an envoy from Ataucusi's colony in the Amazonian province of Chanchamayo came to request that a Bible scholar go speak to a local tribe who had no one to teach them. Not one member of Loje's church offered to go, but Álvaro did. Before visiting the tribe, he traveled to meet Ezequiel in the Amazonian village of San Ramón, where he was then based. They spoke over the course of an entire day. That proved enough for Álvaro to realize that they didn't hold the same beliefs. Ezequiel didn't even use the lunar calendar anymore and had gone back to the Gregorian one. As Álvaro said years later, "He was worse than the Adventists."

Nevertheless, Álvaro had been impressed by the extensive land the church had claimed in the jungle and told his brother so on his return from the excursion. The jungle, particularly the vast area where the Andes meets the Amazon, known as *ceja de selva,* or the "jungle's rim," had been attracting settlers from the highlands since the beginning of the decade—it had become harder to find a lot, to make a living, in the overpopulated coastal cities—and in 1963 President Fernando Belaúnde Terry had announced the construction of the first highway to cut through the jungle, connecting it with cities north and south.[34] That was the answer, Segundo realized. That was the solution: move into the Amazon, closer to God and farther from man. Like Ataucusi, they could claim a remote parcel of land and found their own colony. All they had to do was establish it.

Sixteen volunteers accompanied Segundo on the expedition in the winter of 1967. There were veterans, like Demetrio Guerra, as well as younger folks, like Julio Raza, who had been with Israel of God only a short time. Julio was from El Cortijo, on the outskirts of Trujillo. His parents were Adventist farmers, and as a boy, if he wasn't helping them with the harvest, he listened to the pastor's sermons and remained unmoved. One Saturday morning while walking down a street in the neighborhood of El Alambre, he heard a booming voice that made him stop. What a crowd must the man have had before him, to be speaking that way, Julio thought, and followed the sound to a door. Looking in, he saw José Aguilar smile and keep speaking in his stentorian tone while amiably waving him in. Julio stared incredulously into the room, empty save for one lone woman sitting directly in front of the preacher, listening to every word with rapt attention.

How much passion must this man have felt, to speak like that for just one person? Julio wondered. He sat down and listened to the end. Aguilar spoke about the people of Israel and their passage from Egypt. It was a story that Julio especially loved, for it transported him to his own birth, or to the tale his mother had told him about it: on returning from a day in the fields, she'd given birth to him, alone, on the ground, with no midwife, like a doe or—he thought—like the women of Egypt.

When the sermon ended, Julio asked Aguilar how many people he regularly met with. Just the sister, he responded. How extraordinary, Julio thought as he was leaving, to dedicate so much passion week after week to a single parishioner. A few Sundays later, on his twentieth birthday, he was playing soccer and broke another player's tibia and fibula with a violent tackle. It had been such a dangerous foul that he was jailed for it. In the cold cell, Julio commended himself to God: "If you look after me, I promise I will obey." He was sentenced to two years in prison, but granted provisional release since he had no previous criminal record. Julio went straight to the home of the man he'd injured, offering him a plate of food and his apologies; both were accepted. Julio told himself there was no such thing as coincidence. What had happened was a sign from God. He returned to El Alambre in search of Aguilar and that very day joined Israel of God.

And so it was that out of faith, and need, seventeen men set off from Cajamarca. Leaving behind the crowded, immovable city bristling with churches and priests, they trekked up mountainous roads, through clean, familiar air, to the dense, hot, rainy forests of the northeast.

A bus left them in Bagua Grande, where Segundo hired two local brothers as guides. They took a boat across the river Utcubamba, a branch of the Marañón—which itself was a tributary of the Amazon—and made their way into the jungle on foot. They kept walking until they hit a wall of vegetation, a tangle of wild fuchsia that could be navigated only by hacking their way through with machetes. Making any headway at all was an exhausting endeavor. Not only did they have to clear a path using the strength of their arms, but the jungle was not flat, as they'd imagined; instead, as one of the seventeen said, it was a "land of profundities" that climbed steeply and then came to sudden vertical drops. The ground was a quagmire covered in dead leaves, a slippery surface on which simply keeping their balance was a feat. They trekked through a tunnel of thick vegetation so dense there was no sky, in hot pungent air filled with bloodthirsty flying insects. Sudden rains drenched them without warning, and then just as suddenly the sun would emerge, scalding the earth. They continued to make their weary way, clothes stuck to them like a second skin, knees aching, skin burning, hands covered in calluses.

For an entire day they lurched and stumbled their way along, heading toward the river Tafur, a tributary of the Utcubamba. A plague of locusts had devastated the place years earlier, and it was now property of the Peruvian government, which is to say it had no owner, or at least in their view. Segundo was in the advance guard of the expedition, along with the Bagua locals. One brother led the way, armed with a machete. Behind him, shotgun on his shoulder, came Segundo. His wiry, muscular body moved rhythmically through the foliage, strong arms pulling aside the vegetation like a native.

Behind Segundo was the second brother, also armed with a shotgun. Close, perhaps too close. The others weeded their way along the rear guard, widening the path for their return. On the second day, they were startled by the sound of a shotgun. Were they being attacked? Frightened, with not enough empty space to see what was going on, they ran ahead in search of Segundo. And they found him on his knees, body doubled over, his back stained with blood. The second brother's shotgun had fired, he claimed, accidentally (María Teresa would doubt this claim; she suspected the brothers didn't want the Cajamarcans to occupy the land); the shot had hit Segundo's scapula.

They laid him out and tried to stanch the bleeding. Segundo told them not to bother.

"My life is leaving me," he said. It was what God had ordained, and they should not fight it.

"Trust in the Lord, brother," Castillo encouraged him.

The guides ran off in search of mud and matico leaves.

"Israel is the people of God. God is One. This is one more test," Segundo recited.

Suddenly horrific shrieking filled the jungle. In terror, they realized that the uproar was coming from the treetops. The scent of blood had attracted a troop of monkeys who, howling and breaking branches, were now rushing toward the clearing in search of their prey. Fearing for their lives, the Israelites fired into the air, shouting at them. The monkeys fled. But how long until they returned?

In that moment of unease, Segundo stood and began to walk. Julio Raza looked at him in disbelief, astonished at this resurrection. Segundo mumbled that he was fine, his face as pale as a river-washed stone. But he was unable to remain upright. They helped him lie down once more. The guides covered the open edges of his wound with matico sap and bandaged his chest tight. Using a blanket and two branches, they fashioned a stretcher and laid him on top of it. Then they took turns carrying him.

On the trip back, Segundo was delirious with fever. They walked for days, hacking their way through with machetes, not getting anywhere. They didn't recognize the terrain; so deep in the jungle, they had no perspective or sense of direction. Why was it taking so long? Too late, they realized that their guides, unsettled by the accident (or was María Teresa right?), were leading them deeper into the jungle rather than back to Bagua.

Perhaps they'd never find their way out.

Perhaps Segundo really would die there.

One night, exhausted after climbing a muddy hill, they laid a blanket of twigs over the swampy ground and went to sleep.

Suddenly the roar of pumas woke them.

"Danger! Everyone on alert!" the guides shouted.

They picked up their patient and began rushing down the hill at top speed, stumbling in the dark. The roars drew nearer. Segundo commanded them to stop.

"Our Lord is testing us, our Lord will help us. Fear not!"

And he began to sing Psalm 121. The others joined, singing as loudly as they could:

> I will lift up mine eyes unto the hills, from whence
> cometh my help.
> My help cometh from the Lord, which made heaven
> and earth.
> He will not suffer thy foot to be moved: he that
> keepeth thee will not slumber.
> Behold, he that keepeth Israel shall neither slumber
> nor sleep.
> The Lord is thy keeper: the Lord is thy shade upon thy
> right hand.
> The sun shall not smite thee by day, nor the moon by
> night.
> The Lord shall preserve thee from all evil: he shall
> preserve thy soul.
> The Lord shall preserve thy going out and thy coming
> in from this time forth, and even for evermore.

When they stopped, the humming of cicadas was all that could be heard in the jungle. They returned to their twig-covered beds, afraid to sleep, but overcome by exhaustion.

Segundo asked Julio Raza if he was tired. He said he was not. Could he keep watch? "I don't see why not," Julio replied. "Then watch over me," Segundo said. He explained how to fire the shotgun, handed him a flashlight, and went to sleep.

Several minutes went by. There was no sign of the pumas, no sign of the monkeys. With the shotgun resting over his shoulder and a flashlight in one hand, Julio began to nod off.

A rustling in the bushes a short distance away woke him. Frightened, he fired before thinking. But there was no explosion. Instead, the flashlight lit up the face of one of the Israelites. Staring into Julio's eyes, the man lamented he couldn't sleep. Julio had "fired" the flashlight; he was ashamed. And yet God had protected him: he'd failed as a lookout, but since it wasn't the shotgun in his hand, he'd been saved from killing a man.

The following morning, they continued on their journey. They were nearly out of *panatela,* the rice-and-sugar paste that had been their only sustenance since the accident. Three long days later, after climbing a huge tree, one of the guides glimpsed a house in the distance. We'll arrive tomorrow, he announced.

They did, and kept the Sabbath in that house, where a local family lived. On Sunday, they transferred Segundo to Bagua Grande. A local checked out his wound: the matico sap had kept it from getting infected. Once back in Cajamarca, sitting on a chair in his mother's house, he had fifteen pellets removed from his back. Segundo withstood the procedure with no anesthesia.

When he'd recovered, Segundo recruited more men from among his acquaintances in Rodacocha and returned to the jungle. The group traveled the same treacherous path: leaving Bagua Grande behind, they crossed the Utcubamba and walked along the trail that they themselves had cleared. When they reached the place in which Segundo had been shot, where the first expedition had ended, the men unsheathed their machetes and kept going. Thus they extended the path, step by step and blow by blow, until they reached the shore of a stream.

And there they stopped, not because it was the ideal setting, but because most of the men could not, or would not, go any farther. It was a remote and hostile place. Yet they were sure they'd reached the land where God wanted them to be, the place where, like King David, they could establish if not a kingdom, then at least a settlement, a place in the jungle for Segundo to hammer the sign of his church, a place he called, after 2 Samuel 5, Hebron.

After measuring the land, they divided it into twenty-one equal plots, one for each of the men who would settle there with their families. (A similar number of the faithful chose not to go, whether for lack of adventurous spirit or to keep from losing their jobs in Cajamarca and Trujillo.) Each plot ran perpendicular to the stream and was 330 feet wide, giving them all direct access to water. It rained several times a day, and the land would yield crops twice a year; all they had to do was weed, sow, weed again, and then harvest.

Three months it took them to clear the land. On their plots, each of them built a small wooden house with a calamite roof, raised up on stilts to keep the snakes out. On finishing the workday, they would cook yucca and rice over a campfire they lit in the rocks. On Fridays, when the sun went down, they threw water on the fire, prayed, studied, and discussed the Bible, just as they had in Cajamarca and Trujillo. They spent their first Feast of the Tabernacles there.

Next, they worked together to erect a small oak and cedar house on central land. Inside, they built a room where they would gather for Bible study and discussion and to celebrate feast days and pray three times a week. Another room was built of logs to house a small school where they would teach children up to the third grade. The older children would go to school in Naranjillo, the closest town. Others would stay in Cajamarca—including María Teresa and Segundo's children, who stayed in the care of Raquel, the eldest sister—and travel to Hebron only for the most important feast days.

When the work was done, the men returned to their respective cities to gather their possessions and their families; most of them were married and had children, except for Víctor Chico, who lived with his mother and three siblings, and Castillo, who was single and lived alone. They brought them into the jungle on burros and horseback. Once settled, they dug furrows and planted purple corn, beans, plantains, sugarcane, coffee, and yucca. They learned to prevent malaria, avoid dehydration, treat sunburn. What they planted and raised actually grew. Each family had their own turkeys, roosters, and hens; Demetrio Guerra had fourteen cattle. They fished in the stream. Castillo proposed that they set up a cooperative and share everything equally, but the others insisted on keeping separate accounts. Carpenters, employees, workers, drivers, and traveling salesmen from the highlands had, through sheer willpower, become small farmers in a hot jungle.

They all continued to celebrate feast days the way they'd learned from Loje. During the Feast of Tabernacles, they slept for an entire week in huts made of branches and leaves, even in torrential tropical downpours. They did not cook or heat food for eight days during Passover, eating only fruits, sweet potatoes they'd cooked in advance, and uncooked porridge they flavored with lime. The night of Holy Saturday no one slept: they studied the Bible, sang, and recited psalms until the break of day.

The families who had remained in Cajamarca traveled to

Hebron for feast days, on exhausting perilous journeys. Julio Raza once got lost along the way, the night before Tabernacles. He ran all day until coming upon a house in the middle of the jungle, thinking he was saved. But when the woman of the house caught sight of him, Julio saw her run to begin sharpening her machete. The locals didn't take any chances. The Aguaruna were a tribe who had ruled the area until Peru forced them deep into the jungle; they made tsantsas, shrunken human heads, and had never been conquered by the Incas or the Spaniards. Outlaws and fugitives roamed the area, too. "Look, I've got my Bible right here," Julio implored. But the woman did not trust him. So Julio spent the night alone in the jungle, not sleeping. The following day he started on his way and, in an act he attributed to the grace of God, finally made it to Hebron.

Despite the difficulties, they were happy. They had made it. They plowed the land and kept their animals, selling what they didn't consume in the nearest town. They lived true to God, with no one to judge them, tempt them, or keep them from their path. With no ruler, bishop, neighbor, or school principal to keep them from worshipping God. No false idols, churches, pastors, or prophets. Alone with God and His Book.

Because they lived so far from other churches, preachers, and prophets, there was only the Book to give them answers now. Segundo turned to it again and again, only to be confounded by the same questions, the same mysteries that had obsessed him for twenty long years.

About a year after he settled in Hebron, he traveled to search for answers in more Bibles. It took him two days to reach Lima, including eight-hour treks through the jungle, but he made them happily in order to visit the Bible Society. He would get off the bus, walk through Lima's stately Parque de la Reserva, and reach the big old house on the corner of Avenida Petit Thouars and Avenida Alejandro Tirado. It had once been a family home but was now a bookstore. In what had been the reception hall, there were now display cases; the bedrooms had been turned into meeting rooms and lecture halls. The society had all kinds of Christian Bibles: some more luxurious, others cheaper, some with watermark inscriptions, others printed in Braille, and even some that were illustrated for children. There was one Bible for Catholics, another for Mormons, and others for the various Protestant credos. They had no specialized literature of any kind, but the regulars—a handful who came to attend lectures—shared information and recommended expert treatises to one another.

Segundo had read all of the Bibles he could. He would go from one to another comparing the same verse. In the various versions, God was called Jehovah, Elohim, or a more generic Lord; He was "tender" in one and simply "merciful" in another. The men in one Bible "honored" Him and those in another "feared" Him; they either were ineluctably guided by their own "flesh" or were mere victims of their "weak nature." Depending on which version he looked at, the sound of "harps" might become the sound of "sitars," a "plant" turned into a "bush," "vapor" became "water," and "waters" became "waterfalls." Segundo understood that some of these discrepancies were the product of doctrinal difference. The Catholic Bible, for instance, included the so-called deuterocanonical books (Tobit, Judith, Ecclesiasticus, two books of Maccabees, Wisdom, Baruch), which the Protestants branded as "apocryphal" and, even if they read and studied them, did not consider them sacred. In his German translation of the Bible, Luther had placed them at the end of the Old Testament with a warning: "Apocrypha: these are books which are not held equal to the Holy Scriptures, but are useful and good to read." Other variations seemed to have no explanation and were added to the mysteries to be solved. Such were the disquisitions that Segundo lost himself in during his visits to the big old house on Avenida Petit Thouars.

Álvaro, too, often visited the society and on one occasion found a pamphlet inviting people to a lecture about the first complete Spanish translation of the Bible. The history of this Bible, the pamphlet said, went as far back as the origins of the Protestant Reformation.

The Bible had been the principal weapon in the war between Catholics and Protestants. In it, according to the Protestants, the faithful could find all of the errors and lies told by the popes; in it they could discover the truth of Christ for themselves: that was why it had to be made available in all languages. The first Bible to come out of the Reformation was the one Luther himself translated into German, based on Hebrew and ancient Greek texts. But to the Catholics, maintaining control over who read it and how it was interpreted was critical to fighting

Segundo Villaneuva's childhood home in Rodacocha, 2016.

The Peruvian Andes near Segundo Villanueva's birthplace, 2016.

Abigail Correa, Segundo Villanueva's mother,
Peru, 1960.
Courtesy Yehoshua Tzidkiya.

Segundo Villanueva, Peru, 1950.
Courtesy Yehoshua Tzidkiya.

Segundo Villanueva and friends, Cajamarca, 1955.
Courtesy Yehoshua Tzidkiya.

Segundo Villanueva and María Teresa Correa, Peru, 1960.
Courtesy Yehoshua Tzidkiya.

Members of the Bnei Moshe community in El Milagro, Trujillo, 1987.
Courtesy Yehoshua Tzidkiya.

Segundo, second from right, in the Bnei Moshe synagogue,
El Milagro, Trujillo, 1989.

Courtesy Yehoshua Tzidkiya.

A group of Bnei Moshe celebrating Sukkot in El Milagro, Trujillo, 1988.
Courtesy Yehoshua Tzidkiya.

Segundo and a group of Bnei Moshe during Sukkot, El Milagro, Trujillo, 1988.
Courtesy Yehoshua Tzidkiya.

Zerubbabel Tzidkiya in Elon Moreh, 1990.

Courtesy Yehoshua Tzidkiya.

the Reformation's heresy and defending their authority. If "the Sacred Books are permitted everywhere and without discrimination in the vernacular, there will by reason of the boldness of men arise therefrom more harm than good,"[35] their priests claimed. Between 1545 and 1563, at the Council of Trent, papal delegates, cardinals, patriarchs, bishops, and archbishops met and determined that the only authorized version of the Bible was the Vulgate, translated into Latin in the fourth century by a monk later canonized as Saint Jerome. All other versions were banned.

In conquered America, where the church aspired to keep hold of its monopoly on faith, which had already been lost in Europe, this meant eliminating the Spanish translation undertaken by Casiodoro de Reina, a monk from the Order of Saint Jerome.[36] Shortly after joining their monastery in Seville, Reina had rebelled and converted to Protestantism. Luther's German translation of the Bible had already been published, as had an incomplete English translation, and Bibles were coming out in Danish, French, and Belorussian. But in Spain there was no place for heresy. Reina had been forced to flee the convent with a dozen other monks who'd been denounced to the Inquisition. His first complete translation of the Bible into Spanish was published in Basel, Switzerland, in 1569, with the books ordered exactly as they were in the Catholic Bible. The Vatican immediately included it in its catalog of banned books.

The Bible, banned by the pope. Was this not the greatest proof of its authenticity? Segundo must have wondered. Yet in the prologue to this first edition[37]—reproduced in the pamphlet Álvaro had picked up at the Bible Society in Lima—Casiodoro de Reina explained that he'd based his translation, to the extent possible, on the original texts of the Old Testament, in Hebrew, and the New Testament, in ancient Greek. But because those texts were old and, in some cases, impossible to obtain, he'd had to complement them with other versions, including Saint Jerome's Vulgate and an earlier, preliminary Spanish edition of the New Testament. Each of them had defects, he admitted. The Vulgate, in particular, was "full of errors" that altered the original meaning "countless times." Even his own translation should be distrusted, he warned, even though he had considered every possible interpretation.

Segundo knew, of course, that the Bible had been translated. But since all his life he'd spoken, written, and read only one language, it had never occurred to him that the transfer from one to another could constitute a problem. On one side of his prologue, Segundo read, Reina noted that he'd added "the various interpretations that we could not include in the text, so that the reader might take the one that seems best, should the one we selected not be pleasing." Errors? Various interpretations? The reader should "take the one that seems best"? This was a scandal. The Word of God was one, infallible, and true. How could a man change it at will?

That was the problem: the translator. Men and their interpretations, disobedience, not adhering strictly to the letter of God. Was it "And on the seventh day God ended His work which He had done, and He rested on the seventh day from all His work which He had done," as one translation said, or was it "By the seventh day God had finished the work he had been doing; so on the seventh day he rested from all his work"? In the first case, it seemed that God had also worked on the seventh day; in the second, that He'd spent the entire seventh day resting. These interpretations opened a chasm between divine meaning and human understanding, between the will of God and the action of men. And only the original words, those that contained the meaning God intended, could close it. What was required was to dispense with the translations, dodge them like obstacles, and go back to the original word, as it had been pronounced for the first time and was intended forever.

What was vital, he realized, was learning to read the original: the Bible in Hebrew. The society's museum had one on show in a display case. Until then it must have seemed to him a historical curiosity, sitting beside a copy of the Gutenberg Bible, printed in Germany and translated by Luther, or the Bibles translated into Indigenous languages, or the battery-operated Bibles you could listen to like radios. But that was the only Bible he wanted, the Bible in the original. The true Bible. Where could he get it?

But it wasn't only a matter of obtaining it. Even if he had it in his hands, how would he read it? He knew the Hebrew alphabet. He'd read it in Psalm 119, in which each verse began with one of its letters.

"Aleph. Blessed are those whose ways are blameless, who walk according to the law of the Lord.

"Beth. How can a young person stay on the path of purity?

"Gimel. Be good to your servant while I live, that I may obey your word."

And so on. In Spanish, this made no sense: a word without a meaning, which in fact was the transliteration of a Hebrew letter, followed by a text praising God. In the original Hebrew version, however, the first word of each verse began with that Hebrew letter, as if the letter itself created the word and the verse, as if the entire alphabet served to praise God. Similarly, in the Hebrew Bible, each book of the Pentateuch was named for one of the first words in that book. Genesis, for example, was called *B'resheet,* which in Hebrew meant "In the beginning."

How many other mysteries might be thus resolved? Once back in Hebron, Segundo had both the children and the adults of Israel of God begin memorizing the alphabet and on a subsequent visit to Lima bought a Bible in Hebrew.

But what for, if there was no one who could read it? He could touch it, skim through it, strike it with his fingers, but its message remained just as elusive.

Segundo set off again, on a crucial expedition to Lima. As usual, he headed to the Bible Society. This time, however, he asked not for new versions of the Book, or for scholarly works about it, but for someone who knew Hebrew.

Hebrew? "The Jews," they responded.

The Jews.

Of course. The Jews!

But where, in Peru, could he find authentic Jews? Where were the descendants of the people who had made a pact with God in the Sinai Desert, the people from whom Jesus descended? He had searched in vain for them in the past. Years earlier, he'd sent Álvaro to Celendín, in the highlands, near Rodacocha. Celendín was the place where they made the toquilla straw hats people wore in Cajamarca; it was also the place his father was headed when he met his death. According to an ancient legend, a town full of tall white men with light hair and eyes had hidden there, after the Inquisition, and those men had been Jews. Álvaro searched and searched, but on his return reported that he'd seen nothing but Peruvian mountain people who looked no different from anyone else.

In Cajamarca, Segundo had managed to find one: José Goldstein, owner of a bazaar near the main square. Goldstein lit candles on Fridays at dusk, rested on Saturday, and celebrated certain feast days, alone. But he was married to a Catholic, and his daughters attended Catholic school. After speaking to Goldstein about the Bible, Segundo had invited him to spend a few Saturdays with Israel of God. Goldstein was appreciative: "You are my brother, through Adam and Eve." But he was just one man, with no community or church, and was nothing like the men and women of the Book.

Where could he find *authentic* Jews?

Two blocks from here, they said.

Segundo left the Bible Society, walked down Avenida Petit Thouars, crossed Avenida Alejandro Tirado and Calle Mariano Carranza, and came to the corner of Calle Enrique Villar. There stood an unassuming two-story building from the 1930s, nothing to distinguish it but a sign that stated it was the headquarters of the Sephardic Jewish Charitable Society.

Segundo knocked on the door.

It was opened by a man with a black beard and curly hair, the crown of his head covered by a small circular cap, knotted tassels dangling out from under his shirt. Segundo introduced himself as leader of the Israelites. The bearded man introduced himself as Rabbi Abraham Benhamú.

Segundo told him the story of Israel of God and the founding of Hebron in the Amazon, recounted the way they kept the Sabbath and observed feast days, and the way they ate, following the teachings of the Bible. The rabbi listened, moved and yet feeling a secret, growing unease. What was this highlander doing in a synagogue? What did he want?

To learn Hebrew, Segundo finally explained.

Relieved, the rabbi went to his office. He had designed a way to learn Hebrew in four lessons, a method that was used to teach children, and he'd written it down on a few sheets of paper. He gave them to Segundo. Benhamú also told him how to find the Hebrew teacher at the Jewish school who could help him obtain a Hebrew-Spanish dictionary. And he explained how to get to Stadium bookstore, in San Isidro, Lima's most upscale neighborhood, where they sold a book called *Jewish Traditions and Customs,*[38] which children used to prepare for their bar and bat mitzvah, the rite of passage marking the start of adulthood at age thirteen.

The book would make clear who was Jewish and who was not, why a highland Peruvian, a *cholo,* was not, and *could not* be, Jewish.

Benhamú sent him off amiably, expecting never to see him again.

Segundo had to beg the Hebrew teacher for a Hebrew-Spanish dictionary. The books were hard to come by in Lima, and the teacher clung to the few copies he had but, at Segundo's insistence, finally agreed to sell him one. On the secular shelves of Stadium, Segundo found a paperback copy of *Jewish Traditions and Customs,* its cover lettered in brown and white.

He spent the long journey back to the jungle reading it. The lunar calendar, the Sabbath, the feast days, Israel. It was all there.

On reaching Hebron, Segundo announced the good news.

They were Jews.

Jews!

Part Two

They had been mistaken; they had read but not under-stood. Circumcision was a matter not of the heart, as they'd believed, but of the flesh. Just as God had told Abraham, men must cut their foreskins to mark themselves as members of his people. To be an Israelite, to be part of Israel, was to be a Jew; therefore, because they were Jews, they had to live and act as such. This was explained in *Jewish Traditions and Customs:* circumcision was the first of the "Foundational Ceremonies in the Life of an Individual," one of "the most important moments in the private lives of the Israelite."

Some were horrified. Others felt lost. They expected guidance from Segundo, but this . . . To confuse matters further, they learned that Víctor Castillo, who had gone back to live in Trujillo to find a wife and start a family (he would end up mar-rying Víctor Chico's aunt), disagreed.

A crucial matter of doctrine was unsettled. The scope of this issue was so great that it soon extended beyond the orders of Israel of God. Honorato Vásquez, a friend of the two leaders who himself led a group of Loje's followers in an Amazonian hamlet called Arrayán, a few hours from Hebron, requested clarification. And so the entire council—Segundo, Castillo, Álvaro, José Aguilar, and Demetrio Guerra—set off for the neutral territory of Arrayán. It was a difficult situation, and the assembly got right down to business. Segundo explained that he'd finally understood that, as stated in Genesis, men of the house of Abraham—the people of Israel—were required to cut their flesh: "And the uncircumcised man child whose flesh of his foreskin is not circumcised, that soul shall be cut off from his people; he hath broken my covenant."

Castillo countered with the New Testament. Paul had said that there was no difference between the circumcised and the uncircumcised: after the sacrifice of Jesus, all were equal before God. "For he is not a Jew, which is one outwardly; neither is that circumcision, which is outward in the flesh: But he is a Jew, which is one inwardly; and circumcision is that of the heart, in the spirit, and not in the letter; whose praise is not of men, but of God."

Cutting the flesh was not required for salvation. What's more, Castillo said, our bodies will not be present in the form they are now at the Last Judgment, since they will immediately be transformed to be in the presence of Christ. Therefore, circumcision could not be of the flesh and could not be part of the plan of salvation.

Segundo, as usual, would not cede. Once convinced of something, he was nearly impossible to dissuade. In addition to the Bible, he quoted from the book the rabbi in Lima had recommended to him.

To avoid a greater confrontation, Castillo—only twenty-nine, while Segundo was forty-one—said that he accepted circumcision for reasons of hygiene and allowed that some might even do it out of principle, but said it should not be imposed on all as an obligation.

But Segundo refused to compromise on matters of divinity. The tone grew hostile. Something greater than circumcision was at play. A confrontation between the two had been brewing for some time. To Segundo's frustration, Castillo's name had been drawn from the bag two years in a row, which meant he had not led the council for two years despite being older and considering himself the true leader of Israel of God. Segundo thought that Castillo, young and still single, could not and should not occupy that position; a minister, which is what they were, should be married. The second time the scrap of paper had been drawn with Castillo's name, Segundo had been unable to mask his frustration. Why, how, did Castillo dare to compete with him? "Brother Castillo," he'd said, in front of twenty-odd Israelites, "I opened the doors of my house to let you in, but they are also open to let you out." Castillo had replied, "Do not worry. I know that what is open to me are the gates of heaven." For his part, Castillo thought that Segundo, though very knowledgeable and more advanced in his understanding of the Book, was too rigid, sometimes plain stubborn; he resisted any opinion that was new or different. That was why Castillo got on better with Álvaro, who was always open to innovation.

The Arrayán caucus went on for three days. On the last of them, tempers frayed. Segundo, bewildered, began to stutter. In a flash of anger, Castillo called him a "traitor of Jesus." There was an uncomfortable silence. The attendees stared at both leaders, astonished: this was an insult impossible to come back from. But Castillo did not budge, to Segundo's surprise, nor did the others, who were unexpectedly supporting Castillo. Segundo had tested the limits of their faith, these men who had followed him into the jungle. Not merely their faith in him, their teacher, but in God Himself. Their foreskins, their mortal bodies, thus, were the limit of their faith.

Segundo departed, followed only by Álvaro and Demetrio

Guerra. His brother and his cousin, like when he'd first opened his father's Bible. He had just lost his church in the depths of the jungle, and with it his place in the world.

Or he'd begun again.

The group returned to Hebron split into two unequal parties. Castillo's Israelites, faithful to Segundo's original ideas, were in the majority and continued to serve and obey as they had. The few who'd sided with Segundo, now calling themselves Jews, would have to learn new ways. Both sides were once again living in the same situation they'd escaped by moving to the jungle: among neighbors who saw their ideas as an offense to God.

What's more, they were all reaching the limits of their strength. Despite all their efforts, they had not quite adapted to the Amazon, to its oppressive climate, to their feet being forever swollen by mosquito bites, to the snakes, to the impossible terrain. Nor were they prospering. The land in Hebron was fertile, but in order to sell their harvest, they had to transport it to Bagua Grande, which meant taking burros and horses along muddy, bug-ridden trails full of bandits. And because they had not accepted Castillo's proposal of a cooperative, each family had to do it on their own, shouldering all of the costs and the problems. A few had started to trickle back to the city already. Having lost his leadership, Segundo, too, saw little sense in staying in Hebron. Shortly after the split, he returned to the family home he'd maintained in Cajamarca.

Before, the children used to crowd around when they saw him sit beneath the peach tree, knowing that he was going to tell them a story. Now they found him with his nose in a book, repeating over and over again, *lechem, lechem, lechem.* Bread, in Hebrew, he taught them.

Lechem, lechem, lechem, the children repeated.

Nisan, Iyar, Sivan, Tammuz, Av, Elul, Tishrei, Heshvan, Kislev, Tevet, Shevat, Adar. Those were the months of the Hebrew calendar, the *luach,* which they would use to mark time from now on. The first day of the month was *Rosh Chodesh.* Saturday, the Sabbath, was no longer *sábado* but Shabbat. Passover was no longer Passover but Pesach. Pentecost was no longer Pentecost but Shavuot. Tabernacles was not Tabernacles but Sukkot.

The feast days they had celebrated for so many years bore no relation to Christ, as they'd learned from Loje; rather, they marked moments in the history of the Jews. And there were other festivities for which they had no name in Spanish, ones they knew nothing about: Lag BaOmer, Chanukah, Chamisha Asar BiShvat, Purim. They had to learn.

The handful of families still following Segundo were given photocopies of *Jewish Traditions and Customs.* They were to learn everything in its pages. There were names, expressions, and songs in Hebrew that had been transliterated into Spanish, enabling them to praise God in the original language of the Book. They were given a glimpse inside a Jewish home on Shabbat and could compare it with their own. "In half an hour the sun will set," they read. "With the devotion of one performing a rite, the mother lights the candles; the light signifies that a day of rejoicing draws near. Then she pronounces the blessing, the berachah: Blessed are You, the Eternal, King of the Universe, who has sanctified us with His commandments and commanded us to kindle the light of the Shabbat. As their lips form the words of the blessing, the matron covers her eyes with her hands, as if to concentrate and banish daily concerns."

On the table was a tray with two loaves of bread made from wheat and covered with a small cloth. The loaves were called challah. The Jewish family then went to the temple for the ceremony. They sang not the songs of praise sung by Israel of God but something new called *Lecha Dodi*. Víctor Chico, the orphan who had joined Segundo's family in 1958, learned to play it on the guitar by reading the stave in *Jewish Traditions and Customs*. Everyone learned it by heart with him.

After the ceremony, the Jewish family returned home. The father blessed his sons—"May God make you like Ephraim and Manasseh"—and his daughters: "May God make you like Sarah, Rebekah, Rachel, and Leah." And they all sang a song called "Shalom Aleichem" (the lyrics were not included in the book).

The family read Proverbs 31:10–31. Sitting at the table, the father recited something called kiddush, a prayer that expressed Israel's gratitude to God for having dignified the people of Israel with his benevolence, honoring the holy Shabbat, recalling creation and their liberation from Egypt. He had a glass of wine in his hand. On finishing the prayer, he passed it to the others to drink; he cut the challah, sprinkled salt on it, and shared the pieces with all, while reciting another prayer called a *motzi* (though the book contained the exact content neither of the kiddush nor of the *motzi*).

All the families in Israel of God learned to keep the Shabbat in this way. They made small, narrow wooden cases called mezuzahs that held pieces of paper (in lieu of parchment) with the beginning of the prayer Shema Yisrael, which meant "Hear, Israel." Josué, the eldest of Segundo's sons, by then a teenager, built tefillin, following the indications printed in the book: two small leather boxes containing four specific verses of the Torah, each box attached to a base with a small opening through which a leather cord ran. During the prayer, the cords had to be wrapped first around the arm and then around the head.

And then there was the Brit Milah, the circumcision that had led to the permanent rift between members of Israel of God. "Circumcision represents the individual's first contact with the tradition of his parents," the book explained. The ceremony was carried out eight days after a boy's birth, for God had said to Abraham, "And he that is eight days old shall be circumcised among you, every man child in your generations." The cutting of the flesh was undertaken by a specially trained man called a mohel.

Segundo set off in search of Lima's mohel, accompanied by Álvaro and a handful of other Israelites, this time to enter not the Bible Society's familiar doors but those of the synagogue. This time, they were told that they needed to cover their heads to enter. Since they had no skullcaps, they improvised with handkerchiefs tied at the four corners. Benhamú again came to meet them.

Segundo explained: they wanted to be circumcised and were in need of a mohel.

What the rabbi had initially feared was indeed happening: they wanted to be Jews.

Benhamú would later say he'd never doubted the sincerity of their aspirations. On the contrary, he would avow that they moved him then, and they still moved him. How could he not be moved by the fervor of a man who had gone nine days without working to observe Pesach despite being so poor that not working meant he couldn't eat? How could he not be moved by these men's genuine passion to be Jews? But if he had one mission in that far-off, faithless community where he'd ended up, that mission was to defend it from outside corruption.

Benhamú was thirty-two, and he had children; he wasn't heartless. But if he accepted more Gentiles, the already tenuous identity of Peruvian Jews[1]—the colony, as they called themselves—would eventually vanish. The colony comprised three thousand men and women who'd seen extraordinary success in Peru. They'd arrived in three waves—from Germany in the second half of the nineteenth century; Turkey, the Balkans, and Thessaloniki in the early twentieth; and Poland and Bessarabia shortly after that. They were part of an exodus of millions of Europeans pouring into the Americas, including hundreds of thousands of Jews who were fleeing war, poverty, and anti-Semitism. Most of them chose the United States, Brazil, and Argentina—more accessible destinations than Peru, so far away from the Atlantic Ocean. Those countries also offered land, jobs, or financial opportunities sponsored by private organizations or the state, none of which was offered in Peru. But a few thousand Jews, most of them single men, arrived nonetheless, salesmen, teachers, jewelers, and engineers, looking for opportunity. They were welcomed with open arms by a country that had honored the white man and reviled "Indians" and mestizos since the days of the conquest. The inauguration of the first Ashkenazi congregation in Lima, in 1934, was attended by both the city's mayor and an aide representing the president.

Whether rich or poor on arrival, the majority of Lima's Jews amassed fortunes over the course of a single generation and went on to form part of the capital's upper class. They left the working-class neighborhoods where they'd first lived behind and moved to the residential areas of San Isidro and Miraflores, on the Pacific, where almost the entire colony ended up settling eventually. Even today, there is a bustling, labyrinthine Lima full of colonial buildings and narrow sidewalks, small houses and street markets selling food and spices; and another Lima, that of Miraflores and San Isidro, with wide boulevards and clean streets overflowing with jasmine, an abundance of flowers lining the sidewalks, exclusive restaurants serving customers from all over the world, a park with olive trees dating back to the sixteenth century, cliffs overlooking the sea where young people paraglide over the surfers below, and a golf club ensconced behind high brick walls where the only people who can even see the rolling green hills are the golfers themselves and residents in the surrounding glass high-rises guarded by private security and doormen.

For the Jewish community, integrating had been so simple and so advantageous that they'd ended up taking on the customs and habits of the local elite. Add to that the fact that there were so few of them, and it was logical that the majority ended up marrying Gentiles. So common was the practice that when Benhamú arrived in Lima, he found out that his predecessors had accepted as Jews many husbands and wives who had never gone through the process of conversion, which according to Jewish law was the only way a person not born Jewish could become a Jew. The law clearly stated that the children of marriages where the mother neither was born Jewish nor had converted were themselves not Jewish. And yet the sons of non-Jewish mothers had been circumcised by the mohel and buried in the colony's cemetery as though they were Jews.

Benhamú put an end to these practices. No more irregular marriages and burials. He had to be strict even at the risk of making himself unpopular among those whose support he relied on. How, then, could he say yes to these rustics who had no connection whatsoever to the people of Israel?

He sided with Castillo: stay as you are, he told them, you're fine this way.

But they insisted. They were going to be circumcised. All they needed was the colony's mohel. The mohel couldn't help them, Benhamú replied, since he only circumcised newborns. One of the men with Segundo was eighty years old. Circumcision, at his age? "Abraham did it when he was ninety-nine," the man replied. "Why not me?" The rabbi winced. If only those in the colony had one iota of these men's faith.

But no: the mohel could not help them.

Who, then, if not the mohel? Segundo learned that there was a surgeon, Rubén Kogan, who performed adult circumcision. Though he was a Jew, he did it not as an act of faith but as a job: he charged sixty dollars per person. It was not until 1971, after struggling to raise the money, that Segundo, his son Josué, and Álvaro had the operation. After cutting their flesh, Kogan allowed them to use his office to celebrate the ritual described in *Jewish Traditions and Customs*. They recited the prayer of thanks: "Just as you have entered into the covenant, so may you grow to study the Torah, form a happy family, and practice good deeds." Then they toasted with a glass of wine. When they were finished, each one took his foreskin with him to bury.

Some time later, having saved enough for the journey to Lima and the operation, thirteen more men turned up at Kogan's office. The doctor had told them to arrive an hour before opening time and operated on them all, one after the other. The men asked permission to stay and conduct the ceremony in the waiting room, and on finishing, they lay down on the floor in pain. Which is where Kogan's surprised patients found them when the office opened. From his spot on the floor, Víctor Chico, suppressing his laughter, mused that they probably looked not like the men of the Bible they compared themselves to but like characters on some television comedy.

They were circumcised, they could finally celebrate the Sabbath as God intended, but what about worship? What about the temple? The priests? The rituals? They had found their way to the people of God yet at the same time been deprived of everything. They were Jews, yes, but beyond the basic notions they'd taken from one slim volume, they didn't know *how* to be them.

So they began to travel to the Lima synagogue whenever possible, to attend services on Shabbat and holidays. There they would learn to serve God properly, after having done so improperly for so long. There they would learn the tune to the songs in *Jewish Traditions and Customs* and find out how they ended; they would finally be able to pronounce the words of the kiddush and *motzi,* be able to hear and perhaps even—one day—read the Hebrew prayers.

But on entering, they were greeted with an uncomfortable silence, scornful looks, erect backs—that same invisible wall they'd been met with all their lives, reminding them that even if they'd entered the house of God, they were still living in Peru. The colony wanted it no other way. Assimilation had, on the one hand, made them forget their religious orthodoxy—to Benhamú's despair—and, on the other, steeped them in the values of the city's upper classes. Considered white by national taxonomies—even the darkest-skinned Sephardic Jews—they too rejected lower-class, provincial mestizos. Back when the colony had no school of its own, the first generation of Jewish children had attended wealthy Presbyterian (the boys) and Methodist (the girls) schools, since there they could avoid mixing with other social classes, a feat that would be impossible in public schools. It was for this very reason that these lax practitioners had sought a rabbi as strict as Benhamú: to safeguard the community's *formal* (read: class) purity, despite being unwilling to comply with the religious rules he tried in vain to impose. So when Benhamú prohibited local conversions, Catholic brides began traveling to the United States to be converted. On their return, they were more observant than the husbands who'd asked them to accept—but not practice—their religion.

When the "Cajamarcans"—as the members of the colony called them, as a reminder of where the newcomers came from—entered the synagogue, the men and women who were casual about their religion but strict with regard to their class could not hide their displeasure. After all, what, if not the desire to climb the social ladder, could bring such people to their synagogue? Or perhaps they were like Ataucusi's Israelites, a sect of fanatical lunatics. Many would have closed the doors in their faces, but they couldn't. The military government of Juan Velasco Alvarado (1968–1975), a peculiar mix of authoritarian nationalist politics and center-left progressive measures, had ruled that no house of worship—or school, public or private, including Jewish—could bar anyone from admittance. The colony took this measure as a new attack by a hostile regime. Velasco's government symbolized the deluge of *cholos* from the poorest regions, the mountains and the jungle. Under his rule, new actors had entered the political arena—including Jews for the first time—but the majority of the colony had sided with the establishment. "We were united: we had the same interests, the same problems and the same enemies," said Moisés Levy, son of Ashkenazi immigrants.[2] More than a thousand Lima Jews immigrated to the United States and Israel, fleeing Velasco and his government. Unable to kick the Cajamarcans out, they had to make do with scorning them. To make it clear that they were nothing like the Cajamarcans or Ataucusi, the entity comprising the colony's three organizations officially changed its name from the Association of *Israelite* Societies, as they had been founded in the 1940s, to the *Jewish* Association of Peru.

Segundo and his group had no choice but to put up with it, for how could they form part of the people of God without going to His temple? At least Benhamú spoke to them—a little. He didn't have the heart to tell them they'd never be Jews no matter how hard they tried. He should have, he knew that. But when he recalled the story of the man who'd stopped working for nine days to observe Pesach . . . the intensity of that faith moved him deeply.

At least until Segundo came to speak to him about Christ. There was something Segundo didn't understand: What did the Jews think about the Messiah? Why didn't they accept Jesus as Savior? "I believe the Messiah has already come," Segundo said, not seeing any contradiction between his Judaism and his faith in Jesus Christ. Benhamú replied that, no, they were still awaiting the Messiah, and suggested he read Isaiah more carefully: "The wolf also shall dwell with the lamb, and the leopard shall lie down with the kid; and the calf and the young lion and the fatling together; and a little child shall lead them."

But Segundo had read Isaiah, not once, but many times, in many versions. And not only Isaiah but all the prophets. He could quote them by heart—and did. The rabbi began to worry. Had this man actually come to convert *him*, to convert the entire colony? Was that what Segundo was, a proselytizer? Benhamú sought out Lima's other Orthodox rabbi, who led the Ashkenazi synagogue. They decided to tackle the matter together and summoned Segundo to a meeting. Excited, he recounted his story, described his studies and his path, and concluded by invoking Isaiah's prophecy foretelling the day when all men would be members of the people of Israel: "For I know their works and their thoughts: it shall come, that I will gather all nations and tongues; and they shall come, and see my glory."

The rabbis grew alarmed. The man was messianic! Judaism had resisted supposed messiahs and their followers for many centuries, but the Protestant Reformation had ushered in a new species: Christian Hebraists, Protestants who learned Hebrew in order to comprehend the Book and ended up becoming convinced that it was necessary to convert all Jews as some sort of precondition for the Second Coming.

Shaken, the rabbis sent Segundo off and sequestered themselves in council. "I want nothing to do with him," Benhamú announced. The Ashkenazi rabbi agreed. They told Segundo he was persona non grata and cut off all contact with him.

What had he accomplished, what had he obtained, with his decision to become a Jew? He'd lost his church, his leadership, and his foreskin. In exchange, the people he declared himself a part of rejected him, their rabbi refused to speak to him, and only as an intruder could he attend the rituals that no one was willing to teach him and were conducted in a language he didn't understand. But that was the path, those were the people of Israel, and *true* people of Israel, the descendants of the sons of Jacob, the only ones to say their prayers in the language of the Book; their rabbis were Aaron's legitimate successors. God had chosen them. And how could He be mistaken?

Still, hadn't Jesus come to spread his grace to all men of faith, and thus to Segundo as well? Isn't that what was said in the Gospels, isn't that what Paul explained? "Then said he, Lo, I come to do thy will, O God. He taketh away the first, that he may establish the second. By the which will we are sanctified through the offering of the body of Jesus Christ once for all." How could Paul be wrong? How could Jesus?

Segundo made sense of it thus: Jesus had not fulfilled the prophecies on his First Coming. Therefore, they had to wait for the second one for him to become the Messiah *in action*. In short, the First Coming had been a failure, but the Second Coming would be a success.

And yet the Old Testament made very clear what man had to do in order to be saved: obey His law, universal and everlasting. Did Psalm 119 not say, "So shall I keep thy law continually for ever and ever"? Was Romans 2:12 not unequivocal? "For as many as have sinned without law shall also perish without law: and as many as have sinned in the law shall be judged by the law."

God had told Moses that His law was everlasting, so how could it expire? Why had Christ changed the law after he'd promised it was everlasting? Why had Paul written "For all the law is fulfilled in one word, even in this; Thou shalt love thy neighbour as thyself"? And Acts of the Apostles went even further; there the law was replaced by mere faith, "because the promise, that he should be the heir of the world, was not to Abraham, or to his seed, through the law, but through the righteousness of faith." And in Romans 7:2–4 it was dispensed with entirely: "For the woman which hath an husband is bound by the law to her husband so long as he liveth; but if the husband be dead, she is loosed from the law of her husband . . . Wherefore, my brethren, ye also are become dead to the law by the body of Christ; that ye should be married to another, even to him who is raised from the dead, that we should bring forth fruit unto God."

So, was His law eternal? Or had it been carried out and expired?

Two years went by before Segundo found the answer on a

bookshelf at Stadium, the San Isidro bookstore where he'd first bought *Jewish Traditions and Customs* and to which he often returned in search of lay books to explain what the Bible could not. There he'd found, for instance, an illustrated encyclopedia of religions in which he read about Hinduism and Buddhism. On this trip, he found a paperback with an intriguing title: *Judaism and Ancient Christianity: From Antiochus Epiphanes to Constantine.* The authors were two French historians, Marcel Simon and André Benoît,[3] who set out to explain how Christianity had emerged *from within Judaism itself.*

At the time Jesus was born, Segundo read, the Jews believed that the coming of the Messiah—a savior who would restore Israel's independence, lost six centuries earlier with the fall of the Kingdom of Judea to the Chaldean king Nebuchadnezzar—was imminent. And although the Temple of Solomon still stood in Jerusalem, the political and religious capital of the Jews, many had scattered in a diaspora that included the most important metropoles of the Roman Empire: Carthage, Rome, Alexandria, Antioch. In those days, Judaism was still a proselytizing religion, meaning it encouraged the conversion of Gentiles. The main instrument of conversion was the Book, translated from Hebrew into Greek, the region's lingua franca. That translation, known as the Septuagint Bible, had been completed in the third century before Christ. Many pagans celebrated the basic tenets of Judaism but resisted adopting certain laws—circumcision, for one. So, they embraced Jewish rites and customs without being circumcised. Therein lay the dilemma: Should the rules be relaxed in order to fill the ranks of the people of God?

Over the centuries to come, Segundo read on, this dilemma turned existential. The territory that had in ancient times belonged to the Kingdoms of Israel and Judea was subsequently controlled by other empires, first the Seleucid and later the Roman—with the exception of a brief period from 135 BC to AD 37. The Seleucids profaned the Temple with their pagan gods; the Romans accepted the faith during a short lapse but then punished it, leading to the total destruction of the Temple in the year AD 70 and to Rome expressly forbidding its subjects to convert to Judaism.

These two catastrophes decided the answer. As an act of self-defense, the Jews renounced proselytizing, deemed the Greek translation of the Book illegitimate, and made their laws stricter. To seal the matter, Jewish priests transcribed their oral laws in a series of books known as the Talmud.

The sect led by Jesus, however—arising during the short period of independence—continued advocating the opposite strategy: carry the faith to all men. For a time, the sects coexisted within the religion as Judeo-Christianity, but this evangelizing spirit was in conflict with the new restrictions. Since the Talmud was like a wall dividing the Jewish and the non-Jewish worlds, Christians wrote their own texts: the Gospels. Like Segundo, they confronted the contradiction between eternal, undisputable Jewish law and the teachings of Christ, which often either negated it or relaxed ritual obligations to the point of annulling them completely and then countering with a new moral rigor. Those Gospels, the French historians explained, had not been written by direct witnesses, but they were the only existing written sources on the life and teachings of Christ. The authors did not doubt their veracity but warned that they could not be taken as exact accounts and should be treated with caution. They reflected the preoccupations of an early church that was separating from Judaism, and as a consequence some events had been deformed. The authors then listed the same incongruencies between the various Gospels that Segundo had been observing since his early readings. So imprecise were they that it was impossible, even, to ascertain the exact years in which Jesus had been born and died.

For the third time in his life, at forty-six, Segundo was hit by the full force of revelation, brought on by the pages of a book. Here, finally, was the explanation to all that was unexplainable: obeying and not obeying the law, the importance of circumcision, the translation and non-translation of the Bible, the coming of the Messiah, everything at the very core of Christianity that Segundo had accepted as truth. None of the prophets had said that the Messiah would come twice, first to fail and then to triumph. Jesus had not been, and could not be, the Messiah. His messianism had been a human invention, well intentioned but false.

The Messiah had not yet come.

His name was not known.

They had to wait.

The New Testament was false.

The Old Testament, the Jewish Bible, contained God's only true message.

One by one, Segundo took the treasured Bibles from his library and proceeded to rip from them the false, Christian portion. And in doing so, he ripped from his heart the entire life of Jesus as recounted in the beautiful, contradictory versions of Matthew, Mark, Luke, and John; the exciting, miraculous, yet false story of his resurrection; the epic beginnings of his church; the dramatic biography and impassioned letters of Paul, whom he had so loved and who had guided his thinking for so long; the feverish visions of the Second Coming that had so moved him while he was with the Reformers. With this false portion of his Bible went Acts, Romans, First and Second Corinthians, Galatians, Ephesians, Philippians, Colossians, First and Second Thessalonians, First and Second Timothy, Titus, Philemon, Hebrews, James, First and Second Peter, First, Second, and Third John, Judas, and Revelation. Half of his life and his faith, years of Bible study, whether alone or in groups, his discussions with the Reformers, the joyful days of Hebron.

Those who were with him did the same and, as with their foreskins, unhesitatingly buried the severed New Testaments in fresh soil.

Founded in 1535 by Francisco Pizarro, who named it for the region in Spain where he was born, the city of Trujillo was—and still is—on an extensive coastal plain in the Northwest, bathed by the river Moche on the south and the Pacific Ocean on the west. It had once been home to two pre-Incan civilizations, and a mud-brick city called Chan Chan still survived from that time, as did temples to the Sun and the Moon that brought tourists from all over the world. It had also been the first Peruvian city to declare independence from Spain, in 1820, and was the cradle of a peasant-student-worker uprising against sugar plantation owners in 1932. Twenty years later, it had reemerged as the industrial hub of the north, bustling with factories and businesses, a historic center teeming with travelers, car horns, and street food hawkers. A decade later, countless peasants who'd come down from the hills had begun to set up on land on the outskirts of town, forming *pueblos jóvenes* that lacked paved roads, electricity, running water, and sewage. The city doubled in size and then doubled again, forging north in its battle against the dusty brown desert.

In one of these young towns Segundo would start again. He'd abandoned his own church, the jungle, and even Jesus Christ himself. His Bible, guiding light of his life, was unrecognizable; it had been reduced nearly to half, thirty-nine of the sixty-six books it had started with, and, though those thirty-nine were the same, in Hebrew they were ordered differently. So, for instance, the last eleven books of what he'd known as the Old Testament—Joel, Amos, Obadiah, Jonah, Micah, Nahum, Habakkuk, Zephaniah, Haggai, Zechariah, and Malachi—were now in the middle, as part of Prophets. And those that had been in the middle, like Nehemiah and

First and Second Chronicles, were at the end. It was, in fact, another Book: no longer the Bible, but the Tanakh, an acronym for Torah (Teaching), Nevi'im (Prophets), and Ketuvim (Scriptures), which were its only three parts. There seemed to be no Spanish translation of this Bible in all Peru. He had to make do with his circumcised Bible.

Once again, he was leaving it all behind. Once again, he would have to reinvent himself. When he couldn't be a civil guard, he'd become a carpenter; after renouncing Catholicism, he'd become an Adventist; expelled from their church, he'd created his own; isolated by intolerance and poverty, he'd left the city for the fields.

He'd returned to his home in Cajamarca, but now it was the city that had left him behind rather than the other way around. On leaving for Hebron, Segundo had dismantled his workshop and didn't have the money required to open a place in the center of town. Nor could he win back his old customers; Cajamarcans now preferred cheap new industrial furniture, and an artisan couldn't compete with that.

He'd have moved to Lima, the only place he and his community could learn to live both as Jews and among Jews, and yet he knew they were not welcome there.

His daughter Noemí suggested he do once more what he'd always done: try out a solution devised by others. Noemí was the second of his daughters but the first to marry, and through her husband, Pepe Rengifo, she knew other people who had left Hebron and found a way to reinvent themselves without losing their religious community.

César and Pepe, brothers, had been born in a remote village in the province of Bolívar, on the eastern slopes of the Andes. Their father belonged to a small Adventist community and had read the Bible to them, recited the commandments, instilled in them the importance of the Sabbath, and stipulated the foods that were pure and those that were impure. César, the older of the two, had not been swayed and, as a consequence, had grown up with no religion and no God. Years later, doing his military service in the army, he'd fallen ill; he was told he'd need to have a kidney removed. César begged the doctors not to operate and spent the following three months in a hospital bed experimenting with herbal treatments and natural medicine. His kidney, however, continued to swell, until one day he was able to see it and even feel its shape, a sort of morbid mound growing out of his side. One morning, the pain was so intense it knocked the breath out of him. Perhaps he would need to have it removed after all. In that lonely, desperate moment, he heard birds singing and was moved by the beauty of their song. There is a God, he thought. He jumped out of bed and walked out of the hospital in his pajamas to stand under the heavens, and there he made a promise: "If you heal me, if I leave this place with my health, I will serve you forever more."

Months later, his kidney healed, César bought a Bible and began to study. But he didn't like this Bible. Known as the Reina Valera 1960, after its translators and the year of its publication, it used the term "repose" instead of "Sabbath," the word he'd learned as a child. So he found another that used "Sabbath" (the Reina Valera 1909) and stuck with it. He'd been studying for some time when he met a woman in Trujillo who told him about a church led by another man who studied the Bible, a man named José Aguilar. And it was Aguilar who brought him to Israel of God, taught him to preach, and in 1967, before the first expedition to the jungle, took him to Segundo's house in Cajamarca.

César liked what Segundo had to say, liked his emphasis on the written word. He liked the fact that he encouraged him to study the Bible deeply: its laws on hygiene, on men and women, on which animals to eat and which to shun. He was one of the seventeen on the first voyage into the jungle and one of those who first moved to Hebron. He'd visited Rabbi Benhamú with Segundo. But when the church split over the circumcision issue, he'd sided with Castillo. And later, when Castillo stepped down from the leadership of the Christian Israel of God, César was elected as his successor.

He was, therefore, part of the larger group of families in Hebron when Segundo, in the minority, left the jungle. But soon César, too, began planning his departure. The struggles of surviving in the Amazon were many, and their farming micro-economy hadn't really panned out. He was faced with the same dilemma as Segundo: Where to go? He had tried the mountains and the jungle. The only place left to try was the coast, so he set off to do just that—in Trujillo.

César settled on a plot in a *pueblo joven* known as La Espe-ranza, which he preferred to call Jerusalem, and many Israelites had followed him there. Then he opened a small factory manu-facturing straw brooms that he gave the brand name Natacha and set out to sell in nearby coastal towns, with great success. His ensuing prosperity seemed to indicate that he'd made the right bet, and the church grew: César became the leader of more than a hundred. In order to differentiate his congregation from Segundo's Jews, he changed their name; they were now called the Israel of God Christian Church. In time, it would produce new leaders who would open branches in Lima, Cajamarca, and other Peruvian towns, and their members would grow to number one thousand—enough for a rift to emerge, leading to one group breaking away and founding its own church, the Evangelical Congregation of Israel of God, which also grew.

Encouraged by his brother's success, Pepe Rengifo resolved

to follow his example. Pepe, being married to Noemí Villanueva, had been a member of Israel of God and was now one of Segundo's Jews. He opened a broom factory similar to César's in the *pueblo joven* nearest to La Esperanza. And it was there that Noemí invited her parents to join them in 1973.

The place was called El Milagro, "the miracle." It was, and is, set up on a grid, dirt roads crisscrossing in the desert far from the sea, the river, and the colonial center. Far, in fact, from everything that made Trujillo, Trujillo. There were very few trees or flowers and certainly very few plazas. Junkmen traveled through on horse-pulled carts and still do, now being narrowly missed by moto-taxis zooming past. The houses resemble ruins, though there was never a time when they were anything but what they now are: half-built constructions, with unpainted walls, metal or plastic sheeting in place of doors, packed-dirt floors, and—occasionally—a much-desired second floor.[4]

Segundo chose a lot close to the exit for the Pan-American Highway, which bordered both their *pueblo joven* and La Esperanza, as though somehow determined to keep the lost members of his church as close as possible. There he built a house with dirt floors, whitewashed brick walls, a wood-fire stove, and a latrine. Together, everyone helped build a thatch-roof construction supported on wood beams, under which they set up their broom factory, which they named Star of David: its logo was a six-pointed star. The children sorted the straw, and the adults cut it and tied it to wooden sticks. Under the same roof, they kneaded dough for challah, the braided Sabbath loaf.

At the time, Segundo was leading only eleven families. Several more had stayed behind in Cajamarca with Víctor Chico; theirs was a single community separated by 180 miles, but they met up to observe the Jewish high holidays.

They had one another, and that was all: no rabbi, no town, and, apparently, no prospect of attracting others. They'd returned to the city but were more isolated than they had been in the jungle.

One night in 1980, more than a decade after they had found Judaism, Víctor Chico was fiddling with the dial of a short-wave radio, in search of music and news, when a woman's voice made him stop: "Coming to you from Israel." He'd happened upon the Spanish broadcast of the international service's Voice of Israel, on Israeli public radio. News *from Israel;* now that was news. But there was more: the voice announced that the Israeli government was hosting an international contest on biblical knowledge in all the countries where it had embassies.

Like Peru.

Like Peru!

Víctor Chico asked a sister-in-law who lived in Lima to go to the Israeli embassy and find out the rules. The terms stated that any Peruvian, regardless of religion, could participate. There would be three elimination rounds of written exams and a final round, which would be oral and public. Questions were limited to Genesis, Exodus, Deuteronomy, First and Second Samuel, First and Second Kings, Isaiah, Jeremiah, Hosea, and Amos.

The purpose of the contest was to find common ground between all of the religions based on the Bible—"Let constant Bible study bring us ever closer," the organizers proclaimed—which was why the jury would include one Jew, one Anglican, one Catholic, one Methodist, one Lutheran, one Presbyterian, and one Adventist.[5]

The winning prize would be an all-expenses-paid trip to Israel to compete in the world final.

Víctor Chico informed the Israelites of the terms. He intended to sign up and wanted to know who else did. They'd do better to multiply their chances. Julio Raza decided to sign up, as did Josué Villanueva, Segundo's oldest son, and Pepe Rengifo, his son-in-law. Segundo himself, surprisingly, announced that he would not compete. No one asked him why. Víctor Chico figured Segundo didn't want to risk losing. Being eliminated would be a dishonor, he reasoned. Or perhaps he was ashamed of his stutter. Josué concluded that his father didn't want to compete against his children.

In December, they presented themselves for the qualifying exam, held at the imposing auditorium of Lima's Universidad Peruana Cayetano Heredia. More intimidating still was the competition, which they had not foreseen: three hundred Peruvians from numerous churches and creeds were hoping for the same prize. Each of them received a form on which they were to respond to multiple-choice questions. They were also given a typed page of instructions.[6] And a final warning: "Albeit obvious, we remind you that the exam is individual and the Lord will be Witness to the honesty with which it is taken."

Víctor noted that some questions offered multiple versions of the quoted verses, corresponding to different Bible translations used by the churches represented there. For instance: "Now King David was old and stricken (advanced) in years; They were a (protective) wall to us day and night. And they shall beat (hammer) their swords into ploughshares, and their spears into pruning (cutting) hooks. And I was no prophet, neither was I a prophet's son; but I was an herdman (a shepherd), and a gatherer of sycamore fruit (took care of sycamore-fig trees)."

He knew them all.

The multiple questions had four possible answers each, only one of which was right. "What words does the Bible use to explain the significance of Moses's name?" Was it "Because he is the father of a great people"? Or, "Because I drew him out of the water"? Or maybe, "Because he will take us from the dishonor of Egypt"? Or perhaps, "Because God has looked upon my affliction"?

Víctor got right down to work.

After finishing all twenty-five questions, the nervous Israelites handed in their sheets and returned home.

Only the top thirty—10 percent of contestants—would move on to the second round. Their names were to be announced the following Tuesday.

Víctor and Josué were among them.

Two months later, on February 26, 1981, the semifinalists arrived at the small auditorium of a Lima academy. This time, only the first part of the exam, sixteen questions in all, was multiple choice. For example, "Who said to the people, know in all your hearts and in all your souls, that not one thing hath failed of all the good things which the Lord your God spake concerning you; all are come to pass unto you, and not one thing hath failed thereof?" Was it Moses? Saul? David? Or Joshua? The second part of the exam consisted of six statements, each of which had two questions, the first about a character and the second about a circumstance. Who was the king who first called the children of Israel "people"? And why did he distrust the people of Israel? The third part contained dialogues between two people that the contestant was to identify.

The winners' names would be published the following Tuesday. There were seven. Víctor and Josué were among them.

The final written exam took place on May 14 at the Anglican

church of Lima. Víctor and Josué arrived at nine o'clock in the morning, along with the five other participants. They were given breakfast and then spent the rest of the morning studying and battling their nerves. After lunch, they were taken to a Catholic school, where the tests were handed out.

The first section once again consisted of multiple-choice questions. The second part contained brief accounts, followed by two questions each. And in the third part, dialogues had been transcribed and the contestants were to identify the speakers. Who said, "Blessed be thou of the Lord; I have performed the commandment of the Lord"? Or, "What meaneth then this bleating of the sheep in mine ears and the lowing of the oxen which I hear?"

Víctor thought he'd answered all of the questions correctly. Exultant, he finished quickly, handed in his answer sheet, and left the room before anyone else. Segundo was waiting for him outside. "It was so easy," Víctor told him, surprised. Then why hadn't the others come out? Why hadn't Josué come out? Segundo asked, perplexed.

The others took some time to emerge. When the last contestant had finished, they were all brought back to the Anglican church to rest before the final round, the verbal duel. Josué, Víctor, and another friend used the time to quiz one another and practice further. Víctor realized that in his haste he'd made a mistake on the last question, identifying who had spoken: he'd put Abraham and King David in the same dialogue. Now he felt discouraged: there would be no way to win.

They kept practicing anyway. "How many years did Enoch live?" Víctor asked. Three hundred sixty-five. "Which king burned himself while setting fire to his palace?" the third friend asked. Josué didn't know the answer. Nor did Víctor. The friend informed them: King Zimri, 1 Kings 16:9–20. Víctor read the story: Zimri, an army official, had killed Elah and succeeded him as king of Israel. But the army opposed him, proclaiming their commander, Omri, king instead. The army laid siege to the city of Tirzah, where Zimri was reigning. As Zimri realized that the city had been taken, he set the royal palace on fire and died in it.

By the time the organizers came to look for them, Víctor had lost all hope. They were taken to the auditorium at Santa Úrsula School, in San Isidro, which was packed to the gills. They were given places up on the stage, in front of everyone. When it was announced that the president of Peru, Fernando Belaúnde Terry, who had been overthrown by the Velasco Alvarado military coup in 1968 but had returned to power the previous year, in July 1980, had arrived—surrounded by bodyguards and ministers, to the sound of trumpets—Víctor lost what little confidence he'd regained. He could hardly concentrate when it was his turn to select an envelope of questions. The envelopes bore numbers indicating the difficulty of the questions therein: five points for easy questions, seven and a half for difficult ones. Víctor reasoned that easy and difficult were relative terms: what was easy for one might be difficult for another. He selected only difficult envelopes.

The jury were up on the stage, beside the contestants. Immediately after each answer, they announced whether the response was correct or incorrect. Points were tallied on an electronic scoreboard that everyone could see. Josué didn't score high enough and was eliminated. But Víctor made it through to the next round. He had missed a few questions and was so nervous he was trembling, but he was still in the running. In fact, his score on the written questions was highest.

And then he realized that only one other contestant was still onstage with him—one he knew and feared.

Manuel Palomino was leader and founder of one of the smallest churches in the world: his worshippers could be counted on the fingers of one hand. He called himself Reverend, dressed in a white tunic, and wore a breastplate inlaid with colored gems. Some time ago he had invited Segundo and his brother Álvaro to visit him at his home in Lima. He'd shown them the tiny bronze altar where he made offerings and burned incense. Segundo pointed out that burning incense was forbidden. It is allowed, Palomino retorted, citing the prophet Malachi. But only the descendants of Aaron, granted priesthood by the Law given to Moses in the desert, Segundo said, were authorized to make offerings. Palomino didn't care; he followed his own line.

Segundo explained that their Israel of God offshoot wanted to convert to Judaism. Palomino warned him that they were making a mistake. They were going to lose, he said. They'll be joining a people among whom they'll be anonymous. They would lose their authenticity, their originality. "Here, on the other hand, you can create a community with plenty of worshippers and be famous."

They were not looking for fame, Segundo replied disdainfully. They were looking for the truth.

Misguided or not, Palomino knew the Bible exceedingly well and had a phenomenal memory. It was said that he could recite the whole of Leviticus, word for word.

On the platform of that packed Lima auditorium, standing before his friends, the authorities of several churches in Peru, the president of the republic, and the Jewish leaders he wanted so badly to accept him as equal, Víctor Chico resigned himself: he had no chance against Palomino.

The contestants selected their final envelopes. Out of nervousness, Víctor answered a question incorrectly. It was Palomino's turn. He replied correctly. That was it, it was all over, he thought.

The final question was asked to Víctor. Sent like a ray of light from heaven: "Which king burned himself while setting fire to his palace?"

Once he answered, the scores appeared on the big screen for all to see. Víctor had won by a margin of two and a half points.

The audience erupted in cheers: "Cajamarca! Cajamarca!"

President Belaúnde came up onto the stage. Like most of Peru, the president was Catholic; this was an ideal opportunity to garner some press attention. Not only because Peruvians were a religious people and the Bible bridged ideologies, or because the Bible was a book, which gave him a chance to announce his new literacy campaign aimed at teaching one million Peruvians to read in the following five years.[7] No, it was the perfect moment to speak of religion and tolerance, just one day after Pope John Paul II had survived an assassination attempt in Rome. "At this moment, when the world is suffering over yesterday's attack, when everyone condemns violence," Belaúnde intoned, "I believe His Holiness, Pope John Paul II, has, with his sacrifice—a sacrifice wrought by constant contact with the people—achieved the utmost victory over violence, for if we gain one thing from the bloody events of yesterday, it is proof that violence engenders nothing, as a great statesman would say, and only love is fecund." The president congratulated the contestants and finalists and, in closing, handed the winning certificate to "the brilliant, victorious Víctor Chico."[8]

Segundo and the Israelites in the crowd leaped for joy.

A few yards away, the colony's representatives struggled

to overcome their disbelief. Not because they saw the trip to Israel as a dream come true; on the contrary, most would have preferred a trip to the United States or Europe—places where they presumed they'd fit in more naturally.[9] But the winner of the contest was to have been, ought to have been, one of the students from León Pinelo Jewish School who had signed up convinced of victory. León Pinelo prided itself on the quality of its Tanakh classes, and the colony's leaders, of course, had pictured themselves on the dais with the president, accepting the prize. Instead, it was going to be taken by a Cajamarcan. This was unacceptable. It had to be prevented.[10]

A group of leaders from the Jewish Association of Peru resolved, privately, that although they could neither annul the results, given that they'd been announced publicly, nor take back the president's words, they could deny Víctor Chico the prize: the two-week trip to Israel to participate in the world final. The money to cover the round-trip flight had been donated by a colony businessman, Menachem Mandel. All he had to do was refuse to pay it. But when they proposed as much, Mandel replied that he'd do whatever the Israeli ambassador decided. The leaders then went to speak to Ambassador Gideon Tadmor. They had to avoid having this Cajamarcan act as Peru's representative in Israel; that much was obvious, and the ambassador would no doubt understand. But Tadmor disagreed. From the start, the contest had been open to other faiths; the process had been clear and transparent. His victory was public. They had to accept the result, even if they didn't like it.

Unaware of this failed conspiracy, Víctor Chico, the orphan whose father had been crushed by a rock, the child who'd become like a son to Segundo, the boy who'd accompanied him on every venture, for better or for worse, was preparing to undertake his first great adventure solo. He'd spent so many years with the Israel of his readings that the prospect of actually going was overwhelming. How many verses could he quote from memory about the glory of the land about which God had told Abraham, "I will give unto thee, and to thy seed after thee, the land wherein thou art a stranger, all the land of Canaan, for an everlasting possession." He, a Cajamarca boy, would soon walk through Jerusalem like in the book of Isaiah. As in the prophecy of Obadiah, he would see the desert of Negev and the fields of Samaria.

That biblical Israel, he knew, was also the modern utopian nation described with Zionist romanticism in *Jewish Traditions and Customs,* the one that had, with its creation, fulfilled the words of the prophet Amos. It had been thirteen years since that decisive encounter between Segundo and Benhamú, since they had dreamed of this Israel, the land of Jewish renaissance, where everyone observed the Sabbath, where on Friday afternoon every business, store, and office shut down, public transportation stopped, "and a veil of holiness descended over the cities." On Saturday afternoon, people were out on the streets, singing in jubilation, chatting leisurely, walking to literary gatherings and music festivals. Before sunset, crowds gathered to bid the Shabbat farewell in communal public ceremonies.

Everything there, he had read in *Jewish Traditions and Customs,* was special, idyllic. On Simchat Torah, the second day after the end of Sukkot, when the scrolls of the Torah were removed from the sacred arc of every synagogue and passed around the altar, the congregation erupted in song and joyful cries each time they passed. In a town called Meron, on a mountain of the same name, at midnight on Lag BaOmer a bonfire was lit to commemorate the death of a great rabbi. The settlers fed the flames, and men danced around them, singing psalms and sacred songs until dawn. The glow from it illuminated the night. All over Israel, children danced around bonfires in merriment such as the Israelites of Peru had never seen.

And on Shavuot, the Feast of Weeks, farmers brought their harvest to cities, as in the past they'd brought their offerings to the God of Israel. Schoolchildren joined the caravan, dressed in white, adorned with leaves and flower garlands, and young people from the new farming colonies brought ears of wheat, jars of honey, fowl, and lambs.

But that wasn't the only Israel. The country where Víctor Chico arrived in the northern autumn of 1981, the Israel that prided itself on having conquered the desert, given ancient biblical Hebrew a second life, founded a nation where Jews never were nor ever would be persecuted, was also a country constantly on the brink of war with its Arab neighbors and the Palestinians who'd inhabited the land since before the nation's founding in 1948. Many different organizations, just like the one behind the Bible contest, financed trips to Israel for groups from all over the world. Visitors were taken around the country, received instruction about its form of government, economy, and customs, and welcomed by officials and leaders from each of the political parties. The group Víctor traveled with, which included the thirty-eight winners of the Bible contest from each of the countries where it had been held, were given this royal treatment. Prime Minister Menachem Begin and President Yitzhak Navon congratulated them on their victories. "For many students of the Bible, Jerusalem is in heaven, in the air," the president told them. "But you, who have come, can see that Jerusalem is a city on earth that needs water and electricity."[11]

Víctor could, indeed, see the modern Jerusalem Navon was

talking about, but in his heart shone the New Jerusalem rebuilt, a walled city with thousands of pilgrims arriving at its gates from every part of the planet. "Jerusalem will extend beyond its walls from the sheer multitude," he wrote in his travel diary. He'd been transported to the book of Ezekiel to witness the rebuilding of the Temple, just as the prophet had been taken by God to the top of "a very high mountain, by which was as the frame of a city."

He'd been brought as a witness, to share all he saw with his brothers and sisters in Peru. He visited the Dome of the Rock and saw the place where Abraham had offered his son in sacrifice. In the Ayalon valley, he recalled, "spake Joshua to the Lord in the day when the Lord delivered up the Amorites before the children of Israel, and he said in the sight of Israel, Sun, stand thou still upon Gibeon; and thou, Moon, in the valley of Ajalon." He saw the place where God had slain the lion that attacked Samson and Samson found a "swarm of bees and honey in the carcase of the lion." He stopped before Rachel's tomb. He visited Beit Shemesh, the city founded in 1950 that has ruins of the Beit Shemesh of Joshua and Samuel, the city in Judea set aside for priests of the tribe of Levi, site of the battle between King Amaziah of Judah and King Jehoash of Israel.

At the Western Wall, the only surviving wall of the Second Temple that was destroyed in 70 CE, Víctor predicted that the Messiah would soon arrive to erect the Third Temple, as it was written, and that this one would never be destroyed. With the help of a rabbi praying at the wall, he wrapped the tefillin properly and covered himself with a tallit, a white prayer shawl with black fringe.

Overcome by emotion, he thanked God for the beautiful vision he'd been given. The words of Isaiah sprang to his mind:

"I have graven thee upon the palms of my hands; thy walls are continually before me." In his mind's eye, he saw the Temple of King Solomon that the wall he prayed at had once made complete, and he saw the atrium reserved for non-Jews, those who were as he had once been.

Moved, Víctor thanked God for the privilege of being there—actually being there!—on behalf of his brothers and sisters.

What more could he ask for?

Just one thing.

On a small slip of paper, he wrote: "God of Abraham, of Isaac and of Jacob, if you allow it, make it so that I return with my family and the members of my community."

He searched the cracks and crevices in the crumbling stone wall packed with messages until he found a tiny hole.

Then he rolled his wish into a scroll and slid it deep inside.

In 1985, four years after Víctor Chico's trip to Israel, a new rabbi arrived in Lima, a young Argentine named Guillermo Bronstein who knew very little about the colony or Peru. He came to lead the 1870 Synagogue, named for the year of its founding, which served the oldest, but also the smallest, Jewish community in the country. Bronstein had studied at the Latin American Rabbinical Seminary in Buenos Aires, the leading rabbinical preparatory center in South America. Unlike Benhamú's temple, which was Orthodox Sephardic, or Lima's other synagogue, the Israelite Union of Peru, which was Orthodox Ashkenazi, the Latin American Rabbinical Seminary was Conservative.

Orthodox Jews and Conservatives diverged in their views on how to adapt Jewish tradition to modern-day life. Their dissent dated back two hundred years to the French Revolution, when, for the first time since their defeat and scattering, Jews were given the opportunity to be equal citizens with equal rights. Many Jews in Europe embraced this opportunity and abandoned traditional practices, beliefs, and laws—dietary restrictions, Hebrew prayers, traditional clothing—to adapt to their modern, westernized surroundings. This movement was known as Reform. Orthodox Judaism, which vowed to stay true to traditional Judaism, arose in response. Conservatives emerged from those two movements aiming to preserve essential elements of tradition, but maintaining that the Torah could and should be reinterpreted in light of changes in the world; that, from the moment God handed it to Moses in the Sinai Desert, it had begun to change and evolve; that, in the same way, Jews themselves could and should evolve and adapt to modern life.[12]

As part of being open to the non-Jewish world, Conservatives adopted a more tolerant policy on conversions. In Lima, neither Orthodox synagogue would conduct them; the 1870, however, did. There were only a small handful of aspiring candidates each year, nearly always Gentiles who wanted to marry a Jew.

Shortly after his arrival, Bronstein heard the story of Víctor Chico and his controversial victory. At a later date, someone from the Jewish Agency for Israel told him that Víctor wanted to meet him to recount the history of his community. Bronstein took an immediate liking to the man. He found him so honest and dedicated to the study of Judaism that at the end of their conversation he asked him to come visit the synagogue, along with the rest of the community. They would always be welcome, he informed him, and if they wished, Bronstein would convert them.

This was everything Segundo and his followers had wanted: a synagogue, a community, a rabbi with whom to discuss the Tanakh and Jewish rituals. And yet, to Bronstein's surprise, Víctor replied, "Thank you, but we're looking for an Orthodox conversion."

The offer had come too late, when Segundo and his followers were no longer seeking the acceptance of the colony, hoping to be welcomed by any synagogue in Lima, or longing for anything Peru could offer them. It had all changed with the Bible contest. Until that moment, they'd believed that their Judaism was a personal matter, between them and God; they lived and obeyed as they saw fit, with God as their only judge. To them, that was what being Jewish entailed: being worthy of His approval. Obtaining that approval would make them part of the chosen people.

But at the reception the Israeli embassy held in honor of Víctor's victory, Segundo's son Josué had mentioned to the first secretary, Rafael Barak, that his younger brother, Oseas, was planning to do military service in the Israeli army.

Israel does not accept volunteers, Barak had informed him.

Volunteers? Josué was shocked. A volunteer was a stranger, a foreigner. It felt like a slap in the face. Did they not see them as equals? Did they not understand that, to them, serving in Israel was a mitzvah, a divine commandment?

Josué had gone to Benhamú, who agreed to speak to him despite refusing all contact with Segundo. Benhamú had, for example, helped him confirm that the Hebrew Bibles they'd finally found in Lima indeed contained the correct text, despite not having been printed by publishers deemed legitimate by Orthodox Judaism and thus not being kosher. The rabbi liked the young Villanueva for his intelligence and gentle tone, for always being open and inquisitive. Benhamú confirmed what Josué had understood at the reception: to *true* Jews, they were not Jews. How could that be, Josué protested, citing Esther from memory: "And in every province, and in every city, whith-ersoever the king's commandment and his decree came, the Jews had joy and gladness, a feast and a good day. And many of the people of the land became Jews; for the fear of the Jews fell upon them." "You said you were Israelites!" Benhamú claimed, obfuscating. They were not Jews and never would be without conversion.

When Josué had returned with this news, Segundo had not shared his desolation. It was not the colony's laws they had to follow and obey, he'd said; they wanted to be accepted by God, not by men. But Josué had insisted that it was men who had to convert them, not God: that was the condition required to reach Israel. The others agreed with him. They now aspired to live in Israel; Víctor Chico had brought that dream with him from Israel and they all were dreaming it. He hadn't even wanted to return from his trip, but they'd explained to him in Israel that he couldn't stay. It made no difference what his religion was called or what rituals they practiced: to live in Israel, he had to be accepted as a Jew by Jews. He wasn't one by birth, which meant that the only alternative was conversion.

Finally, Segundo gave in.

But converting was a complicated matter.[13] The Conservative conversion Bronstein offered was enough to *get* to Israel. They'd understood this much from a conversation with Zvi Netzer, the head of Lima's Jewish Agency, which was charged with handling immigration to Israel by Jews from all over the world. Netzer had attended the Bible contest and admired Víctor Chico's biblical erudition. They'd met several times since his return; Netzer had called his superiors in Jerusalem, asking them to help find a way for Víctor to emigrate, but nothing had come of it. When Netzer acknowledged his defeat, Víctor consoled him: it was God's will. Netzer wasn't religious, but the response moved him. He'd also met Josué Villanueva and found him brilliant. He had liked Segundo's earnestness and called him an "exceedingly interesting" man. When the president of the agency himself was passing through Lima, Netzer sat him down with Segundo, Josué, and Víctor. They told him their story and asked questions they'd brought written down on slips of paper. Josué asked why he must not carry a handkerchief in his pocket on Shabbat. Netzer marveled at the sophistication of the question, for which he had no answer.

The agency, he explained, accepted all converts as potential Israeli citizens, regardless of the rabbi who performed them. But

Israel's religious authority was in the hands of the Orthodox, and they accepted only those who'd been converted by their rites. All others were denied the right to a religious wedding—the only kind valid in Israel—and the right to be buried in Jewish cemeteries. In other words, the right to have their children fully accepted as Jews by the state and the community.

The Chief Rabbinate was the Israeli religious authority, headquartered in Jerusalem. That was where they'd have to present their case. Josué had written to the Chief Rabbinate, in his questionable Hebrew, recounting the story of the community and their desire to live in Israel. Víctor had taken the letter with him, but he didn't understand enough Hebrew to find the Chief Rabbinate's address and actually mail it. So on his return, he'd given it back to Josué, who finally managed to find the address and post it from El Milagro. Obtaining no reply, he then wrote another letter and sent that. And then another, and another, a dozen letters in the course of a few years.

To Segundo, the idea of being half-accepted was inconceivable. What's more, his understanding of God's message was, by definition, the Orthodox one: adherence to the letter of the divine message. Hence, they had to be Orthodox.

But how? What did that require? What obligations did it entail, beyond those indicated in the Tanakh? With no guidance from the Chief Rabbinate, how could they even find out?

Víctor found the answer to these questions as well, in the same place Segundo would have: the pages of a book. It was unavailable at any bookstore in Peru but came into his possession via a Peruvian Jew who had a copy at home. The softback tome with its brown and white cover was called *Abbreviation of the Shulchan Aruch.*

Written four centuries earlier by a scholar named Joseph

Karo, the *Shulchan Aruch* was, according to the prologue to the Spanish edition, the most important compendium of codes of conduct in the Jewish religion. Karo had finished writing it in 1563—thirty-one years after the fall of the Inca Atahualpa, six years before Reina published his Spanish translation of the Bible—to address a need similar to the one Segundo felt: that for a clear and standardized guide on how to lead a *proper* Jewish life. The context, naturally, was quite different. In the sixteenth century, after having been expelled from Spain and Portugal, Sephardic Jews had gone off to live either among Ashkenazis, who had different customs, or among Gentiles in strange lands. Many had questions, or no idea how to obey the law in this new world, or didn't know whom to turn to in case of controversy. Karo's life itself was an example of these dilemmas. He'd left Spain as a young boy in 1492, the first year of the Christian conquest of America undertaken by Spain and later Portugal. He had moved to Constantinople and later to Safed, in Galilee. When the rabbi of Safed died, Karo had assumed spiritual leadership of the community. Discovering that they lacked any sort of codex for that purpose, he decided to create one.[14]

In Hebrew, *Shulchan Aruch* means "set table"; that is, it's a menu ready to be consumed by the pious Jew. This was Karo's aim: to write a comprehensive instruction manual for all Jews in all parts of the world. He drew on the Talmud as well as texts written by the greatest Sephardic authorities of the day: Maimonides, Jacob ben Asher, Isaac ben Jacob Alfasi. When he came across a discrepancy in the interpretation of a law, he opted for whichever one had been backed by at least two scholars. The result was four thick tomes of instruction, written in simple language aimed not at learned men like himself but at the Jewish community of the entire world. After its initial publication, a contemporary of Karo's, the scholar Moses Isserles, added glosses to the text, noting where Ashkenazi practices differed. With these additions, the *Shulchan Aruch* became the legally accepted code of both communities and continues to be so centuries later, though only ultra-Orthodox Jews follow it to the letter today.

The book Víctor Chico obtained was a 228-page abridgment, translated into Spanish.[15] Víctor read aloud from it to the followers in Cajamarca at their Saturday gatherings. Segundo did the same in El Milagro, attempting to explain each passage. Both groups together would then discuss how to put the rules into practice. Though the abridgment was far shorter than the original version, there were so many instructions, written in such detail, that each family needed their own copy to study and consult. Photocopies were expensive in Cajamarca; in Lima, however, they could be made for far less. So Víctor asked an uncle who traveled to the capital regularly to order eight complete sets for the families that could afford to pay.

There were instructions for every time of day. As soon as they opened their eyes, before even moving from bed, they had to recite, "I am thankful before You, living and enduring King, for You have mercifully restored my soul within me. Great is Your faithfulness." This was the only prayer they could recite before washing their hands, because it made no mention of God. They had to wash their hands before taking a step—a jar of water had to be kept by their beds—and another prayer accompanied the wash. For drying their hands, a different prayer.

There were many rules around the washing of hands. Before each meal, before breaking bread, they were to wash their hands the same way as they did each morning, pouring water three times from a vessel. The vessel could have no scratches or holes.

The water could not be salted, cloudy, or bitter. They had to wash their hands on rising, on leaving the bathroom, after cutting their fingernails or hair, after brushing their hair, taking off their shoes with bare hands, touching anything dirty. And each morning and afternoon they had to ask forgiveness for their sins with a prayer called Tachanun: "And David said unto God, I am in a great strait: let us fall now into the hand of the Lord; for his mercies are great: and let me not fall into the hand of man." They were to recite it with head lowered and face in the bend of one forearm: the right one in the morning, the left one in the afternoon.

They learned that every Jewish temple was required to have a Sefer Torah, a handwritten scroll containing the Torah, the first five books of the Tanakh, which they'd seen the Jews in the Lima synagogue take from a cabinet—the ark. Each Monday and Thursday, after they recited the Tachanun, the Sefer Torah was to be taken from the ark and three men were to recite blessings. The one called to read from the scrolls was to wear a tallit, take the shortest path to the table where it lay (though on returning he was to take the longest path), look at the passage to be read, and say, holding the scroll with two fists and never touching it with a bare finger and instead only through the tallit or holding it by the rollers, "Barechu et Adonai ham'vorach, Blessed God, who is the blessed one." The response was "Baruch Adonai Ham'vorach l'olam va'ed, Blessed be God, the blessed one forever and ever."

The morning service was called Shacharit; the afternoon, Mincha. Mincha was to be prayed at three thirty, that is, nine and a half hours after the day began. Before praying, they were to wash their hands up to the wrist. Then they were to read the Ashrei—Psalm 145—wrapped in a tallit, and recite the Kaddish, one of the most important prayers. At night, they were once again to recite the Shema, and more psalms and Bible verses about God's mercy. It was imperative, at that time, to search their conscience for any fault or sin committed during the day and repent, forgive those who had offended them, and in turn beg forgiveness from God.

Before bed, they were to take off their clothes and lie on one side, never on their back faceup or on their stomach facedown.

Their homes were to be consecrated. On the right-hand side of door frames, with the exception of the bathroom door, they were to hang the mezuzahs they'd had since their early readings of *Jewish Traditions and Customs*. On nailing them to the doors, they were to say a specific blessing. Each time they entered or exited the home, they had to kiss the palm of one hand and touch it to the mezuzah.

They learned different prayers for each type of food: one for some types of bread, another one for others; one for some types of fruit, and a different one for others; one for mushrooms and another one for olive oil, for wine, for sugar, and many different ones for a variety of drinks. And if they'd eaten various types of foods, they were to combine the prayers in a certain order. There were blessings for leaving the table after a meal, and they differed according to how many people were present.

There were prayers giving thanks for fragrances, and on receiving good news for oneself or another. Other prayers were recited when building or buying a house, wearing new clothes, purchasing articles for the home, receiving gifts, or seeing a parent, dear friend, or teacher after a separation of thirty days (if the separation had been twelve months, there was a different prayer).

In Cajamarca and El Milagro, the Israelites read, took notes, and memorized all of this and more: instructions on how to interact with others, on how to be and act at home and in the world; details on the foods allowed and those forbidden, festivities, fasting, and circumcision; rules on intimate hygiene, on clothing, on conduct and morals, on the treatment of animals; steps to follow on visiting the sick and on mourning the dead.

They had to remember and recite complicated prayers, like "Asher natan lasechvi bina, who has given wisdom to the rooster." Knowing Hebrew was not necessary in order to say the prayers, the *Shulchan Aruch* noted; what mattered was thinking of God and being humble of heart while reciting them, despite not understanding what they said. That wasn't easy. The Shema Yisrael, which included blessings for the dawn and dusk, love for the light of the Law, and God's redemption of Israel, contained 248 Hebrew words, each of which had to be learned through transliteration.

Not only that, they were also required to perform corresponding actions while reciting the prayers. The Shemoneh Esrei, also referred to as the Tefila and the Amida, had nineteen blessings, and they had to stand when saying one, and take three steps back or forward when saying another. Then they were to place their feet together, bow slightly forward, close their eyes, bend their knees, and rock back and forth four times at the beginning and the end of the first blessing.

There was no way to abbreviate, simplify, or deviate. The *Shulchan Aruch* cautioned, "We must take extreme precaution to never pronounce any blessing in vain." Eventually, after endless repetition, the prayers became habit, and in the end they memorized them all.

Maybe that was enough for God. But was it enough for the Chief Rabbinate?

Probably not. They had to prove they'd changed not only on the inside but also on the outside. They could no longer call themselves Israel, because Israel was the country they wanted to take them in. They had to form a new community, a community that would make their observance and desire to be Jews clear to *all.*

After much deliberation they chose the name Children of Moses, to signal their acceptance of the Torah's commandments—but in Hebrew, not in Spanish, because it was Israel, or its Chief Rabbinate, whom they were addressing.

Bnei Moshe.

In mid-Sivan of the year 5746—June 1986 in Peru—they drafted the new organization's founding document.[16] The Bnei Moshe wanted to "build a group that was compact in every aspect" so as to ensure "spiritual-material benefit to each of its members, under steadfast and proper ideological guidance." The main objectives were to "praise our Lord in the best way possible and educate ourselves, elders and children alike, in the divine doctrine and in all realms possible."

Leadership was formally democratic, as it had been in Israel of God. Everything was to be decided by majority, but any resolution could be "invalidated in the event that it went against the Torah, [the] Shulchan Aruch," or sought "to do harm." They still called one another brother and sister; a vote by all members would elect the executive committee. At the first election, held one winter night, Segundo's son-in-law Pepe Rengifo was elected president. Segundo, modestly, ran for and was elected spokesperson. Two other family members also ended up on the executive committee: Segundo's son Josué was voted second spokesperson, and his daughter Eva became treasurer.

There were ten "principles of the community," as there were

tablets of the Law given to Moses, which established general moral order: constancy, punctuality, mutual aid, order, responsibility, effort, discipline, respect, organization, and tolerance.

In order to join Bnei Moshe, one had not only to accept Mosaic Law but to "love it, be advanced or moderately so in knowledge of the Torah and practice it to the greatest degree possible," enjoy an honorable reputation, abide by the group's agreements, be over thirteen years of age, and pay a monthly fee. "Attending synagogue on the three high holy days" and observing the Sabbath each week were also required.

As per the *Shulchan Aruch:* "It is the duty of all men to choose a synagogue in which to pray permanently and select within it a regular seat for worship." This mandate occasioned a new dilemma: the Bnei Moshe had no synagogue. But why build one if they were preparing to move to Israel? It was essential to consider what might happen to it once they were no longer there. A synagogue was a sacred place. What if someone turned it into a chicken coop? They could never allow that: if they built one, they had to be responsible for its future. The only solution was to ensure that the synagogue remain in Jewish hands; only Jews would care for it. There will never be a lack of Jews in Peru, Josué said. It didn't matter that the colony didn't accept them as equals. And thus it was resolved. The founding charter of the Bnei Moshe decreed that "in the event that the community's organization is dissolved, everything it possesses in property and everything belonging to the community will be donated in its entirety to the Jewish community of Lima."

On the first of Tammuz 5746—July 8, 1986—the Bnei Moshe met at Segundo's house, where each week they prayed and studied together, where they'd signed their constitution and would congregate from that point on, from 7:00 to 9:00 p.m. on the first of each month, to plan the construction of the synagogue. The first matter pending was its location.

El Milagro was no longer the wasteland they had moved to fifteen years earlier. Now people had to obtain authorization and follow procedures before building. So Pepe Rengifo informed the mayor of the local council that the community wanted to occupy a new lot on which to build their religious center. The mayor denied their permit: the deeds of the families who had taken land were in legal proceedings, and there was no more space for new occupancies.

Laura Tirado Valderrama, who was sister-in-law to Segundo's youngest daughter, Eva, and the only other woman on the Bnei Moshe executive committee, proposed moving forward regardless. No one would kick them out, she ventured. Josué was emphatically opposed to the idea: the land where they built the synagogue needed to be legally obtained; these were matters of God. His sisters Noemí and Jocabeth had two adjacent lots just a few meters away, across the street from where Segundo had built his house; they offered to donate one half each, so the synagogue could be built there. And thus it was settled.

Once they resolved the matter of location, the design was simple. The synagogue would have two rooms: one, a prayer room; the other, a common dining room. What would be trickier, though, was coming up with the funds needed to build. It took them five months to raise enough money for just the bricks required to build the walls. Not only that, they also had very little free time for the actual construction, what with the jobs they had to work to get by and their religious obligations. In September they held a fundraiser to hire a bricklayer but didn't collect enough. Months later, someone suggested that the Bnei Moshe of Cajamarca contribute as well, but that idea didn't take off; Víctor Chico and his followers were struggling to build their own synagogue. All they could do was lay a cement floor in the smaller of the two rooms, the room that would someday become the dining room.

They were poor people living in an impoverished economy. The country was experiencing one of the worst crises in its history: inflation was out of control, national debt had reached record levels, and political tensions had given rise to a bloody armed conflict. The majority of Peruvians lived in miserable edge cities outside the major metropoles, eking out a living as traveling salesmen, craftsmen, and hustlers doing all manner of precarious, marginal labor. President Alan García, who had succeeded Belaúnde, coming to power a year before the founding of Bnei Moshe, announced that he would not pay the astronomical foreign debt, equivalent to 25 percent of the nation's export revenue. The decision, which didn't garner the support of other Latin American countries, led to a debacle: exports plummeted, investment disappeared, and the debt interest skyrocketed. With annual inflation at over 100 percent, entrepreneurs made money buying dollars and goods legally and reselling them on the black market; employees rushed to change their wages into dollars the moment they were paid in an attempt to offset the constant depreciation. A single dollar, in that period of unsuccessful fundraising, cost twenty-four intis—the local currency at the time—one month; forty-two, the next. A few months later, it rose to a thousand intis and then five thousand.

On the first of Adar 5747—or March 2, 1987—eight months after they'd agreed to build the synagogue, the Bnei Moshe met for the first time inside the actual building, or what they'd managed to complete of it: four brick walls enclosing a single room with an unleveled cement floor, no roof, windows, bathroom, plaster, paint, doors, or furniture. Illuminated by candles and three kerosene lamps, the self-declared Children of Moses prayed in the first Jewish temple they could call their own.

Segundo read from a notebook in which he'd taken care not to write out the name of God so as not to pronounce it in vain:

Adonai: G-d of Abraham, of Isaac and of Jacob: there is no G-d like You in the Heavens or on Earth: You who show mercy and keep the covenant with your servants who walk before You with all their heart.

You have kept us to this day in the greatness of Your power and mercy: because You have seen that we want to walk in Your laws: this small house, which is built with the effort of Your children. For the study of your Holy Torah and to pray to Your holy and blessed name. We beg You to accept this small offering from each of us.

Only You are G-d of the spirits, of all flesh, and know the desires of men: we have no merits before You. We do it all for Your mercy. Redeemer and our father, give our souls the strength to learn and practice Your Holy Torah. Make us part of the blessings of Your people ISRAEL. And bring us closer to You. We have felt Your divine presence and the light of Your face guides us to the end. You have redeemed us from darkness.

Merciful G-d: remember where we have come from and lead us always down Your paths of peace. Let this place be for Your Glory. And may men of good faith learn to fear You. May You heal the sickness of spirit. Because You are our Healer.

(Though he continued to receive no reply, Josué relayed this progress to the Chief Rabbinate in his periodic letter.)

They created a rota, to take turns dusting, since dust inevitably covered everything. Segundo donated the bimah—the podium on which the Torah was to be read during services— two corner posts on which to set the kerosene lamps, three long benches, five chairs, and a fabric screen to separate men from women, as required of an Orthodox synagogue. Two brothers promised to provide two benches. They debated purchasing a gas stove on some sort of payment plan but, sadly, concluded that they simply couldn't afford it. Segundo suggested gathering firewood before each holiday instead.

More important than the windows, kitchen, or gas was the lack of prayer books: they had no money to buy them with. Josué copied out a guide including prayers and songs of praise, and everyone made their own photocopies. These were their first siddurim, their prayer books.

Pesach was the first holiday the community celebrated in their new synagogue. Segundo and his children suggested that the seven families take turns, each cooking one day of the week. Laura Tirado complained: "Rather than days of rest and joy, the holidays [become] a worry and more work, because preparing food for [so many] people is dedicated labor." It would have to be voluntary. Segundo and his children Josué, Eva, and Jocabeth each volunteered. For the remaining three nights, when no one had stepped forward, each family donated seventy-five intis to buy food.

Pepe Rengifo recalled that installing windows was an urgent concern, since winter was coming. With eighteen hundred intis, they could buy the metal frames required; they'd worry about the glass after that. But the donation box contained only four hundred intis. The eleven members present donated one hundred intis each; they still needed three hundred. Battered by a wave of hyperinflation, they watched the completion of their temple grow ever more distant.

Once the walls were standing, another problem cropped up. The group's membership had not grown since their decision to choose Judaism, which made following one of the *Shulchan Aruch*'s mandates impossible: they needed a minyan, a quorum of ten adult men, to conduct certain religious services. It was hard to get ten adult men at the El Milagro Bnei Moshe. Though the community had fifty followers, they included women, children, and nonmembers. Throughout 5746, they had eleven members, but that included women; the following year there were fourteen. Fifty more lived in Cajamarca and Lima, led by Víctor Chico and Álvaro Villanueva, but they had Shabbat and said their prayers in their own cities; only on major holidays did they travel to El Milagro.

How could they move forward with no money and no members?

On the other end of the Pan-American, by contrast, César Rengifo was seeing his Israel of God congregation grow ceaselessly; more than 120 people gathered on a regular Shabbat. His broom business was doing well despite the country's economic woes, his temple was full every Saturday, and his command of the Bible kept him firmly—or so he thought—in the plan of salvation. But his physical ailment had returned, and this time it hit not only his kidneys but his liver. Illness forced him to rest completely, and he spent an entire month in bed. Leaving his employees in charge of the factory, he sent his family to a relative's house in the country. Alone, he put himself on a strict diet containing no fat and spent his time reading; the Bible was a given, of course, but also other books on religion that he borrowed from friends and family.

One day César Rengifo took to bed an encyclopedia of the great religions of the world, the same one Segundo had bought years earlier in Stadium, and in it read something he'd never before considered: that Christianity and Islam had both emerged from within Judaism, from the Torah given to Moses on Mount Sinai. Through his illness and isolation, he suddenly saw it all clearly: the other two religions were *imitations* of Judaism. What he had heard and rejected from Segundo was the truth. None of this was chance or coincidence, but divine plan: his convalescence, the book, these truths, they were all a sign of the Everlasting. I've been wrong, he said to himself. That is, he was on the wrong path. If all religions had drunk of Judaism, should he not go back to the original source as well?

To ensure that he was understanding the message properly, he asked his friends at El Milagro to lend him *Jewish Traditions and Customs* and the *Shulchan Aruch*. Everything his brother and Segundo had said suddenly took on a new meaning. It wasn't they who convinced him, he thought, but his faith, sent by God during his convalescence to make him see once and for all. An awakening of the mind, he said to himself.

The following Saturday, he headed over to Israel of God's temple to share the good news with his faithful. "Brothers and Sisters: this is it. I have truly understood the truth of things. I have seen that the Jewish religion is right. No other religion. None. Catholics, Reformers, Witnesses: they all came out of Judaism."

He read them passages from the books he'd studied, quoted prophets, told them the story of the people of Israel. The faithful listened, dumbstruck, scandalized. But Rengifo continued proclaiming the truth that had been revealed to him. Some were persuaded. We agree! they cried. Others doubted, questioned. The discussion embroiled them in debate for weeks.

Those who seemed convinced one Saturday doubted the next. Until César Rengifo announced dramatically that he could not go on like that any longer. If the majority agreed, he said, he would be with them. If they were against him, he would not carry on arguing that way. I will leave now, he announced. Who wants to follow my way, considering Judaism? Come with me.

Forty men climbed aboard his broom truck. They traveled on Shabbat, against the Torah's mandate, because some time earlier, after they'd left Segundo's community, they'd resolved that it was allowed. They drove along the Pan-American and entered El Milagro, braking in front of the skeleton of a synagogue. Segundo emerged from within to welcome them. On realizing what was happening, he embraced César Rengifo. My brother, he told him, you have seen! Everyone will see if you have seen!

With the arrival of these forty, who were soon circumcised, the Bnei Moshe finally had their minyan. With César Rengifo, they also had an enterprising new member of the executive committee who could pitch in with a little money. The three hundred remaining intis required for the windows came from his pocket.

Now they had to raise enough to finish the temple. Someone suggested applying for a loan from Central de Crédito Cooperativo, a savings and loan. They estimated that it would take a deposit of six thousand intis to obtain a loan of twenty-five thousand. Segundo approved: "the ends of construction" justified the means. Rengifo disagreed: the interest rate was too high. Instead, he suggested asking the Bnei Moshe of Cajamarca for the funds. Segundo objected: they were duty-bound to finance their own synagogue. Rengifo reminded him that taking out a loan required collateral and asked if the papers on the land were in order. They were not. What's more, a loan approval took six months. All they'd be able to do was advance on the construction of a cement barrier around the four walls with no roof. Having no solution, Segundo proposed they sing a liturgical poem—a piyyut, in Hebrew—in gratitude for the goodwill shown by all. They sang "Ein Keloheinu."

A month later they had yet to raise even half of the money needed to pay for the roof. They gave themselves a week to raise the rest; Segundo would get an estimate from a brickmaker who was the son-in-law of a Bnei Moshe, to see if he'd offer a discount. They had nearly all of the cement needed for the wall, and the two wooden benches promised had finally appeared. Segundo and his sons, Josué and Oseas, set to building the barrier but were unable to complete it: not enough cement. Nine months later, they still hadn't raised enough to pay for the roof.

When they finally managed, once they'd finally saved up 23,265 intis one by one, there was an iron shortage in Trujillo. Without iron, they couldn't build. Each day they waited, their 23,265 intis lost value due to the constant devaluation and inflation. They should buy the bricks immediately, Noemí Villanueva advised, since the money would continue to lose value if they didn't use it. Why not make the roof from Eternit, a fiber cement sheeting that was so much cheaper than brick? someone else proposed. César Rengifo was thoroughly opposed: a roof for something as important as a synagogue had to be durable. This wasn't any old roof.

Lacking a roof, they turned to another obligation: obtaining a Sefer Torah, without which no building had a right to call itself a synagogue. Eva donated the wood for the Aron Hakodesh, the Torah ark; Segundo built it with his own hands. But what about the actual Sefer Torah? The scrolls needed to be genuine parchment, contain the five books of Moses, and be handwritten by a professional scribe. The Lima Jews paid twenty thousand dollars to import them from the United States, Israel, or Europe. It was an unfathomable amount of money.

Months passed. No Sefer Torah, no roof. César Rengifo finally gave in and agreed to using the cement sheeting he hated. The motion was approved by majority vote. Next, they dug a pit to make a toilet "for women and visitors" but didn't have the money to cover it or install plastic pipes for drainage.

How could they carry on? César Rengifo scandalized the community by offering four thousand intis he'd kept from a collection taken from the La Esperanza Israelites. Jocabeth Villanueva argued that they couldn't accept the money; Rengifo could not donate it without first speaking to the members of his old congregation, to whom it belonged. Another Bnei Moshe warned that accepting it would lead to gossip. Someone else argued that they had to return it. But Segundo disagreed. The amount was "minimal," he said, compared with "the permanent contribution made to his ex-organization" and should be employed "in missionary work." Rengifo took the opportunity to assert that returning the money was not "just, as per the justice of Israel," given that he had done so much for the congregation he left. The funds might be "minimal," as Segundo maintained, but "in light of the other members not being in favor of accepting the donation," he withdrew the offer. The bathroom would be finished using the most economical materials available and the labor of the Bnei Moshe themselves.

If it was ever to be finished at all.

It was in those days of anguish—when it seemed they would never succeed, when the toilet, roof, synagogue, and their own conversion were growing further and further away—that they received the news, and the miracle occurred.

Israel was sending someone to see them.

Eliyahu Avichail invariably dressed in black jacket and trousers, a white shirt with the tassels of his tzitzit hanging down, and a broad woven kippa. His wild, dark beard was flecked with gray. Born in Jerusalem in 1932 to Ashkenazi parents, he'd spent his childhood waiting.[17]

Forty years before he was born, a group of Jewish intellectuals led by Theodor Herzl had affirmed the Zionist postulate: "We shall live at last as free men on our own soil, and die peacefully in our own homes." The dream of a homeland.

Fifteen years before he was born, the British government, which wielded colonial power over the Middle East, had agreed that Jews had the right to a "national home" in Palestine.

But just fifteen years *after* he was born, in 1947, and after six million Jews were murdered in Europe during World War II, the United Nations, the organization created with the aim of preventing another war, decreed the end of the British mandate over Palestine. The territory would be divided into two states, one Arab and the other Jewish.

The future Jewish state was to include the fertile eastern part of Galilee in the north; the Mediterranean coastal plains to the west; and, to the south, almost all of the Negev Desert. The future Palestinian state would include the central and western part of Galilee in the north; another piece of land in the center-east, beyond the river Jordan, including the mountainous regions that had, in the distant past, been Judea and Samaria; and a coastal strip in the south as well as a section of desert along the border with Egypt. Jerusalem, geographically located in the center of the future Arab state and the symbolic seat of the three religions of the Book, would receive special status. The plan was accepted, with reservations, by the Zionist movement and rejected completely by the Arab leaders of the region, including the Palestinians. Arabs, who constituted the majority in the land to be divided, had lived for many years mostly in peace with the small Jewish communities that had been there before the war. But once the British withdrew, Arabs and Jews clashed over the land they each considered theirs.

In the eyes of Avichail, who'd spent his adolescence studying at a yeshiva, the present-day battles converged with those waged by Kings David, Solomon, and Jeroboam. So he quit his studies and joined the army.

The result of that conflict, known as the War of Independence by the Jews and the Nakba, or Catastrophe, by the Arabs, was the State of Israel. Hundreds of thousands of Jews who had survived the concentration camps in Europe or had been expelled from Arab countries began arriving to build and inhabit Israel, displacing hundreds of thousands of Palestinians, who either took refuge in neighboring countries or resigned themselves to forming part of the new country, which expanded beyond the borders established in the original agreement to include all of Galilee in the north and nearly all of the southern border with Egypt. There was no Palestinian state: the narrow Gaza Strip was occupied by Egypt, and the territory east of the river Jordan was occupied by the Kingdom of Jordan. Jerusalem was divided, controlled by Jordan in the east and Israel in the west.

A few Jews saw these victorious events as the sign of a messianic era. One who stood out particularly was Zvi Yehuda Kook, head of Mercaz HaRav Yeshiva, where Avichail went on to earn his rabbinical degree after completing three years of military service.[18] Z. Y. Kook was the son of Abraham Kook, a famous rabbi who had seen the emergence of the Zionist movement in the late eighteenth century as a sign of redemption. Abraham Kook was convinced that the Jewish people were different from all others due to the special relationship they had with God: a holy people who'd been assigned a nation-state unlike any other; one that embodied the Torah. The land of Israel and the Jewish people were, thus, inextricably linked by their equally sacred value. The Jewish state that Zionists were dreaming of, once realized, would be a divine emanation. Its foundation would be the foundation of the kingdom of God on earth. The fact that the Zionist leaders might be secular, or that their political agenda might not consider religious and sacred aspects, in no way affected his reasoning, for the dreams of men did not alter the plan of their Creator.

When he died in 1935, Abraham Kook bequeathed to future generations a collection of texts that would form the basis of a new, religious Zionist movement, and his son, Z.Y., set out, at forty-four, to continue his father's work. Kook senior had asserted that the *people* of Israel were pure in essence; Kook junior shifted this purity to the very *state*. He claimed that possession of the land of Israel was a mitzvah, a commandment from God that outweighed all other Jewish laws, even the one that decreed preserving life. Nothing was more important than populating the land of Israel. Nothing. So even the Israeli army's weapons were sacred.

In Z. Y. Kook, Avichail found a mentor who would guide his thinking and action for the rest of his life and in his teachings found a destiny that needed only to be heeded. As Avichail himself explained, "We are living at the end of history. The redemption of Israel no longer depends on Israel's deeds . . . Divine Providence no longer operates, as a rule, according to Israel's actions but according to a cosmic plan . . . None of the redemptive processes currently under way, processes from which there is no backtracking, are dependent upon us."[19] And although the process could not be stopped, it could be, had to be, accelerated. There was no reason to await the messianic era; there was no reason to wait at all.

Avichail had only one question: What was *his* role in the divine plan? How could he aid in its swift execution? He found the answer where all answers lay: in the Tanakh.

Jacob, or Israel, had had twelve sons, each of whom had given rise to a tribe: Reuben, Simeon, Levi, Judah, Issachar, Zebulun, Gad, Asher, Dan, Naphtali, Joseph, and Benjamin. Generations later, the tribes dispersed and formed two kingdoms: the descendants of Judah and Benjamin formed Judea in the south, and the ten other tribes created the Kingdom of Israel in the north. Around 722 BCE, the Assyrians, at the time the most powerful empire in the world, invaded the Kingdom of Israel and deported its inhabitants. The ten tribes scattered, their traces lost over time.

The prophets had foretold that the twelve tribes would be reunited in the land of Israel with the coming of the Messiah. "And it shall come to pass in that day, that the Lord shall beat off his fruit from flood of the River unto the Brook of Egypt, and ye shall be gathered one by one, O ye children of Israel," Isaiah proclaimed. Jeremiah predicted that the Lord would cause Israel and Judah to return to the land of their forefathers. The same in Ezekiel and Hosea and Amos and Obadiah and Micah and Zechariah.

We are commanded to search for them as the brothers of Joseph searched for him and return them to the land, Avichail wrote.[20] But they weren't easy to find. Avichail believed he'd uncovered clues in the Tanakh, the Talmud, and other contemporaneous rabbinical texts. Among them, a letter from Abraham Kook to the rabbi Simon Zvi Horowitz, the famous nineteenth-century kabbalist and seeker of the lost tribes, in which Kook lamented their scattering as one of the people of Israel's "great losses" imposed "by exile and the results of exile." This loss had resulted in a diminution in the spiritual power and pride of the Jews, he wrote. But he anticipated that this loss would be replaced by the influence of the ten tribes, "whose arrival we expect as a great upright gathering, retaining its complete pride, and with the undiminished might of Israel." (Echoing this, Avichail would state that the true impact of the exile of the ten tribes was about not "the loss of numbers or of land" but "the exile of matter from spirit. This is the true exile that we have lived in for thousands of years.") He also studied books by others on the hunt for the lost tribes. Some, unlike him, were obeying not a divine call but historical or anthropological curiosity, or even simply an adventurous spirit. With the Bible set at the heart of so-called Western culture, believers over the years had attempted to explain surprising cultural traits exhibited by "remote" peoples—that is, those hitherto unencountered by Western colonizers or adventurers—as the presence of some lost tribe or the tribe's descendants. Thus, for instance, the British who colonized Afghanistan were amazed to discover that the members of one local tribe had lighter skin than their neighbors, the men let their sideburns grow long, circumcised male babies eight days after their birth, and did not eat certain foods viewed as impure. Since the British had learned all of this as Jewish tradition, the Afghan tribe *must* have descended from one of Israel's lost tribes.

The truth is, customs akin to those described in the Bible could be found in many parts of the world. In the twentieth century, serious academic studies stopped attributing them to Judaism: the supposed similarities existed only in the minds of those who established them; customs and atavistic characteristics were the result of the communities' histories and experiences, not some fictive transmission. Later, scientific common sense concluded that it was impossible to track down any direct descendants of groups displaced two and a half millennia ago. The idea that lost tribes still existed was, in short, a myth.

Avichail despised that conclusion. He had three dozen Talmud and Bible quotations to back him up: the gathering of the twelve tribes on the holy land of Israel was a requirement for the "physical redemption of Israel." And it wouldn't just happen by accident, or by God's work alone. "In matters of redemption," Avichail wrote, "heavenly intervention will be the result of human initiation." And the ingathering of the tribes needed that human initiation. He was determined to be the man to bring it about.

He'd found some texts that led him to conclude that the Pathan, or Pashtun, were one of the lost tribes. Avichail advanced this theory in a talk at Mercaz HaRav in 1975. When he finished, Rabbi Kook took him aside. It was imperative that Avichail move past mere theories: action was urgently required. "If this is true," Kook said, "you can't just present the idea. You have to do something!"

Avichail opened an office he called Amishav, or My People Return, in Jerusalem and prepared to act. Through his readings, he'd deduced that the regions the ten tribes had set off to were in current-day Afghanistan, Pakistan, Iran, India, China, and Burma. But how could the tribes be identified? Judging by the prophecies of Jeremiah and Ezekiel, Avichail reasoned that they now lived as Gentiles yet must still retain some sign: the use of customs that other inhabitants of the region didn't follow or words that no one else understood; perhaps distinctive physical characteristics, or names used by the people of Israel.

He set off in search of signs. And, as he who seeks shall find, Avichail found.

Indeed, he found the Pathan, approximately fifteen million people living in Afghanistan, Pakistan, Iran, and India. They were Muslim, yet they circumcised their baby boys eight days after they were born; knew about the Sabbath and pure and impure foods; used Jewish names such as Reuben, Naftali, Gad, and Asher; and their language, Pashtun, contained words of Hebrew origin.

He found the Kashmiri, who numbered between five and seven million and lived in the north of India. Their place-names and some people's names were similar to Israeli names; they used a calendar similar to the Jewish calendar; and despite being Muslim, he wrote, they were "sympathetic towards Israel and the Jews."

He found the Bnei Menashe, as he called them, nearly two million people living on the Indian-Burmese border. They kept some customs that resembled Jewish ones; offered sacrifices on public altars, as in the Bible; named their sons Menashe; and used the name in songs.

He found the 250,000 members of the Chiang tribe in China, who followed some Jewish laws and offered sacrifices akin to those in the time of the First Temple.

And he found the Bnei Moshe.

Or perhaps they found him. Gideon Tadmor was the first; he'd been transferred to Colombia as ambassador and, during a meeting in Bogotá, had told the story of the Bnei Moshe to the then president of the Jewish Agency, Mendel Kaplan. "You've got a group of goyim there who are more Zionist than the Jews," he'd said. Kaplan had promised to study the matter, but Tadmor never heard back from him. Which was why, on his return to Israel, Tadmor told the story to someone who he knew would be interested: Avichail.

There was someone else as well. In 1982, David Liss, an Argentine who'd taken Israeli citizenship, had been sent by an agricultural co-op to Cajamarca, to analyze soil and crops. Liss had read in an Israeli newspaper about the curious case of the Cajamarcan who'd won the Bible contest. Intrigued, he'd sought out Víctor Chico in Cajamarca and, on meeting him, taken an immediate liking to the man, as had Bronstein before him. Years later, Liss wrote a letter that he sent to Avichail via Chaim Avni, an academic at Hebrew University in Jerusalem who'd been his professor. The Bnei Moshe were suffering in Peru, his letter stated; helping them get to Israel would certainly be a great act of Jewish kindness.

Avichail knew full well that the Bnei Moshe had nothing to do with the lost tribes. According to overwhelming scientific evidence not even he could deny, no tribe had gotten so lost as to end up in the Americas. By that time, however, he'd decided to broaden his campaign to include the descendants of Marranos, or crypto-Jews—Jews who'd been forced by the Spanish and Portuguese to convert to Catholicism during the time of the conquest. A great number had fled to the New World, where they secretly maintained their Jewish rites. They were descendants of the tribe of Judah, which, although not lost, had been forced to disperse. Hence, Amishav expanded its mission: now it aimed at bringing back to Israel not only direct descendants of the lost tribes but any Jewish souls in the vast Third World, anyplace where the devoted, the persistent, the desperate could be found.

Avichail wrote a letter to the Peruvian community asking for details of their lives and the ways they practiced Judaism. What he was really asking, though not in so many words, was whether they were lost Jewish souls.

Shortly thereafter, a wealthy Jew turned up at his door in Jerusalem, a man who in no way fit the description of the Bnei Moshe he'd read about, yet came to argue fervently for their cause.

This stranger's intercession had its own backstory. In 1985, a woman from the Lima colony named Rebeca Levy had traveled to Cajamarca to visit her sister, who'd married a Gentile. At her sister's home she saw photos of what appeared to be a bar mitzvah, but the rabbi—or person who seemed to be acting as rabbi—was a short man with weathered copper skin, straight black hair, and eyes black as coal; he was draped in a tallit and wore a kippa. A *cholo* rabbi? A bar mitzvah in Cajamarca?

The man in the photo, her sister explained, was Víctor Chico, a friend of her husband's who *practiced* Judaism. Shortly thereafter, back in Lima, Rebeca told the story to David Kiperstock, an old friend who had emigrated to Israel years earlier but was visiting for a few days.

Kiperstock had grown up in the colony but despised what he viewed as their acute materialism and lack of sensitivity to the impoverished majority of Peru. Born in Poland, he'd immigrated to Lima in 1936. Early on, Kiperstock had earned his living as a *cuentenik,* or street vendor, while finishing his secondary studies at night school. As such, he lived in the Peru not of the privileged but of those who, like him, worked all day to support their families and could only attend night school. Kiperstock developed a deep, romantic regard for those men and women, a feeling wholly contrary to the disregard he held for his peers in the colony and what he saw as their racism. In time, he founded a construction company and made a fortune, which he invested in moving his young children—whom he wanted to keep away from Peru's upper classes—to Israel. But he still had business ties in Peru and traveled back regularly.

Kiperstock asked Rebeca for Víctor Chico's address and, before returning to Israel, sent him a letter full of questions. Víctor was delighted to respond, telling Kiperstock of the long road that had led him to Judaism. His tale was peppered with quotations from the Tanakh. Kiperstock marveled that a Cajamarcan who worked sunup to sundown at a street market could have such extensive biblical knowledge and was eager to meet him. If what Víctor Chico was telling him was true, the Bnei Moshe embodied what he'd always believed and admired about destitute Peruvians: that through sheer determination and sacrifice they rose above their circumstances.

The following year, Kiperstock told Víctor he would like to visit him in Cajamarca. And in May 1986, Segundo and the entire El Milagro community traveled to the airport to welcome him. When the doors of his plane opened and Kiperstock stepped onto the airstairs, one hundred men, women, and children broke into "Hevenu Shalom Aleichem" (We come to greet you in peace), the song Víctor had learned to play on guitar in Israel.

Kiperstock embraced Víctor, Segundo, and Josué. They helped him into the broom truck and off they headed, in a caravan, to Cajamarca's central plaza. They took him to eat at the restaurant of a Bnei Moshe they called Zarco, a term used in Peru to refer to people with light eyes. Sitting at the table, Kiperstock listened to Segundo tell the story of the Bnei Moshe.

Later, at Víctor's home, he saw posters for the Israeli airline El Al on the walls and a photo of Víctor shaking hands with President Yitzhak Navon. After lunch, they strolled through Cajamarca and, as evening fell, in Víctor's small prayer room, prayed Maariv together.

Kiperstock spent three days with them. Though he was not a religious man, on the last night he wrapped himself in a tallit and, standing before the Bnei Moshe, recited, "The Lord bless thee, and keep thee; the Lord make his face shine upon thee, and be gracious unto thee: the Lord lift up his countenance upon thee, and give thee peace." Seven Bnei Moshe climbed up on the small dais and, one after the other, delivered a brief prayer that ended with a plea: "David, don't forget us."

One year and seven months later, on December 1, 1987, Kiperstock visited El Milagro. He stayed with Segundo three more days and was moved by the poverty in which the man lived. He prayed in the yet-unfinished synagogue, where a curtain had recently been hung to separate men from women, as per Orthodox Jewish law. Segundo showed him the letter Avichail had sent them. An Israeli rabbi, interested in them! Kiperstock was astonished: this was their way out. Avichail would have the authority to help them in a way he himself could not. When they said goodbye, Kiperstock assured him that their next meeting would be in Israel.

Back in Jerusalem, Kiperstock spent four hours at Avichail's apartment, telling him about Segundo, Víctor Chico, the Bnei Moshe's humility, their poverty and determination, the authenticity of their Judaism, and their devotion. Too busy to travel himself, Avichail told his yeshiva class about the community and asked who would be willing to travel halfway across the world to meet them. One of his students, Jonathan Segal, volunteered immediately.

Segal was an Englishman with a long dark beard, bright eyes, and a sweet voice. In his youth he'd been a left-leaning idealist, an adventurer who traveled the world with his 35 mm and his Super 8. Although now he was a strict observant Orthodox Jew, he hadn't lost his love of adventure. He'd never been to Peru, and this was his chance to visit Machu Picchu, one of the wonders of the world.

He set out in October 1988. After strolling through the historic center of Lima filming *cholas* at their market stalls, he traveled to Cuzco, trekked into Valle Sagrado, and hiked up the Andes to the ruins of the Inca citadel whose beauty was, and is, unrivaled.

Only after all this did he set out for Trujillo. Segal didn't know what to expect; he made no assumptions. He was just an explorer: he would simply watch, listen, and return with detailed notes.

A euphoric entourage of Bnei Moshe welcomed him at Trujillo airport. Segal filmed them as they sang "Shalom Aleichem" a cappella and loaded him onto the bus in which they'd come to pick him up. Although he spoke no Spanish, Josué knew enough Hebrew to carry on a conversation. For quite some time, they bumped along an uneven road in their overloaded bus.

By the time they stopped, night had fallen. Segal had stopped filming some time earlier. Where were they? The darkness was intense, and there seemed to be nothing but desert all around. What were they doing there? Someone removed the vehicle's battery and expertly hooked a couple of cables to it. And then there was light. The floodlight illuminated a single house: Segundo's. Then others. A handful of half-finished brick constructions in the middle of a dusty nowhere. The poverty of it staggered him.

They invited him to visit the synagogue. How could there be a synagogue in such a place? Segal was led to another miserable construction. The would-be door was a metal plate held in place by wires, and the walls were neither whitewashed nor painted. He was unaware of all that they'd had to sacrifice simply to build those four walls. Once inside the space, illuminated by candles, he knew their penury, their determination, and their sincerity.

Then someone said that they should take out the Sefer Torah. Segal marveled. A Sefer Torah? Impossible. How could these poor people possibly have obtained a Sefer Torah? It would cost more than their entire community.

Josué placed it on the modest bimah his father had built and slowly, lovingly opened it. Removing it from its case, he untied the cotton ribbon. Segal looked on in astonishment, questions swirling through his mind. Then very carefully Josué unfurled the scrolls. Segal moved closer to get a better look. Something was wrong. It did resemble a Sefer Torah, but none that he'd ever seen. After a moment he realized why. They'd photocopied the Torah and carefully glued the pages to cloth scrolls.

Later he saw the library, and the women who so painstakingly made challah, and the children who worked in the broom factory. He sang and prayed with them, and he thought about the Shabbat prayer:

He who blessed our forefathers, Abraham, Isaac, and Jacob—may He bless this entire sacred congregation along with all the holy congregations; them, their wives, sons, and daughters and all that is theirs; and those who dedicate synagogues for prayer and those who enter them to pray, and those who bring lamps for illumination and wine for Kiddush and Havdalah, bread for guests and charity for the poor; and all who are involved faithfully in the needs of the community—may the Holy One, Blessed is He, pay their reward and remove from them every affliction.

Segal reflected that it was the first time he'd truly understood the meaning of the prayer he'd said a thousand times before. The very first.

And on realizing that, he began to weep.

Segal returned to Jerusalem convinced that helping the Bnei Moshe was a mitzvah and recounted to Avichail all that he'd seen and heard. He showed him the film he'd made of his trip, in which Segundo recounted how he'd come to Judaism, Josué prayed in Hebrew, women baked bread for the Shabbat, children made straw brooms, and the entire community sang "Shalom Aleichem" in a strange, semidesert landscape. He read Avichail the titles of the books they had in their library and told him of their photocopied Sefer Torah and precarious synagogue and the dusty streets of El Milagro.

It was enough to convince Avichail: he would help them reach Israel; he'd convert them. But first he needed the approval of the Chief Rabbinate, the double authority that determined religious matters in Israel: the Ashkenazi chief rabbi had authority over Jews whose origins were in Eastern Europe; the Sephardic chief rabbi, over Jews whose origins lay in Spain and Portugal, North Africa and Turkey. Though the Peruvians had no Jewish origins whatsoever, as Latin Americans and Spanish speakers they naturally fell more into the domain of the Sephardic chief rabbi, Mordechai Eliyahu.

Born in Jerusalem, Eliyahu was the son of an Iraqi rabbi from whom he inherited a passion for the Torah and Talmud. As a teen, he'd led a religious youth group called Brit Hakanaim, which opposed the existence of a secular state; they had torched the cars of Jews who drove on the Sabbath and set fire to a butcher's selling nonkosher meat. He was arrested in 1951, while the group was plotting to throw a grenade into the Knesset, the Israeli parliament, in opposition to a debate over whether women should serve in the Israeli army. Eliyahu was sentenced to ten months in prison. He did not relinquish his extreme views as he aged and as a religious leader mounted active campaigns to attempt to make Jews who didn't keep the Sabbath observant. He publicly identified with the most extreme right wing of religious Zionism, which used terrorism against Palestinians. With his spectacles and long white beard, Eliyahu was an old man revered by politicians and religious leaders who sat on the far right of the Israeli political spectrum. Avichail got along well with him: they agreed on the coming of the Messiah as a matter of urgency and shared a belief that Jews should occupy *all* of the land of Israel.

As a first step, Avichail sent Jonathan Segal to tell Eliyahu what he'd told him. The chief rabbi knew whom Segal was referring to immediately: over the years, he'd amassed a drawer full of letters written in Josué Villanueva's self-taught Hebrew. He'd also heard about the Bnei Moshe from David Kiperstock, who had told him about Peruvian Jews who had made more sacrifices for their faith than many Jews by birth. But the chief rabbi had his doubts. The Bnei Moshe could claim no Jewish ancestry whatsoever: they did not claim, as other communities did, to be descendants of crypto-Jews, nor did they keep any customs their supposed ancestors had clandestinely passed down. No, the Bnei Moshe made no reference to any past other than that of their faith, any blood other than that which coursed through their veins, any tales of candles lit in secret. They were not a lost tribe, nor did they wish to be. They were, simply, an enigma.

Because if what they said was true, they had almost no historical precedents. Individual conversion, of course, was as old as Israel. The Tanakh recounted numerous stories: the Moabite Ruth, widow of the Jewish Mahlon, had surrendered to the God of Israel and his laws out of love for her mother-in-law. The Syrian general Naaman had asked the Israelite prophet Elijah to cure him of his leprosy and on being cured had declared, "Behold now, I know that there is no God in all the earth, but in Israel." Exodus, Leviticus, Numbers, and Deuteronomy all contained laws for the *ger,* the foreigner, the convert, whom Jehovah commanded his Israelites to love as they loved themselves. And the prophets spoke of *gerim* as well. Isaiah makes the prediction that when all of humanity comes together under the influence of Israel, "the LORD will have compassion on Jacob, and will yet choose Israel, and set them in their own land; and the stranger shall join himself with them, and they shall cleave to the house of Jacob."

After their captivity in Babylonia, as far back as the time of the Second Temple (516 BCE to 70 CE), Jews began to argue over who could be converted and what status, obligations, and rights the converts should have. When the Christians in power began to persecute converts, some Jews were of the view that conversions shouldn't take place, and a polemic arose. Certain scholars argued that anyone seeking conversion was suspect; others, that there was always a possibility they were lost Jewish souls who'd been present at Mount Sinai when God made clear his alliance with the chosen people and, after being lost, had returned to Israel in the bodies of Gentiles. To find out, what was required was a test of their will and determination to return: true Jewish souls would always want to return; nothing would stop them. And thus began the tradition of rejecting those who wanted to convert; if they were truly worthy of conversion, they would persevere until attaining their goal.

These contradictory views were reflected in the Talmud. It is written, "Beloved are proselytes by God, for the Bible everywhere uses the same epithet of them as of Israel." But it is also written that conversion must not be accepted during a period of prosperity, because it could be motivated by economic reasons or a desire for greater social status. And that converts should be rejected under all circumstances, because they delay the arrival of the Messiah. And that converts "are like leprosy on the body of Israel."

In the early third century CE, by which time conversion was no longer embraced, rabbinic law set out that it was in fact one of the legitimate paths to Judaism (the other was being born of a Jewish mother) but also imposed an explicit procedure to be followed: a court (*beit din*) of three Jewish men over the age of thirteen had to serve as witnesses; the candidates, if they were men, had to be circumcised; both men and women were to be immersed in a ritual bath and offer a sacrifice at the Temple of Jerusalem (this final requirement to be suspended until the Temple was rebuilt). Successive Talmudic commentators clarified, although this was nowhere written, that the aspiring convert also had to understand and accept the obligations imposed by Jewish law. Once these steps were taken, the *beit din* issued a certificate of conversion, the *shtar giur.*

This was the way individual conversions were carried out for centuries.

But mass conversions?

History records only a handful of cases, about which there appeared to be no overwhelming consensus or credible documentation. Some historians believed that King Abu Karib Assad of Yemen had established a Jewish kingdom in 350 CE that survived two hundred years, until it was vanquished by Christians and later converted to then nascent Islam. Others thought that something similar had happened with the Khazars, a Turkic people of central Asia who for three centuries in the early Middle Ages controlled the area between the Volga-Don forest steppe, eastern Crimea, and the northern Caucasus. According to this theory, the Khazars converted en masse to Judaism in about the ninth century. Then, for reasons that are disputed, they abandoned the religion before disappearing entirely from the face of the earth.

More consensus existed about Judaizing communities,[21] groups existing throughout history who took on Jewish customs without claiming or seeking any connection to Jews. In Russia, the Subbotniks kept the Sabbath, did not eat pork, denied the divinity of Jesus Christ, and circumcised their boys. As a result, they were persecuted, burned at the stake, thrown into prison, and sent into exile, but they kept their customs secretly, until the mid-nineteenth century.

And yet when, in thousands of years of history, had there ever been a case like that of the Bnei Moshe? Where had there been a community that adopted the Jewish religion entirely and asked to become part of the Jewish people, with no outside influence or any illusions of ancestral connection to Judaism?

There seemed to be only two documented cases that were comparable.

The first was that of the Abayudaya community of Uganda, which sprang from the imagination of the tribal leader Semei

Kakungulu. Born in 1869, Kakungulu was converted to Christianity by a Protestant missionary who taught him to read the Bible in Swahili. In it, Kakungulu found the commandment to circumcise and, later, the commandment to keep the Sabbath. In 1913, he abandoned Christianity and joined a local sect, the Malaki, who rejected idolatry, kept the Sabbath, and held anticolonialist and anti-Western views during the British occupation. Anti-British sentiment was apparently important to Kakungulu's conversion, for his aspiration to become king of his land had been denied by the colonizers.

In 1919, Kakungulu created the Abayudaya community, which, not unlike Segundo's late Israel of God, professed to be Jewish despite conserving some elements of Christianity and following a very personal interpretation of the Bible. It seems that Kakungulu had no contact whatsoever with Jews aside from those in his Bible until the mid-1920s, when he met one or more Jewish workmen employed by the British. They taught him Hebrew prayers, explained the proper way to kill animals following kashrut, the set of Jewish dietary laws, and persuaded him to abandon the sacrament of baptism.

Kakungulu died in 1928, but the Abayudaya lived on, surviving persecution by the Ugandan dictator, Idi Amin, in the 1970s. Conservative American rabbis took the community under their protection, converted four hundred members, and helped them establish a Jewish community that was formally recognized in Uganda. By that time, the community, which predominantly comprised farmers, numbered more than a thousand, and their leader was studying to become a rabbi.

The second case was that of the Jews of San Nicandro in Italy.[22] Donato Manduzio, born Catholic in 1885 to a poor rural family, had almost no formal education: he learned to read while in the hospital recovering from injuries sustained in combat during World War I that left him handicapped for life. At the end of the war, he met a group of Italians who had attempted to immigrate to the United States and failed, but returned converted to Pentecostalism and Adventism. They brought Protestant Bibles and organized Bible study groups. At group meetings, Manduzio learned the Old Testament and studied the messianic prophecies. But if the Messiah had come more than nineteen hundred years earlier, he wondered, what could explain the suffering he'd seen and continued to see around him?

Manduzio formed his own Bible study group with some fifty relatives and neighbors. Soon he announced that he himself was a prophet and that God spoke to him as he did to the other prophets they read about. In 1928, he declared himself Jewish but, for reasons unclear, was never circumcised. Manduzio believed that the Jews of the Bible had been wiped out, until he discovered that they existed, even in Italy. For years he sent letters to the chief rabbi in Rome with no reply.

In the 1940s, Nazism invaded Europe and led to the deaths of millions of Jews, including Italian Jews. At the end of the war, Jewish American soldiers stationed near San Nicandro discovered these strange Italians who had chosen to be Jews during the greatest anti-Jewish persecution of all times. The "Jews of San Nicandro" ended up on the cover of *Time* magazine. Manduzio died shortly thereafter, in March 1948. One year later, his entire community immigrated to the newly established State of Israel.

Should history add the Bnei Moshe to this short list?

Still undecided, the chief rabbi imposed a condition: that a rabbi in Lima support their request for conversion—in writing.

Avichail asked Benhamú, who agreed to sign on the condition that, once converted, the Bnei Moshe would not attempt to join the colony; they would instead be taken straight to Israel. Avichail agreed.

But the chief rabbi was *still* undecided.

So another man came to see him, the Israeli Jacob Krauss, who'd been sent to Lima the previous year as rabbi of the Israelite Union of Peru, the Ashkenazi Orthodox community. He too wanted to tell him a story.

Shortly after his arrival in Lima, a member of the Bnei Moshe had requested a meeting and told him about his community, the way they lived, and their desire to convert and immigrate to Israel. Assuming the Peruvian to be ignorant of the situation, Krauss attempted to explain the complications to him in the simple language he would have used with a child. But the man knew everything he was saying and more. Krauss was intrigued and asked him questions. And more questions. "He knows as much about Israel as I do," he marveled. "And he's learned it all from books."

The Bnei Moshe requested that he spend a weekend with them in El Milagro. Then he could give them his opinion. Krauss agreed. At worst, it would be a chance to do a little tourism. He took his two small children with him.

El Milagro disconcerted him, as it had the other Israeli visitors: he thought it looked like something out of *The Flintstones.* A few hours later, he corrected his impression: not *The Flintstones,* but the Torah. This was how Israelis must have lived in the desert, with however much or little God provided.

Rabbi Krauss prayed, sang, ate, and slept in El Milagro. At the end of the visit, his children didn't want to leave.

Víctor Chico and Josué Villanueva later visited him in Lima.

They brought along a list of questions they'd written in a note-book, very specific questions about words or passages from the *Shulchan Aruch* or the Torah that were unclear to them. Krauss answered one by one, surprised at the sophistication of the issues they inquired about. After some time, he asked how many more questions they had in their notebook. Víctor counted: twenty. So many! Did they want to know the answers, Krauss asked, half jokingly, or did they want to find out if he knew them? They wanted the answers.

"I was there, I saw them," Krauss told the chief rabbi. "And I think we must help them. At least for humanitarian reasons, leaving all else aside."

Finally, Chief Rabbi Eliyahu announced that he was con-vinced.

But then Avichail had to convince the second chief rabbi as well, the Ashkenazi Avraham Shapira, another leader of the religious Zionist movement, and a man close to Z. Y. Kook. Avichail sent word to Josué to make a petition in writing, in his own words. So Josué sent back a letter in which he told the story of the Bnei Moshe and their desire to love God in Israel. Avichail would later tell Josué that his error-ridden Hebrew and simple grammar were what convinced Shapira that their intentions were honest.

And thus the Great Rabbinate agreed to send a *beit din*. As local rabbi, Krauss would preside, with Avichail as the second member. They needed a third. Avichail suggested Mordechai Uriah, an Israeli rabbinical judge who had lived in Argentina and spoke Spanish. Uriah agreed, with a caveat: "I don't prom-ise to convert a single one of them. I'm going to observe."

Uriah's wife, Rivka, wanted to join them. She'd heard about the Bnei Moshe through a classmate at the University of Haifa who had traveled to Peru and taken photographs of them. In one, Segundo Villanueva posed beside the Aron Hakodesh he'd built.

When the news reached El Milagro on 1 Shevat 5749, or January 7, 1989, the Bnei Moshe convened a feverish assembly. They needed to raise six hundred dollars to cover the cost of the rabbis' airfare from Lima to Trujillo. That was a lot of money, and they needed even more, for there were plenty of other expenses: candles for the rabbis' rooms and water for their hygiene; enough food to feed them for several days; whitewash and paint for the synagogue's prayer hall, which was as yet unfinished. Segundo announced that all those wishing to convert had to contribute.

They would also have to study hard to pass the test, especially the newest members to join the Bnei Moshe in El Milagro and Cajamarca. Segundo set out for Cajamarca to study with them.

When the day arrived, the candidates numbered almost 160. A delegation traveled to Lima to welcome the rabbis early Thursday morning on 16 Av 5749, or August 17, 1989: Josué, Álvaro Villanueva, Víctor Chico, the Rengifo brothers, and two families from Lima. They recognized Avichail the moment he stepped out of the airplane: wild beard, woven kippa, black suit, and white shirt. They took him to Rabbi Krauss's home. "This, for us, is a very solemn, very great moment in the history of our lives," Álvaro Villanueva said.

The following morning, Josué, Víctor Chico, Álvaro, and the Rengifo brothers returned to the airport and watched a second bearded man in a black suit and hat step out of a plane: Rabbi Uriah, accompanied by his wife, Rivka.

After Shabbat, the delegation said goodbye to the rabbis and boarded a bus. They traveled all night and the following morning to arrive in Trujillo in time to join the others at the airport to welcome the very same envoys from Israel. Singing "Shalom Aleichem" at the top of their lungs, they helped the visitors onto the broom truck and drove them to El Milagro.

Avichail recognized the desolate landscape, the synagogue, the Sefer Torah: it was all just as Segal had depicted it. The houses lacked plumbing and electricity, but the mezuzahs were firmly affixed to their door frames.

On entering the modest bedroom that had been prepared for her, Rivka Uriah was moved to find beside her bed a pitcher with clean water for her to wash her hands in the morning, as the *Shulchan Aruch* instructed. She didn't have one even at her own home in Israel; only Haredi, or ultra-Orthodox Jews, kept this custom. Who were these Bnei Moshe, she wondered, these people who had nothing, and yet had learned to live so piously?

Josué sang in the synagogue. The rabbis gave blessings. The Bnei Moshe thanked God for having given them life and put them where they were. Josué introduced his father. Segundo thanked the rabbis who, "ignoring our humble condition, have deigned, like our Father Abraham, to help those who passed near his tent." Josué praised the rabbis' nobility, expressed gratitude for their selflessness, and wished them the rewards of the Eternal.[23]

Víctor Chico declared that finding them was a miracle from God, making their long-held dream come true. From the other side of the curtain separating the prayer hall, Jocabeth said they appreciated what they were doing for them. In a trembling voice, her sister Eva added, "We are unworthy of such a sacrifice, of this magnitude, that you make in coming to this place. As women, we bless the Jewish people. We love the Jewish people."

Rabbi Avichail recalled that helping a foreigner in his desire to convert was a mitzvah. Uriah, who served as Spanish translator, confessed that he had come to verify their desire to be Jews as authentic. "The yoke of the Torah is quite heavy," he warned.

In the synagogue's dining room, a modest banquet awaited them. The rabbis apologized: they could not eat the food unless they themselves had had a hand in its preparation, since those who had prepared it were not yet Jews. They asked to be allowed to light the gas stove and warm the bread there; only then did they eat. Everyone sang and prayed with such joy it overwhelmed them.

In the afternoon, when the men were praying, Segundo's wife, María Teresa, took her grandson, only a few months old, out into the cold and wind, heading for the synagogue. Rivka was alarmed, thinking the baby would fall ill. "But he must hear the prayers," María Teresa replied. Rivka was dumbfounded: this was like a scene out of the Mishnah, in the Talmud, which told of the mother of a wise Jew who had taken him, as a babe so young he was still breast-feeding, to the *beth midrash* where the Torah was being studied, because he had to listen.

The time for their exam arrived. The rabbis called up one part of Segundo's family first: Segundo himself; his mother, Abigail; María Teresa; and their unmarried children, Raquel, Josué, Jocabeth, and Oseas.

Uriah asked questions.

"We began our life in Judaism some twenty years ago," Segundo declared solemnly. "We have progressed and progressed. Even when we were Christians, we loved the Jewish people unknowingly. All that was Jewish was beloved by us always."

"What attracted you to Judaism?"

"We progressed in our Bible study. We have been practicing it."

"Did you study the New Testament?"

"Both testaments, to begin with. We know a lot about Christianity. But the New Testament was not as logical as the Old. It contains contradictions."

"What things have you studied? What books?" Uriah had already seen the books in their library.

"We learned Hebrew, we have a great deal of literature, books on Judaism, a great deal of literature."

"Where did you find details on how to practice? They are not in the Old Testament."

"In the *Shulchan Aruch,* in Spanish."

"How do you celebrate Sukkot? And Rosh Hashanah? And Pesach?"

Uriah translated each reply for Avichail.

Next to take the examination were Segundo's married daughters, Noemí and Eva, and four other families. The following day, after Shacharit—the morning prayer—and breakfast, they examined the remaining candidates. Some were insufficiently prepared: the rabbis determined that they needed to study and practice further before being deemed worthy of conversion.

At the end of the examination period, sixty-eight had passed.

To celebrate, the Bnei Moshe and the rabbis marched in procession some four kilometers outside Trujillo. They sang all the way to the temples Huaca del Sol and Huaca de la Luna, in a dusty desert where the volcanic peak of Cerro Blanco loomed in the distance like a mirage. The huacas bore no religious connection to the conversion, of course; they were a world-class tourist attraction, and the Bnei Moshe knew the rabbis would be impressed by their sight. Huaca del Sol, built from more than 130 million adobe bricks, was the largest pre-Colombian adobe construction in the Americas; sacked by conquistadors, only a third of the original structure remained. At Huaca de la Luna, the patios once used by the Moche people for human sacrifice were still intact.

The following day, the rabbis went to inspect the Moche River, which rose in the eastern mountains and crossed Peru, its mouth emptying into the Pacific. The water ran crystal clear and natural, as required for a mikveh, or ritual bath, in which converts were submerged and from which they emerged as new, pure Jews.

At night, after reciting Maariv, Josué and Víctor Chico said the Shehecheyanu prayer of gratitude, to thank the court once more for their presence.

Segundo quoted from Proverbs: "But the path of righteousness is as the light of dawn, that shineth more and more unto the perfect day."

Night had fallen. Rabbi Krauss exhorted them to lie awake, meditating on what the new day would bring: they would be Jews under the law. This was a birth, he told them, and from the pain it caused would come a new being. They should picture the baby in the future, in five, ten, twenty years. "Will he continue to go forth?" he asked them. "For it is very easy to be born a Jew, but it is difficult to live as a Jew."

Krauss spent the night with the men, answering their questions; the women sewed white tunics for their ritual baths. In the early morning, they recited Shacharit. Then the court asked every one of them to express their commitment to live as Jews.

Afterward they set out for the Moche, the women in their white tunics, the bearded rabbis in suits. The men waited at a short distance. The Moche's waters were as cold as winter and took the women's breath away; the rabbis worried for the health of the elderly among them, but their bodies had to be submerged entirely in the river, and they were.

Next, the men recited the blessing: *Baruch Ata Adonai, Eloheinu Melech ha-olam, asher kid-shanu b'mitzvo-tav, v'tzi-vanu al tevilat gerim.*

Last, they each had to pick a new name, their Jewish name. María Teresa chose Miriam; Josué chose Yehoshua; Noemí, Naomi; Eva, Chava; Oseas, Oshea; Jocabeth, Jochebed; Raquel, Rakhel.

Víctor Chico chose Abraham Chicco, an extra *c* added to the last name to erase its Spanish origin. Yehoshua argued that the family should also take a new surname. They would no longer be the Villanuevas of Cajamarca. They were Jews and loved the Torah and loved Israel and loved Hebrew, said Yehoshua, who'd chosen to name himself after Moses's helper, the man who carried on Moses's leadership in the promised land. "Our names must be Hebrew and so must our surname," he said. Of course, they could simply Hebraize Villanueva, turn it into something like Vaicadash or Vidaigarash. But that didn't satisfy them. Yehoshua thought of a verse from Deuteronomy that Segundo often quoted; it was like their father's moral compass: "Justice, justice, shalt thou follow." They took the word justice (*tzedek*) and added the name of God (*iyia*): this was the family's new name. God is just.

Tzidkiya.

When it was his turn, Segundo chose the name Zerubbabel. It was the Hebrew version of Zorobabel, the name he'd chosen twenty years earlier, when he was still an Adventist; the name of the leader who brought the Israelites back from Babylonian captivity, to whom God had said the phrase ("Not by might, nor by power, but by my spirit") that had led young Segundo to renounce his vengeance against his father's murderer.

Immigrants from all over the world arrived constantly at Ben Gurion Airport. Israelis called them *olim,* "those who ascend"; immigration, or "ascension," they called aliyah. Rabbi Avichail had been responsible for the ascension of thousands, from China, India, Ethiopia, Mexico. But the rejoicing of the Peruanim took even him by surprise.

The six months since their conversion in Trujillo had been like a dream—surreal and intense. Only they knew what it had taken to get there: the time, uncertainty, isolation, rejection, and penury; but also the faith, community, certainty, generosity, sympathy, providence, and selfless assistance.

They would no longer be an anomaly. They could live as Jews among Jews, in the land of the Torah.

The moment they stepped off the plane on February 28, 1990, or 3 Adar 5750, they broke into song and began to dance, sweeping others along with them. Avichail, the Jewish Agency workers, airport employees, random passengers, and the welcome committee sent by their future neighbors were all pulled into the dance. Rabbi Avichail got so caught up in the euphoria that, coming upon two Russian immigrant families on the far side of the room lamenting, "Where will we go? What will we do?" he invited them to join. "Come with us!" he cried, and pulled them into the dance.

They celebrated for hours.

Finally, in the middle of the night, off they drove in two buses from which they glimpsed cities glimmering like gold. They drove along a road that led into a desert of rolling hills and sleepy villages. One of the Bnei Moshe asked about the convoy of armed soldiers surrounding their caravan. "This is the way we live here," he was told.

At two o'clock in the morning, their new neighbors, including North American, European, Australian, and Turkish Jews, were all waiting to welcome them. They'd even hung a sign reading "Welcome to Israel" in Spanish.

They served the Bnei Moshe coffee and snacks in a communal dining room, gave them flowers, and recited Jeremiah 31:17: "And thy children shall return to their own border."

Yehoshua thanked them in Hebrew on everyone's behalf, since the others knew only enough to recite prayers. Again they sang and danced; it seemed the Peruanim would dance for the rest of their lives. When it was finally time to sleep, they were led to the trailers that would house them until something more permanent was found. These mobile homes could be loaded onto wheeled platforms and taken to various settlements as needed. Small, temporary residences, they normally accommodated the visitors who came from other towns each Friday to celebrate Shabbat. The bedrooms were small, and each trailer had a little living room, kitchenette, and bathroom. Zerubbabel, María Teresa (now called Miriam), and their unmarried children, Rakhel, Jochebed, Yehoshua, and Oshea, shared one. It was a cold night, but space heaters kept the inside toasty. And full of warmth, their first day in the world of their dreams came to an end.

They awoke to the brilliant morning sunlight. Although the bedrooms were hardly big enough to fit even the beds, they had large windows. The Tzidkiya family looked out over the vast rolling hills, covered in early spring greenery. Villages and olive trees dotted the landscape, and the dawn seemed more powerful, the color different from any they'd seen. In that infinite sky, God felt closer even than He had in the Andes. The intense, unfamiliar smell of flowers and earth brought tears to their eyes. Yehoshua told himself he had no words to describe what he was feeling.

They were in Elon Moreh, a small settlement of five hundred observant Jews located atop a fenced hill surrounded by Arab towns. "And Abram passed through the land unto the place of Shechem, unto the terebinth of Moreh," Genesis said. "And the Canaanite was then in the land. And the LORD appeared unto Abram, and said: 'Unto thy seed will I give this land'; and he builded there an altar unto the LORD, who appeared unto him."

Why Elon Moreh, of all the towns and cities in Israel? David Liss had objected: "I don't like it." Nor did Zvi Netzer, the ex-representative of the Jewish Agency in Lima who had tried to help them. Netzer went to the airport to welcome them but refused to accompany them to their new neighborhood; he wished they'd chosen "another path" rather than this one. Kiperstock, too, lamented their settling in Elon Moreh. He let them know they would always be welcome at his house in the Tel Aviv suburbs, but said that on principle he refused to visit the place they'd chosen to live.

But Avichail had told them it was important that they join a community who obeyed the Torah. Only 22 percent of Israelis practiced the Orthodox Judaism they did, with perhaps 12 or 14 percent being even stricter. Of those who remained, some 40 percent kept Jewish traditions but did not obey Jewish law, and some 20 percent or even 25 percent were totally secular. They had to decide what part of Israel they would live in, among what kinds of Jews. What was the point of leaving Peru to live among others who did not follow the commandments? Avichail asked. Zerubbabel couldn't agree more.

If the Bnei Moshe wanted to stick together, it was also vital to find a community willing to accept them all, and one that had enough space. Avichail had shown them, on a map of Israel, the

Zerubbabel Tzidkiya
and his brother, Alvaro
(Mordechai) by the
Western Wall, 1990.
Courtesy Yehoshua Tzidkiya.

Zerubbabel Tzidkiya, Kfar Tapuach, 2004.
Courtesy Yehoshua Tzidkiya.

The old Bnei Moshe synagogue in El Milagro, Trujillo, 2004.

Wilson Sánchez, an Inca Jew, in El Milagro synagogue, Trujillo, 2004.

Gilberto Aquiles Luján, La Rinconada, Trujillo, 2004.

Women of the Inca Jews community at El Milagro synagogue, Trujillo, 2004.

The kitchen of the Ciudad family, members of the Inca Jews,
in La Esperanza, Trujillo, 2004. The kitchen walls are covered with reminders
of Hebrew words, prayers, and ritual instructions.

Agustín Araujo, Inca Jew, Cajamarca, 2004.

Dora Salazar and her children, Inca Jews, Cajamarca, 2004.

A group of Inca Jewish women, Los Olivos, Lima, 2004.

Inca Jew Iosef Sánchez and his family, Los Olivos, Lima, 2004.

Zerubbabel Tzidkiya's tomb,
Mount of Olives cemetery, Jerusalem, 2016.

handful of places that met those conditions. There was a place here, he pointed, but it had no synagogue: no. There was this other place over there, but it had no factories or jobs: that was out. At the others, there was no way for them to stay together.

But at Elon Moreh, the entire community was religious, there were factories where they could get jobs, and the residents had agreed to accept them en masse. There were enough trailers to house them until they could find something more permanent. Yes, this was where they wanted to go.

Avichail himself had actually gone to Elon Moreh, where some of his yeshiva students lived, to convince the residents. Some had expressed doubts. But when Avichail showed them the video of their conversion in Trujillo, they were moved and agreed.

Avichail had told the Jewish Agency and the Ministry of Immigrant Absorption, which were in charge of immigration-related logistics, that the Bnei Moshe wanted to live in Elon Moreh. That way they avoided the large, government-run apartment buildings where immigrants were housed for their first six months as they took Hebrew classes and learned Israeli history. Avichail had said it would be far better for them to experience "direct absorption," for the community to help them adapt rather than have the government keep them isolated for half a year.

On Sunday, four days after their arrival, the Associated Press reported that a group of "South American Indians" who'd converted to Judaism had celebrated their first Sabbath in Israel: "The tribe's move to the occupied lands comes at a time of growing US pressure on Israel to stop building or expanding Jewish settlements in the West Bank and Gaza Strip, and demands that Israel not settle Soviet Jews in those areas." Elon Moreh was not just some small, welcoming community of religious Jews: it was a symbol, a bastion of the movement begun by Zvi Yehuda Kook, Avichail's mentor. In June 1967, around the time Segundo and his sixteen were first entering the jungle, surprise attacks by an Arab coalition that included Syria, Jordan, Egypt, and Iraq, led to the Six-Day War. At its close, when a victorious Israel began its military occupation of the West Bank, Kook saw it as an unequivocal sign that the messianic era would soon arrive. The occupation, condemned by the international community for its seizure of lands destined to the future Palestinian state, was for him a call to action: the time had come to impose Israeli sovereignty over *all the biblical lands*. It had to be done, Kook said, at the expense not just of Palestinian lives but of their own. "One is required to give up one's life rather than surrender even a millimeter of the land," he proclaimed. Israel was an ontological whole, a unit, like body and soul, indivisible.

A new movement grew out of the first, one with even more radical ideas and an even greater sense of urgency: Gush Emunim, or Bloc of the Faithful, embarked on establishing settlements on what the Tanakh registered as the lands of Judea and Samaria. Members called for direct contact with nature, the actual land of Israel, but also physical aggression and violence as tools in a fight against evil whose objective was "cosmic rectification." "The wars of Israel represent the steps of the Messiah, marching toward his own coronation," wrote Rabbi Zvi Tau, Kook's main disciple and the movement's ideologue.

In 1973, when Israel won another war against an Arab coalition comprising Egypt and Syria that had launched a surprise attack on Yom Kippur, the holiest day of the Jewish year, members of Gush Emunim marched to the outskirts of the Palestinian city of Nablus, in the northern West Bank, and set up tents, an Israeli flag, and a sign: "Elon Moreh." They had identified the place cited in the Tanakh. The original Elon Moreh, it was said, was located near the old city of Sebastia, north of Nablus—or Shechem, its biblical name. The occupation violated international law, and the Israeli army forced them to evacuate. But the settlers, as they were called, moved to nearby land. Seven times they were evicted and seven times they returned, until in 1979 a new government gave them permission to stay. The place they had chosen, however, was part of the adjacent Palestinian village of Rujeib, and the Israeli Supreme Court ordered the colony dismantled. Elon Moreh moved yet again, this time to the slopes of Mount Kabir.[24]

The settlement's inhabitants lived surrounded by nearly 200,000 Palestinians, whom they had to pass each day on their way to Israeli cities. The government eventually built them a safe, high-speed motorway and sent soldiers, this time not to evict them but to protect them.

In the following decade, despite the opposition of Palestinians, most Israelis, and the international community, similar settlements burgeoned throughout the 1967 occupied territories, now with the support of successive governments. Mobile homes were replaced by houses with foundations, plumbing, gardens; the few remaining trailers were used as temporary housing for newly arrived settlers, like the Bnei Moshe. Regular bus routes were set up to connect the settlements to major Israeli cities.

In December 1987, a Jewish man was stabbed to death in Gaza, the occupied territory in southern Israel along the Egyptian border. Two days later, an Israeli army truck crashed into a station wagon carrying Palestinians, killing four. A rumor spread in Palestine: it was revenge for the killing of the Jew.

Accumulated rage exploded, and the first intifada began: young Palestinians threw rocks at Israeli soldiers, burned tires, set up barricades. The soldiers responded with bullets, and prison, and the destruction of the rock throwers' homes.

On April 6, 1988, almost two years before the Bnei Moshe arrived, sixteen teenage boys and girls and two armed guards from Elon Moreh traveled to the outskirts of Beita, a village where some four thousand Palestinians lived.[25] One of those guards was Roman Aldubi, who had been involved in a shooting incident against Palestinians and whom the West Bank Israeli army commander had prohibited from going to Nablus. A group of villagers caught the group by surprise and threw stones at them. The guards opened fire, wounding one young Palestinian. The villagers asked the settlers to accompany them to Beita, where more stones were thrown at them; Aldubi started shooting in all directions, and two young Palestinians were killed. One of the settlers, the fifteen-year-old daughter of one of the founders of Elon Moreh, was also killed. Villagers surrounded the settlers, confiscated the guards' guns, and gave them refuge in their homes until the Israeli army could come for them. Once back in Elon Moreh, the settlers claimed that the Palestinians had stoned the girl to death. News tore through the settlements and was published in Israeli papers. A week later, the Israeli army announced that the girl had been shot by a stray bullet fired by Aldubi. The settlers were furious, and although they couldn't refute the evidence or the categorical autopsy, they continued to blame the Palestinians. The army entered Beita, destroyed fourteen houses, including those of the two murdered Palestinians, and detained and expelled six inhabitants they deemed part of the incident. Many in Israel criticized the army. Why, when they knew that the settlers had been responsible for the girl's death, were they taking revenge on the Palestinians? "If the facts are known, why are houses being blown up?" the newspaper *Hadashot* asked. "It is a political act, blowing them up. This is the price the defense establishment is paying to the settlers."

One year and ten months later, the Bnei Moshe were passing Beita en route to their new home in Elon Moreh, a hotbed of the ongoing war. Inevitably, they were drawn into it. Were they not there, one journalist asked, as part of a "desperate maneuver" consisting in "using the poor from other parts of the planet as cannon fodder" against the Palestinians?

War coverage now spoke of the "Jungle Jews."[26] "The staccato rattle of Israeli army gunfire from a nearby Palestinian city echoes through this windswept hilltop Jewish settlement while a lone F-15 fighter jet maneuvers in the blue sky overhead. But neither seems to bother the young men and women besieging a mail van to buy stamps and postcards to send to their former homes on the other side of the world. 'No. I'm not afraid. This is God's country,' said Gamaliel Cabrera, 22, abruptly dismissing Middle East tensions and the Palestinian-Israeli conflict." Gamaliel was Abraham Chicco's nephew. A journalist from *The Jerusalem Post* found Zerubbabel "sitting in a class on a Samarian hill, studying Hebrew underneath a picture of the first Ashkenazi chief rabbi, Avraham Yitzhak Kook."[27]

But it wasn't solely the war and occupation that aroused suspicions about Jews who didn't represent familiar stereotypes. The Bnei Moshe's arrival had coincided not only with the intifada but with two mass immigration movements that were raising controversy and seemed destined to redefine the identity of Israeli society.

"Not Jewish enough to be saved?" a column in *The Jerusalem*

Post wondered.[28] "An enormous number of Soviet Jewish immigrants are coming to Israel. Practically none of them are being, or will be, settled on the West Bank—no matter what anybody says. On the other hand, I read recently that a group of 55 [*sic*] Peruvian Indians are being settled on the West Bank after being recruited by a right-wing rabbi and converted to Judaism. The very same authorities who admitted these Indians to Israel—with all the rights and privileges of Jews—also require that Jews fleeing the Soviet Union show proof that they are Jews."

Israel had four million inhabitants, and although the country was accustomed to receiving a constant influx of *olim,* the flood of Soviet Jews was overwhelming: sometimes more than 10,000 landed at Ben Gurion in a single day.[29] In 1989, when the influx began, there were 120,000 Jews of Soviet origin living in Israel, most having arrived in the 1970s in search of the Zionist dream. They were educated, middle-class immigrants, professionals who assimilated easily, quickly adopting Hebrew and local customs. But the new Soviets were different. Under the so-called Law of Return, Israel guaranteed citizenship to anyone who had at least one Jewish grandparent—the same criterion used by the Nazis that had cost millions their lives. The Soviets arriving now were families who satisfied the formal requirement with only one Jewish ancestor, but in many cases they didn't follow Jewish traditions or keep customs.

From the start, it was clear that they had no intention of assimilating; they conserved and defended their identity, language, literature, customs, and values. Many didn't believe in the Zionist cause. They came from three generations of a regime hostile to Judaism and had lost their connection to it. They had largely married outside the faith and, in many cases, didn't even consider themselves Jewish.

One segment of the public saw them as a threat to the very nature of the Jewish state. There were also financial concerns. With so many new residents, the cost of living had skyrocketed. What's more, they were a burden on the state: by law, during their first six months in Israel all expenses had to be covered, and then, if they didn't find jobs, they were eligible for three years of soft loans. The Soviets came from rural areas, poor areas, critics argued. What did they have to offer the Israeli economy?

To complicate matters further, a large number of them, one survey showed, were prejudiced against Arabs as well as Moroccan and Ethiopian Jews—that is to say, against people of color—and generally aligned with the political right.[30]

On top of that, Israel was at the same time being rocked by another huge aliyah: that of the Falasha, or Ethiopian Jews. According to their oral tradition, the Falasha were descendants of a chance union between King Solomon and the queen of Sheba, recounted in the Tanakh. Other versions said they were descendants of Dan, one of the lost tribes. In any case, nearly 17,000 Falasha had arrived in Israel during the 1980s, amid the humanitarian crisis triggered by the Ethiopian famine, and they were still coming. Thirty years later, they would number 120,000. Their Judaism, too, was questioned; they, too, were seen as "other."

Even in the face of these bewildering new realities, the Bnei Moshe, whose numbers were minuscule by comparison, were considered stranger than anything else. Neither the press nor Israeli society knew how to describe them. Without realizing how offensive it was to them, journalists called them "Indi-anim." One commentator claimed that their faces "would fit beautifully in a *Life Magazine* photographic essay entitled 'The people of the Andes.'"[31] And the correspondent from *The Jewish Week* observed that "the Peruvian men were outfitted, like other Elon Moreh residents, in jeans, sneakers and colorful knit kippot. Only their dark complexions and distinctive South American features set them apart."[32]

They were an exotic, unclassifiable element in a nation accustomed to splintering into very specific tribes. Very soon they would be forced to pick one.

Elon Moreh's leaders publicly praised the Bnei Moshe. *The Sunday Telegraph* reported the opinion of Mr. David Singer, an Elon Moreh official, who said that the new arrivals "would spend six months learning Hebrew and getting acclimatized. 'We won't presume to tell them what to do afterwards,' he said. 'But I certainly hope that the majority of them would stay on. They are better Jews than you and me.'"[33] Nonetheless, they trusted they could turn them into Jews like the rest as soon as possible. And that process began by making them decide what *kinds* of Jews they wanted to be. For anyone who lacked the ties of origin—tradition, community, family, nationality— there was a wide range to choose from.

Outside the settlements were the secular Jews, whom the Bnei Moshe found distasteful. They shouted when they spoke and didn't seem to care about pleasantries. In Peru people spoke softly, using exaggerated politeness: How are you doing? May you have a nice day, friend; I wish you well, brother. Here, Yehoshua laughed, people got right in one another's faces, as if they were going to fight, even if nothing happened.

Inside the settlements, differences—even among the Orthodox, even within a small settlement like Elon Moreh—could be disconcerting. There were the modern Orthodox Jews, who lived in the secular world and served in the army. Then there were the ultra-Orthodox, the Haredim, who lived in isolation from the modern world: the men dedicated themselves wholly to studying the Torah, and their children did not serve in the army. Some of them opposed the State of Israel, convinced that Israel could exist only after the coming of the Messiah. Others believed that their rabbi, who lived in Brooklyn, was the Messiah: you could tell who they were by the flags with messianic crowns flying from their roofs. There were Haredim who refused to speak Hebrew and instead spoke Yiddish; they lived not in the settlements of what settlers called Judea and Samaria but in other Israeli cities and towns.

And even within both groups there were countless differences, based on place of origin or which rabbi they considered their spiritual leader. There were the Chabad-Lubavitch, the Satmar, the Ger, the Belzer, the Breslov . . . In time, the Bnei Moshe learned to recognize their distinctive signs. The color of their clothes, the type of head covering: for women, the length of skirt or whether they used a scarf or wig to cover their heads; for men, the color and length of their jackets, the color and material of their kippas.

Zerubbabel's children, Yehoshua in particular, decided they felt closer to the so-called *kippa sruga,* or knit kippa. These were modern, nationalist Orthodox Jews; they voted for their political leaders, served in the military, and fought for the appropriation of all of Judea and Samaria. Many lived in Elon Moreh and other settlements. They dressed like them, in jeans, sneakers, and brightly knit kippas. The women wore long skirts, as they had in Peru, and sneakers; they covered their heads with caps or small hats. Only Jochebed, Zerubbabel's daughter, chose a different community: she married Iosef, a Haredi who dressed as if he lived in seventeenth-century Poland, and moved with him to Mea Shearim, an ultra-Orthodox neighborhood in Jerusalem. Over time, all of them—well, *nearly* all—made choices based on personal preference or new relationships.

After six months, when the state subsidies ran out, they had to join the Israeli economy as well. Zerubbabel, who was sixty-four, his mother, Abigail, María Teresa, and a handful of other elderly who had come with them received a pension. The rest looked for work.

Abraham Chicco learned to lay ceramic floor tile but discovered he couldn't compete with the Palestinians, who did it better and cheaper. Like him and other Bnei Moshe, the Palestinians were construction workers, service-industry employees, factory workers. So he got a job in an aluminum factory. Although the owner was Jewish, fifty of the fifty-five employees were Palestinian, including his direct boss. At work, Abraham Chicco didn't hear a word of Hebrew all day. Arabs didn't seem so bad after meeting them in person. But when they left the factory at the end of the day, everyone returned to their own world. At Elon Moreh, the Palestinians were invaders who had to be displaced, usurpers—as the children were taught—of lands that belonged to the Jews by divine right.

Six months after their arrival, Yehoshua was accepted at a yeshiva in Jerusalem. He discovered then that his self-taught Hebrew was good enough to converse and read but not to write fluently. So he made a deal with a Haredi rabbi: the rabbi would help him to improve his written Hebrew, and in exchange Yehoshua would give him the wood and leather tefillin box he had carved in El Milagro. He became a mezuzah engraver, a trade that kept him close to God and earned him a living.

Yehoshua wanted to be a rabbi. This would take years, but while he studied, he would also learn to be a shochet, a ritual slaughterer, and a mohel, a circumciser. His sister Chava was brought to tears when Yehoshua circumcised her newborn son.

The grandchildren of the first Bnei Moshe were called up to do obligatory military service; their families were proud. When one boy confessed, crying, that the army was too hard and he didn't want to return, his father was furious. "Do you want them to think we're not men? You must be a man and serve in the army like a man, and if you must die, you die."

No matter the difficulties, they were grateful to be in Israel. They had their homes, their gardens, and their incomes, and they were welcome in synagogues. They had everything they'd longed for. Happily, it seemed that Zerubbabel had fulfilled his mission, that the search he'd dedicated his life to was over. He'd taken his people out of Peru to Israel.

Like Moses out of Egypt.

Like the first Zerubbabel out of Babylonia.

And yet the new Zerubbabel often wore not a woven kippa but his narrow-brimmed black felt Peruvian hat. He didn't accept the local identities that other Bnei Moshe, including his own children, had taken: they seemed cut off from God, from the Tanakh, from his faith, from all that had brought him to Judaism. Those groups gave a human, a rabbi, the authority at every step to judge what was right from what was wrong, something only God could do. Some groups he found flat-out idolatrous, like the Chabad-Lubavitch, who believed their rabbi in Brooklyn was the Messiah. Zerubbabel refused to join any of them. Together with Mordechai, who had once been

Álvaro, he visited the Ashkenazi synagogue, then the Sephardic one, then the Teimani temple of the Yemenite Jews, and the two of them spoke to everyone, as they always had. One day, the chief rabbi of Elon Moreh, Eliyakim Levanon, called them to his office. Together Zerubbabel, Mordechai, Yehoshua, and Abraham Chicco went to see him. Rabbi Levanon had told them to bring their prayer books. "Put them on the table," he instructed when they sat down. He pointed to the books, one by one. "This is Sephardic. This one is Ashkenazi. This one is Mizrahi." They had to pick which rite to follow, he said. Then he outlined the differences, as though they did not know them, and recommended they choose Ashkenazi, his branch.

Yehoshua, in his good Hebrew, politely but firmly rejected his counsel. "This division pains us. We want there to be unity among the Jewish people."

In light of the rabbi's intransigence, Yehoshua announced that they would choose the branch of Judaism that combined the most existing rites. They knew there was another option that Levanon had not mentioned: the Sfard followed by some Polish, Ukrainian, and Romanian Jews, which combined the Ashkenazi tradition with Sephardic rites and was therefore considered the closest thing to a neutral solution. Levanon was not satisfied, but they had made up their minds.

The other Bnei Moshe, however, did not support them. Most picked one rite, one group—Ashkenazi, Sephardi, Mizrahi, Chabad—each doing what they wanted without requesting permission from the old leaders.

Leadership, in fact, was at the heart of the conflict. What Zerubbabel and Mordechai could not accept was the authority of the rabbis. They questioned both their teachings and their practices. One of them had admitted, or so Mordechai and

Zerubbabel understood, something that Zerubbabel found as unacceptable as Segundo would have: that he was solely guided by the Talmud, the compilation of oral rabbinical tradition. What value could the Talmud, written by men, have when compared with the Book of God? The rabbis were not interested in entertaining their objections to the Oral Law. The brothers' defiance first took them by surprise, then irritated them.

It wasn't just a question of losing his community. The search that Zerubbabel had begun as Segundo was not over. He refused to simply abide by the rabbis' dogma, which didn't always seem devoted to the letter of the Book. He wanted to keep investigating, both in books and in dialogue with those in other sects and other churches—all other readers of the Book. And this was the most vexing source of conflict: the rabbis forbade certain pursuits and, more than that, certain contacts.

Two years after having moved to Elon Moreh, around the time of Sukkot, in open disobedience, Zerubbabel and his brother went to meet the Karaites of Ramla.

The Karaites were a sect that claimed to be Jewish but did not recognize the Talmud's legal authority.[34] Some experts claimed the movement had come out of Baghdad during the Middle Ages, specifically as a response to an Islamic interpretation that said Jews had renounced monotheism on accepting rabbinical authority as divine law. Others held that their origins dated as far back as the Sadducees, a Jewish sect from before the Talmud was written. When, in 1950, they began arriving from other Middle Eastern countries, the Chief Rabbinate tried to impede their entry: they were not Jews. But the attempt failed, and thirty-five thousand of them now lived in Israel.

Karaite means "reader" in Hebrew. To the Karaites, only the written Torah, the first five books of the Tanakh, was divine law.

Only the Written Law had been given to Moses by God, they reasoned. Rabbinical Judaism responded that Oral Law had been dictated by God to Moses during the exodus from Egypt and that the Jewish people had passed it down from generation to generation until it was finally transcribed by rabbinical authorities. The Karaites turned to the book of Joshua, who "read all the words of the law," to refute this assertion.

The Karaites' main synagogue and rabbinical council were in the city of Ramla, in central Israel. One of the rabbis received Zerubbabel and Mordechai in his home, inviting other rabbis to come and converse with them as well. Then they took them to visit the synagogue, in which there were neither benches nor chairs but only rugs on which they sat for worship.

Just like the Bnei Moshe and Israel of God before them, the Karaites allowed no light or fire of any kind to be lit on Shabbat. Rabbinical Judaism, on the other hand, allowed that if the fire or light had been lit before the start of Shabbat, there was no need to put it out: in Israel they ate hot food on the Sabbath. But Zerubbabel refused, for this contradicted what was written in the Torah.

He saw that the Karaites practiced what was written in the Torah, just as he had. And although he did not join them, meeting their rabbis fueled his rebelliousness. The Talmud might have value, but it could not be the *same* value: only Scripture had divine worth.

Scripture, yes. But which one? They studied Hebrew. And despite having chosen the Hebrew name Zerubbabel, old Segundo from the Andes could never really learn it, not enough to speak and listen to others. His readings, nonetheless, served for him to discover something alarming: even the Tanakh might contain errors. Yes, it had originally been written in Hebrew, but after the Israelites' exile in Babylonia, it had been expanded and rewritten in Aramaic. Were there differences? What were they? Was there perhaps some original Scripture that didn't correspond even to the Jewish one?

In search of that original text dictated by God, Zerubbabel and Mordechai took another forbidden trip, this one to the small town of Kiryat Luza, the Samaritan town on Mount Gerizim.[35] Karaites were seen as an enemy sect but still Jewish; not so the Samaritans, who didn't even claim to be Jews themselves. Not because they didn't recognize God or his Book, but because they claimed to be the *authentic* descendants of the original tribes of Israel, possessors of the *authentic* Scripture and guardians of the *authentic* place of worship that had once been Canaan.

Rabbinical Judaism denied and repudiated each of these claims. As a result, everything related to the Samaritans was a matter of dispute—even their name. The Samaritans called themselves Shamerim, which in their type of Hebrew means "keepers" of the Torah, and professed that the word had given rise to the name of Samaria, their region. Jews, on the other hand, called them Shomronim, identifying them as mere "inhabitants of Samaria" and implying therefore that it was the region that had come first and not the people. The Samaritans claimed to be direct descendants of the tribes of Ephraim and Manasseh. According to them, they'd survived the destruction of the Kingdom of Israel by the Assyrians in 722 BCE and had managed to remain on their land, while the other tribes were forced into exile. In the Samaritan account, they had preserved the text of the original Torah in Hebrew, while the captives in Babylonia had transcribed it into Aramaic and added the other books that make up the Tanakh, which in their eyes were illegitimate and the result of foreign influence.

Whatever their origins might have been, the Samaritans still claimed Mount Gerizim as the authentic site of worship, which rabbinical Judaism sited in Jerusalem. This was a critical difference, one that was not only theological but political: the city was claimed by three religions and two peoples, and the subject of constant dispute. Defending the sacredness of Jerusalem was essential to the Jewish state.

The Samaritans had been reduced to four large families numbering some eight hundred people in total, living in Kiryat Luza and in the seaside town of Holon, on the outskirts of Tel Aviv. Zerubbabel and Mordechai were received cordially on three separate occasions. They asked questions, studied, contemplated. If the original Book, or its most faithful copy, had survived with the Samaritans, how many erroneous things had they learned from the other ones? And how much new knowledge remained to be learned?

Reading some Hebrew had, for instance, led them to discover that there was no passage anywhere stating that Adam and Eve had passed on their original sin to humanity. And to understand that "Messiah" came from a Hebrew word that referred to those kings or priests anointed with a special oil and not to a divine being or envoy of God. And to learn that "Satan" actually meant "adversary," not some being who was the opposite of God or a fallen angel. These were all Christian inventions that they'd ripped from their Bibles in Hebron so that only the Tanakh remained.

But now, according to the Samaritans, the Tanakh itself had to be cut. The Scripture that they used contained only the first five books: the Torah, or Pentateuch, the original text dictated to Moses. The rest was a later creation, the result of historical circumstances, of exile—as had been the case with the Gospels, albeit under different circumstances and out of other interests.

Many books had not come from God: Joshua, Judges,

Samuel, Kings, Isaiah, Jeremiah, Ezekiel, Hosea, Joel, Amos, Obadiah, Jonah, Micah, Nahum, Habakkuk, Zephaniah, Haggai, Zechariah, Malachi, Psalms, Proverbs, Job, Song of Songs, Ruth, Lamentations, Ecclesiastes, Esther, Daniel, Ezra, Nehemiah, and Chronicles. The only worthy part was the one that had moved young Segundo Villanueva the first time he'd opened his father's old Bible: the tale of creation, the flood and reconstruction, God choosing Abraham, the beginnings of Israel, captivity in Egypt and freedom, the encounter at Mount Sinai, the writing of the laws, Moses's tribulations, the exodus, and reaching the land of Israel.

There, in those five books written in ancient Hebrew, was the only truth revealed by God.

The brothers prayed at Mount Gerizim, where Joshua, in the book of Joshua, had sworn his loyalty to God. Mordechai began celebrating Rosh Chodesh, the start of every lunar month, there with his brother and children. Mordechai was convinced that the Samaritans were telling the truth, and he told the rabbis so. The rabbis were indignant. "What are you talking about?" It was ridiculous! Their visits to the Karaites had incited exceptional outrage given that they'd explicitly been prohibited from speaking to them. When it was learned that Zerubbabel and Mordechai left no lights on nor did they eat hot food on Shabbat, the rabbis became convinced that the two were a bad influence and let the other Peruanim know that meeting with them would be frowned upon.

There was no longer a place for them in Elon Moreh. Four years after having arrived, Zerubbabel moved to the nearby settlement of Kfar Tapuach, which had large new homes with gardens.

For the first time in many years, his family were the only ones to follow.

Fourteen miles southwest of Elon Moreh is a place that links the entire network of northern West Bank settlements to Jerusalem and Tel Aviv, a strategic spot where the Israeli army has set up a checkpoint. Each day, the Palestinians living in the area who have to pass the checkpoint on their way to work, or to their olive groves, or on the way back from their villages are subjected to long waits in the sun. Eventually, the soldiers will allow someone to move forward. Before being allowed to pass, the people must have their documents inspected and endure a body search.[36]

Other men and women, however, wait casually for the bus. If it's late, they hitch a ride. Either way, the soldiers make no objection. These lucky souls are neither coming from nor going to the nearby villages; nor are they traveling to Nablus, which they call Shechem. They climb off the bus, or get out of the car that brought them there, and meander down a narrow white road that climbs an adjacent hill. On top of the hill, where the road ends, is a gate guarded by men with long guns. Huge yellow letters painted on the cement announce that this is Kfar Tapuach. Beyond the gate is a sign, a quotation from 1 Maccabees: "It is not foreign land we have taken nor have we seized the property of others, but only our ancestral heritage which for a time had been unjustly held by our enemies. Now that we have the opportunity, we are holding on to the heritage of our ancestors."

Beyond that lies what looks to be a tranquil, middle-class suburb with shiny asphalt streets, clean wide sidewalks, neatly landscaped flower beds, and well-groomed trees. Cars are parked in front of white-tile-roofed A-frame houses with gardens. There is a plaza with brightly colored slides, a community center, a mini-market, a parchment factory, a honeybee farm, and a mechanic's; there are three playgrounds, two mikvehs, and four synagogues.

A van drives around the sleepy town, its back doors open so the music pouring from its speakers can be heard at full volume. This is both a celebration and an advertisement: today, the Chabad-Lubavitch synagogue will receive a new Sefer Torah. The van stops beside a house with a crowd gathered outside. Inside, as custom dictates, the final words of the Torah have just been transcribed onto the parchment. In the garden, a group of men in black suits, tzitzit dangling from their white shirts, rock forward and back as though in a trance. They are praying.

As night falls, the whole town emerges. The inscription has been finished; the Sefer Torah is carried in procession to the synagogue. The sacred scrolls go first, beneath a moving chuppah, or canopy. The men carrying the scrolls take turns kissing them in the torchlight; the women walk behind, chatting and laughing; groups of children run around them, playing. All are guarded by young soldiers armed with heavy machine guns. Music blares from the speakers, floods the valleys and nearby hills outside the settlement, and ascends into the starless sky.

A feast is awaiting in the synagogue. The men eat in one room, the women in another. Once the meal is over, the women will return home to put the children to bed. The men will remain, singing well into the night.

Kfar Tapuach was built in 1978, but the first Tapuach appeared in Joshua. It had been part of the Palestinian village of Yasuf until Jewish settlers appropriated it. Today, Kfar Tapuach is known by many in Israel as the settlement where Meir Kahane followers live.

Kahane was an American-born Orthodox rabbi who committed and called on others to commit acts of terrorism against those he viewed as "enemies of the Jewish people": the Soviet Union and Arabs.[37] In 1971, he immigrated to Israel, where he founded a political party that endorsed imposing religious law as the basis for all law. In the country Kahane envisioned, only the observant would have the right to citizenship, everyone would be forbidden to marry or have sexual relations with non-Jews, and all biblical territory would be taken after forcibly expelling the Palestinians living on it. An Israeli law expressly forbidding racist policies outlawed his party, and in November 1990, when the Bnei Moshe had been in Elon Moreh for less than a year, Kahane was killed by a sharpshooter in New York. The last campaign he launched before his assassination was an open call to American Jews to immigrate to Israel "before it's too late." Chief Rabbi Eliyahu, who was sympathetic to Kahane's ideas, publicly lamented his death and officiated at his funeral. Some time afterward, he stated that the life of just one yeshiva student was worth "more than the lives of 1,000 Arabs."

Important followers of Kahane's, including his son Binyamin, who overtook his father's organization, settled in Kfar Tapuach and opened a museum in his memory there. They also opened a dog breeder's where they trained German shepherds as attack dogs. The dogs were provided to nearby settlements as protection from "Palestinian infiltrations."

Kfar Tapuach, thus, became a bastion for the cause. When the U.S. president Bill Clinton banned Kahane's followers from fundraising in the United States, they moved their money into a bank account created to support the Kfar Tapuach yeshiva. Authorities were well aware of the fact that that was where the heart of the movement lay. More than once, secret service and

Israeli army officers raided the settlement in search of Kahan-
ists accused of committing terrorist attacks on Palestinians. In
2000, Binyamin Kahane and his wife were killed by Palestinian
snipers in an ambush near Ofra, a settlement on the way to
Jerusalem.

But others lived in Kfar Tapuach as well: more moderate
Zionists, a group of Chabad-Lubavitch followers, and a small
minority of secular Israelis who'd moved there in search of not
Greater Israel but cheap housing. Because it was subsidized by
the government, rent, the cost of supplies, and taxes were all far
lower than in Israel proper.

And then there were the Peruvians. The bright purple corn
growing in the garden of Zerubbabel's daughters Naomi and
Chava stunned their neighbors, amazed at the soft and deli-
cious cooked kernels, the sweet juice. How did the Peruanim
dye their corn? they wondered. The seeds had traveled halfway
across the world and sprouted brilliantly on that hill, while the
yucca beside it inevitably froze in the short cold winter.

Inside her large tiled living room, Naomi knit a little dress
for her baby granddaughter. Her mother sat beside her, a little Andean *kolla* hat atop her head. Rakhel and Oshea's wife
lounged there with them on comfortable armchairs. They sat
watching *The Clone,* the afternoon soap opera that Israeli television aired in Portuguese with Hebrew subtitles. In this particular episode, the protagonist, the teenage daughter of a Muslim
family in Rio de Janeiro, sobbed because the time had come for
her to begin wearing the veil. All four women wept along with
her in that Tapuach living room.

Abraham Chicco, for all intents and purposes Zerubbabel's
son, had moved to Kfar Tapuach along with the rest of the
family. He'd gotten a job as a handyman and did rounds in

his white overalls fixing anything in the village that broke. He liked to stop and gaze out through the wire fence surrounding the settlement at Mount Ebal and Mount Gerizim, so close he could still hardly believe it. One to the north, the other to the south, the two mountains flanked the valley surrounding the Palestinian city of Nablus, which he insisted on calling Shechem, as it was in the Torah. The vista always made him think of the passage in which Moses said to the Israelites,

> Behold, I set before you this day a blessing and a curse: the blessing, if ye shall harken unto the commandments of the Lord your God, which I command you this day; and the curse, if ye shall not hearken unto the commandments of the Lord your God, but turn aside out of the way which I command you this day, to go after other gods, which ye have not known. And it shall come to pass, when the Lord thy God shall bring thee into the land whither thou goest to possess it, that thou shalt set the blessing upon mount Gerizim, and the curse upon mount Ebal.

Abraham never carried weapons. Although the Israeli army had provided him with them, for use against possible Palestinian infiltrations, he preferred to leave them at home. The intifada that had been under way on their arrival ended in 1993, with the signing of a series of peace agreements between the Israeli government and Palestinian authorities. Two years later, a young admirer of Kahane's ideas had assassinated Prime Minister Yitzhak Rabin for having signed those accords. Some residents of Tapuach celebrated the prime minister's death, which traumatized the rest of the country.[38] The international community began to view the settlements as one of the major obstacles to peace. Yet they continued to spread, in open defiance.

Five years after Rabin's death, on September 28, 2000, Ariel Sharon, leader of the Israeli opposition, visited the Temple Mount, a site in Jerusalem where observant Jews believe that the First and Second Temples were erected and the third and final Temple will be built. It is also the site of Al-Aqsa Mosque, the third-holiest site in Islam. Sharon had been a commander in the Israeli army from the time of its creation and had fought in every Israeli war since 1948; he was seen by one sector of the country as a national hero. He was also leader of Likud, the Israeli right-wing political party, and a driving force behind the construction of Jewish settlements in Palestinian territory. To Palestinians, he was a war criminal, responsible for the deaths of hundreds, perhaps thousands, of Palestinian and Lebanese civilians in Lebanese refugee camps in 1982.

The Palestinians saw his presence on the site of Al-Aqsa as a deliberate humiliation, a public declaration that Israel would never recognize their rights. Some protested, and their protests were quashed. The following day, riots broke out in Jerusalem's Old City. Rocks rained down on those praying at the Western Wall; the police responded with rubber bullets. When Jerusalem's chief of police was knocked unconscious by a rock to the head, the police switched to live ammunition. The day ended with seven Palestinians dead and three hundred injured. On the other side, some seventy police officers were wounded.

Thus began the second intifada. There were protests and riots throughout the Palestinian territories, in the West Bank and Gaza. By the end of the first month, 141 Palestinians and 12 Israelis had been killed, and nearly 6,000 Palestinians and 65 Israeli Jews injured.

The imbalance in attacks and deaths continued until 2001, the year Sharon was elected prime minister and suicide bombings began. A Palestinian militant would drape his or her body in bombs, board a bus or walk into a restaurant or any other place where a large number of Jews congregated, and detonate the explosives, killing him- or herself along with as many Jews as possible. There were knife attacks as well. The Israeli army responded by destroying the bombers' homes and neighborhoods, arresting people en masse. Settlers out on the roads became targets for snipers. In Tapuach there were widows. Abraham Alon, César Rengifo's brother-in-law, was the first of the Peruvians to be shot. In his austere black Haredi suit, with his long beard and sidelocks, Abraham worked as a bus driver on a route that looped through the settlements. One day he was on his way back from taking a teacher to the school where she worked when a bullet entered his chest and then hit his liver. He entered a coma; no one knew if he would survive. The second victim was Samuel Hilario, also a driver. A bullet struck him as he drove the settlement route, leaving him handicapped.

Most of the Peruvians accepted that their lives, as well as deaths, were determined by divine design. Hadassa, Zerubbabel's granddaughter, liked to walk along the Tapuach fence, gazing out at the landscape dotted with Palestinian villages. A visitor asked if she was not scared of being hit by a sniper's bullet, and she replied, "If God wishes, it will be so." With no more thought than that, they carried on with their lives as ever, driving the highways or traipsing up the little road that led to the entrance to Tapuach.

The girl's father, who had been Pepe Rengifo in Peru, said that it all boiled down to disagreements among the Jews themselves. He blamed the Israelis opposed to the settlements, who didn't understand that the land had been given to them by God and they needed to occupy it. Why was living there seen as wrong? "We don't bother anybody," he said. The Arabs should be relocated to Jordan, Egypt, or Syria. Anyplace but Israel. Take them to countries where their people were. When all Jews understood that the Arabs needed to be displaced, that would put an end to the conflict.

Only Chava, Zerubbabel's youngest daughter, feared for herself and her children. She stopped watching the news, which talked only of attacks and the horrific deaths of young settlers: two teenagers had been kidnapped by Palestinians who, after stoning them, had used their blood to paint the walls of a cave in the desert of Judea; a Palestinian sniper had shot a ten-month-old Jewish baby in Hebron; two army reservists had been eviscerated by a mob in Ramallah. Chava no longer dared to go out.

That was when Zerubbabel, who rarely came out of isolation, asked to meet with David Kiperstock, his old benefactor. Kiperstock lived in a wealthy suburb of Tel Aviv. Since the Bnei Moshe's arrival in Israel, they'd exchanged phone calls, holiday greetings, and wedding and bar mitzvah invitations, but Kiperstock still refused to enter the settlements, whose existence he repudiated. So Zerubbabel visited him at his apartment, on the tenth floor of an elegant building. When Niela Kiperstock, David's wife, offered him a cup of coffee, Zerubbabel hesitated. "Forgive the question, but is this a kosher household?" Niela, slightly offended at a convert questioning her Judaism, assured him that he could drink the coffee safely.

As he did, Zerubbabel explained that he feared for his life and that of his wife. "Mr. David, how can we . . . ? We are old. My children are patriots, but we . . . we'd like to leave." And by leave, he meant leave the West Bank settlements and move to a city like the one where they now sat conversing.

Kiperstock told him it was too late to get them out of there.

Where would the money come from? Segundo no longer received any government aid, aside from his modest pension. Life in Israeli cities was far more expensive.

"Unfortunately, you can't," Kiperstock replied.

Zerubbabel went back to Tapuach and shut himself up in the house, in his mind, his thoughts, and his readings.

Was it fear? Was that truly what he felt? He who'd conquered the Amazon jungle with nothing but a machete? He who had been prepared to die from a gunshot without so much as a whimper? Who had endured having pellets removed from his back with no anesthesia?

A few months later, he announced to his family that he was going back to Peru.

Part Three

N o, we weren't afraid," his brother Mordechai would later explain. He personally traveled all over, passing through Shechem—Nablus, to the Palestinians—with no fear whatsoever. It had never occurred to them to take up arms. No, it wasn't fear. "We didn't leave because of the Arabs," he said. "We left because of the Jews."

Mordechai left first. For five years, he'd tolerated life in Kfar Tapuach. There was nobody to talk to about the Torah there, not the way they liked to talk; there was no discussion, only dogma, only what the rabbis said. He moved his family close to Haifa and didn't come back.

Zerubbabel was alone. Although at Elon Moreh he'd finally obtained his first Tanakh in Spanish, for the first time since opening his father's Bible, he had no one to talk to, to instruct, to convince. Besides, he couldn't speak Hebrew. He'd never really learned. So how could he carry on a dialogue? He needed Peruvians. But his people were content to accept the rabbis' dogma. He felt betrayed. They had renounced the search they'd all been on together for so many years.

He needed a new circle, a new assembly, other men and women willing to listen and study, people to whom he could impart all that he'd learned and discovered. For if he wasn't a teacher of the faith, what was he?

He knew there were others following in his footsteps. Just a year after they'd moved to Elon Moreh, a second *beit din* traveled to Peru to convert the ninety-one Bnei Moshe who hadn't passed the first examination. The most recent members, they hadn't been with the community long enough; Avichail, Krauss, and Uriah had told them to study hard and practice much more before attempting to retake the conversion exam. But in late January 1991, a cholera epidemic, the first to hit the Americas in more than a century, ravaged the Peruvian coast. It was a plague like the wrath of God itself: by April, more than 1,100 had died, and 150,000 were infected. Like so many others who lived without running water or sewage, the Bnei Moshe were among the most vulnerable. From Lima, Krauss appealed to Chief Rabbi Eliyahu: a collective conversion in Trujillo and Cajamarca was critical for humanitarian reasons. They could shore up their Judaism in Israel. The chief rabbi agreed.

Krauss, however, did not form part of the *beit din.* The first one had earned him the enmity of a good part of the colony. People at his synagogue had protested: What was he doing converting *cholos* but not their own girlfriends, who came from good families? Nor did Avichail go, because he was in India, converting a group of Bnei Menashe. So Uriah presided over the court, accompanied by two other Israeli rabbis.

These new converts, too, were taken to settlements. And their joy was so great that they felt the need to share it with parents, siblings, nieces and nephews, aunts and uncles, cousins, and friends from Peru who hadn't even wanted to become Jewish. They saved up to pay for their airfare and hosted them in their new homes, which seemed so luxurious. One of these visitors found a yeshiva where the rabbi agreed to convert the visitors. Many did convert, and therefore managed to remain as new settlers in Judea and Samaria.

Their success encouraged more. And then even more. And more still. There were always, always more. And Zerubbabel went in search of them, in search of that new congregation awaiting him in Peru. Was that not where he needed to be, where those searching for a true faith were?

Nothing, however, was as it had been. His house in El Milagro had been reduced to rubble: a rectangle surrounded by broken bricks. The broom factory, not even that. Only the synagogue remained as it had been upon his departure fifteen years earlier: still unfinished, though it did finally have a door. And a growing community of aspiring converts making a pilgrimage there, morning and evening.

The door, however, could only be opened with Dominga Sánchez's authorization. Just as the key to the Holy Sepulchre is placed in the custody of a single family in Jerusalem, so too was the key to El Milagro synagogue placed in the custody of Segundo's cousin Dominga. It was a prized possession, a source of constant jealousies and intrigues.

Zerubbabel stayed at her house. He had only to walk two blocks to get to the synagogue and find the hopeful. Among them were old acquaintances: some of those who had abandoned him when he chose Judaism, preferring Christ, Víctor Castillo, and their foreskins, were now more than willing to do the opposite.

One, for example, was Julio Raza, who had succeeded César Rengifo as leader of Israel of God in La Esperanza when César left the church for El Milagro and Judaism. The parable of the Bnei Moshe had led him to reflection. Was Israel the reward God had given Segundo and those who followed him for having chosen the correct path? What reward had they received, for having stayed with Christ? His old friend Víctor Chico sent effusive letters from Israel, which he signed "Abraham Chicco."

One day, Julio Raza was finally convinced and, like Rengifo before him, abjured Israel of God and began a group to study the *Shulchan Aruch*.

Julio's younger brother, Luis, had followed Segundo when Israel of God was first starting up, but the long trips he made through the Andes as a traveling salesman had kept him from religion. It was as if a flame had been extinguished. But his brother's decision stirred him. While he was still processing this internal conflict, he was invited to his son's school to have a talk about the boy's First Communion. The teacher asked those present which children would take it. All of the parents raised their hands—except one. "And you?" asked the teacher. "Isn't your son going to receive his First Communion?" With all eyes on him, Luis heard himself reply, "No, miss. I don't believe in such things." Back at home, he argued with his wife and went to speak to his son, who wept disconsolately. Suddenly convinced, he told him that there was only one God, that his laws were strict, that Israel existed. He told him that since he was his son and his own blood, he had to respect his beliefs. They began to spend Saturdays with his brother Julio, studying Judaism and learning to keep the faith. At first, his wife refused to accompany them. But one day she announced she would cook for Shabbat. Later, she learned to light the candles. Finally, she adopted the rites. The flame had been rekindled: faith had returned. Luis got circumcised, celebrated the holy days, allowed himself to dream of Israel. "If Israel didn't exist," he confessed one day, moved, "I might not have so much faith in the Eternal."

But it wasn't only penitents who attended synagogue in El Milagro. There were also unfamiliar faces, people who went because of the things they'd heard from relatives and friends about the only way to Israel—the way out of Peru.

Gilberto Aquiles Luján, for instance, lived not in the dust of El Milagro but in the mud of another *pueblo joven* precariously established at the foot of a hill on the opposite side of Trujillo. The revelation had come to him in a letter from his father, Próspero, who had gone to Israel in the second, "cholera" aliyah:

> May the eternal God of Israel see that you receive this letter in good health, together with all your family. We are all here by the grace of Hashem and in perfect health. Son, I will tell you a bit of the story of our journey, which was extraordinary from the moment we boarded the plane. The food, all kosher, and almost twenty hours in the air. Good stopovers. When we arrived, they asked for our documentation and gave us a document they call *teudat oleh* and money for expenses. Then they took us to a place where we saw a very large room, for seven hundred or a thousand people. Many important men, including all the rabbis, lots of people, so many children, and a beautiful Hassidic orchestra enlivened our welcome so joyfully. So much food and drink. Then they took us to the place where our homes were all ready for us and I couldn't contain my tears on seeing a house with every essential amenity. Like we'd worked five or eight years! And the key in the door.[1]

In his tiny dirt-floor house with no running water, electricity, or sewage, Gilberto Aquiles burst into tears. He desired Israel with all his heart. He began to study Judaism.

Something similar happened with Arturo Vergara, who years earlier had been invited by his sister to attend an assembly of César Rengifo's Israel of God congregation in La Esperanza. The religion hadn't taken hold. He then served several years in the army. After returning to Trujillo, he had seven children, drove a taxi, and worked as a money trader, exchanging tourists' dollars for soles in the Plaza de Armas. Out on the street one day, he bumped into César Rengifo, who this time invited him to study Judaism. "It will be for the good of your family," he said. The suggestion that he renounce Christ offended him. "Who are you to say this to me?" Arturo protested.

Not long after, they bumped into each other in the Plaza de Armas again. "I'm moving to Israel, brother. It's all settled," Rengifo announced. Some time later, Arturo received more news: César now went by Binyamin Dayan; he lived comfortably and had work and a new house, everything he could possibly need. Someone like him, just like him, in the holy land of Israel; it moved Arturo.

He began to read about Judaism. He got hold of a *Shulchan Aruch* and studied it word for word. He began to keep the Sabbath, memorized Hebrew prayers, and learned the rites. He got circumcised, as did his sons. He told his wife that from then on they would eat kosher. She resisted, clinging to Jesus, to what was familiar. Besides, Judaism was a lot to take on, too much: the prayers, the meal preparation, the isolation. But Arturo was determined. Either she convert, or they would divorce. She conceded.

On one trip to Lima, Arturo went to the colony's market in search of a kosher chicken. They were out, but someone suggested he try the place in the new Chabad-Lubavitch community, which was tiny but had a rabbi and also sold kosher meat. The rabbi was friendly and open; Arturo began to visit him on trips to Lima. One day, his friends in Trujillo saw him return in a new black suit, tzitzit hanging from his waist. He stopped greeting women with a kiss, taught his wife the rules of Haredi personal hygiene, and forbade his children to play with other kids because none of them was Haredi. What future could those kids possibly have in Trujillo? How long could they go on living that way? It was vital that they get to Israel.

Binyamin Dayan also sent letters to Wilfredo Ciudad, an old friend of his who lived in Trujillo. Wilfredo had found God as a boy, when the Pilgrims' Church came to his town. A rumor spread that a giant devil-goat appeared at their ceremonies and the lights went dark. Wilfredo went to see for himself, taking care to sit by the exit. But instead of the devil, God appeared in a song: "This world offers nothing, Christ offers salvation." Wilfredo became evangelical.

Years later, he fell gravely ill with liver trouble. The doctors could not cure him. God sent an Adventist missionary to offer him the Sabbath and a vegetarian diet. Once cured, Wilfredo became an Adventist.

These letters from Israel, he saw, were a new divine message: he needed to become Jewish and immigrate to Israel. So he got a kippa and persuaded his wife to cover her head with a small hat, which in Hebrew was called a *kova*. Together they learned to make challah. They hung large cards with recipes in Hebrew on the walls of their modest Trujillo kitchen and, in the refrigerator and pantry, little signs saying "meat" and "milk" in both Spanish and Hebrew, so as never to make the mistake of mixing them. They hung a Star of David on the door frame of the room where Wilfredo made the peanut candy he sold for a living.

Others had even greater clarity about the reach of their faith: all they wanted was to make it to Israel, in whatever way possible. Near the historic center of Trujillo, in El Alambre, the neighborhood that had once been José Aguilar's stomping ground, three sisters were counting down the days until their departure. Their father, Hernán Valderrama, had been a follower of César Rengifo in La Esperanza, and when César moved to the Bnei Moshe, he followed along and accepted Segundo's leadership. Valderrama had failed the first conversion exam but had passed the "cholera" examination, as did his wife and five of their children. His three daughters, however, had been turned down because their husbands did not practice, and the court only accepted complete families.

The sisters stayed in Trujillo awaiting a new conversion court to come and take them to Israel. One, Lucy, was a money changer in the Plaza de Armas. One day, an Israeli backpacker asked her if she knew of any cheap hostels where he could stay; he didn't mind sleeping on the floor. Lucy offered him her house—humble, she admitted, but kosher. The Israeli was so happy that he passed the tip along, and Lucy's modest house became a pension for the many young Israelis backpacking through South America who came each year, after completing their military service. With the help of a loan that her husband, a police officer, obtained, Lucy built new bedrooms, a dining room, and a large kitchen. Hers was the only kosher hostel in all Trujillo, the only one where they kept the Sabbath, celebrated Jewish holidays, and spoke broken Hebrew. Backpackers got there assuming that the Valderramas were Jews by birth and were then shocked to find that some parts of prayers that should have been sung were instead recited, or that they sang the wrong melodies.

Despite the confusion, the hostel prospered. But Lucy kept dreaming of Israel. Her dream turned desperate when her oldest son, who was eleven, began hanging out on the streets of El Alambre with kids she didn't want him associating with: she had to get him out of there. Her father, already in Israel, suggested that he adopt him as his own and take him. They could wait for her there. Lucy agreed.

It took two years for her to save enough money to meet them. She traveled to Israel with her three other children, one of her sisters, and the sister's children. They planned on entering as tourists and, once there, finding a way to convert, as so many others had done.

But the Chief Rabbinate had found out about this shortcut. Relatives, fiancées, friends of the Bnei Moshe, were taking advantage of an agreement between the two countries allowing Peruvians to travel to Israel without a visa and find rabbis there who were willing to convert them. Worse still for the Chief Rabbinate was that many Russians, who were still the center of a nationwide polemic about who was truly Jewish, were doing the same. As far as the Chief Rabbinate was concerned, the scheme was deceitful, and the conversions were deemed invalid. The Ministry of Interior decreed that only Israeli citizens could convert to Judaism in Israel; foreigners had to either do so elsewhere or petition a special tribunal to consider their case.

Lucy, her sister, and the children spent two years in the land they'd promised themselves, but in the end had no choice but to return to Trujillo. There would be no similar opportunity: for reasons unrelated to the conversions, the visa agreement between Israel and Peru had been canceled. All they could do was wait for the arrival of another *beit din*.

In La Esperanza, the Yparraguirre family was losing patience. When César Rengifo emigrated and became Binyamin Dayan, he'd taken his wife, Andrea—now Ruth—with him and gotten her parents, her three sisters, and their respective husbands and children to travel as tourists and convert to Judaism in Israel. Her parents, in fact, had died in Elon Moreh. But the four Yparraguirre brothers and their families had remained behind, having taken longer to accept the faith.

One of them, Cipriano, explained it this way: "These days, since we have so many relatives in Israel, those here are worried about their families. Those of us who were Christians see that we were wrong. We are now taking this path, which is the path; there is no other way. We're going to be descendants of our father Abraham. So that's the reason why maybe we are not from here, but from there." One of the impatient Yparraguirre wives summed it up more succinctly: "I'd rather die in Israel than live in Peru."

Dominga Sánchez, too, thought about Israel day and night. One morning she awoke crying. A young foreign woman had appeared to her in her dreams and placed a check in her hands. "With this you will reach Israel," she'd said. The check then turned into a piece of paper, like a conversion certificate. "I wish you the best," the young woman said, turning into an old man with a flowing white beard.

In Cajamarca, too, they awaited the court to work its magic. Agustín Araujo, a traveling salesman who had succeeded Víctor Chico as head of the local synagogue, was struggling to persuade his wife to keep the Sabbath. Agustín had come to Judaism by accident. He was working as the foreman at a construction site in Trujillo in the mid-1970s when, on a lunch break, he heard some workers talking about the Bible. The group included Adventists, Pentecostals, and Ataucusi Israelites. Agustín didn't know anything about the Bible, because his parents were Catholic. He liked the passion they spoke with. One day, they asked him what religion he was. Catholic, Agustín said. Tell us something about Catholicism, they requested. But he had nothing to say; he'd never learned about his religion. That Sunday he began to attend Mass, where he knelt, imitating the others' motions and recitations, but he felt no joy whatsoever. Why was that? He was concerned.

Around that time, his father-in-law, an Adventist, gave Agustín's wife a Bible, and Agustín began to read it. He didn't like the fact that it said the day of rest was Saturday, since he was accustomed to it being Sunday, and it annoyed him that the owner of the dump truck company who worked with him on the site, a man named Amílcar Reina, stopped work Fridays at one and didn't show up the entire next day. Agustín complained to the builder in charge of the project, who gave him permission to hire another dump truck company. It didn't take long, however, for him to realize that Reina got more done in five and a half days than the new contractor did in seven, and, regretting his mistake, Agustín rehired him. Still, he couldn't help himself and said, "Listen, Reina, don't be a fool. The day of rest is Sunday." Reina replied, "Tell me your name." "Agustín Araujo." Reina continued: "If you expect to convince me, show me your documentation." So Agustín did. Then Reina said, "If you believe Sunday is the day of rest, you'll need to show me documentation for that as well. Because you say the seventh day is Sunday, right? Check the dictionary." When he got home, Agustín checked the dictionary, and saw: "Sunday: the first day of the week." This left an impression on him. Reina was right: Sunday was not the last day of the week; Saturday was.

Agustín began studying the Bible with Reina, who invited him to breakfast. They read and discussed together. Then he met César Rengifo, whom he let borrow his truck to deliver brooms, and joined Israel of God. Later, he moved to Cajamarca and became friends with Víctor Chico. But Agustín traveled constantly for work and stopped attending. In time, he drifted away from the religion. Until Víctor Chico moved to Israel. Then he began studying once more. His wife, though, found it very hard to abide, and they argued constantly. At the time of the second aliyah, he decided not to appear before the conversion court because his mother was elderly and he didn't want to leave her in Cajamarca. But his mother was dead now, and he was ready to emigrate.

Despite the number of people waiting, the court did not come. There were no conversions, no airfares bought to Israel, no houses with wooden doors and ceramic floors, no tiled bathrooms. So Lucy and her sisters, Gilberto Aquiles, Julio and Luis Raza, Wilfredo Ciudad, Arturo Vergara, Dominga Sánchez, the Yparraguirres, and many other families, friends, and acquaintances resolved to organize, as the Bnei Moshe had.

They couldn't take the same name, but they chose one similar: Bnei Abraham. They formed study and prayer groups in El Milagro, in La Esperanza, in Cajamarca, and even on the outskirts of Lima, and just as the original Bnei Moshe had done, they asked Avichail for help. But Avichail didn't think their faith was sincere: they were searching not for God, he thought, but for a way out of poverty. Next the Bnei Abraham turned to Krauss, who wasn't even interested in meeting them.

One person who was interested in meeting them, however, was an American rabbi named Myron Zuber. He was an old man who wore gray slacks and a white shirt. He came from Monsey, a Hasidic community in New York. Zuber had become interested in the Bnei Moshe a few months prior to their conversion and visited them in El Milagro. He'd gone to see Krauss in Lima, telling him he was an envoy of the Rebbe Lubavitch, the highest authority of the Chabad-Lubavitch in Brooklyn, the one that his followers thought was the Messiah himself. Krauss let him stay in his guest room but, mistrustful, asked a friend with contacts in the organization to verify what the man had said. When the friend found out that the Rebbe had not sent him, Krauss kicked him out and said he never wanted to see him again. Zuber had also gone to Avichail to propose that they raise funds for the Bnei Moshe together, but Avichail had refused. Some time later, though, he heard a rumor that Zuber had requested funds on behalf of Amishav.[2]

Despite being refused, Zuber had managed to obtain support from an American organization called Kulanu, which also had the mission of taking lost Jews to Israel from anywhere in the world. Zuber had sent out a letter to his network of contacts, requesting donations for the Peruvian Jews who were following in the footsteps of an "Inca Indian" named Segundo Villanueva, a man who had suffered persecution at the hands of the Catholic Church in Peru and been forced to flee to Spain, where he'd studied Sephardic thinkers; once back in Peru, he had educated an Indigenous community in Judaism.

In spite of Zuber's erroneous and questionable statements, the Bnei Moshe had never spoken badly of him. Once in Israel, they recalled him fondly, as they did all those who'd supported them in one way or another. So the Bnei Abraham, too, received Zuber with open arms: after all, he was the only rabbi who showed an interest in them.

Luis Raza trembled on seeing Zuber for the first time. He'd never spoken to a rabbi before and felt as if he were in the presence of a being from another world. Zuber moved to El Milagro to teach them Judaism. The Bnei Abraham covered his room and board. Though he looked old and fragile, Zuber climbed hills and swam in rivers with the vigor of a young man. And even though he claimed to be Haredi, he shook hands with women and let men and women dance together at weddings and celebrations, which the Bnei Abraham who had studied Haredi laws found wrong. After a few months, Zuber, who had arrived a bachelor, chose a young woman named Margarita to be his wife. Margarita became Margalit; her friends told her how lucky she was. Zuber took her to Monsey, and they never saw him again.

Then another American Jew, younger but also Haredi, came to El Milagro. His name was David Balban, and he was not a rabbi. He called himself a *talmid chacham,* or scholar of the Torah and laws. He lived with them for a year. He taught them songs, prayers, and recipes; he read the Torah with them. Then he went back to the United States.

After Balban came a brief stint by a third American Jew named Robert Lande; he was the director of Kulanu, the organization that had sent out Rabbi Zuber's letter. Next was a friend of his, also American, named Bryan Schwartz. Maybe *he* could get them to Israel? Schwartz traveled the world conducting interviews and taking photos of unusual, isolated Jewish communities; he wanted to publish a book. Schwartz offered to help them raise funds and attract the attention they would require if they wanted to make it to Israel.

First and foremost, they needed another name. Bnei Abraham was no good. What if they called themselves the Inca Jews?

"I'd rather be the son of Abraham than of an Inca," Luis Raza muttered. They found the name offensive. But they had to make it to Israel, and Schwartz knew the world better than they did—or knew *that* world better, the one he came from and the one they wanted to reach.

So from that moment on, they became the Inca Jews.

That was when Abraham Alon awoke from his coma in Israel in 2003.

The Ashkenazi chief rabbi, Israel Meir Lau, came upon him at the hospital, where he was visiting the survivors of Palestinian suicide bombings; there had been forty-four just the previous year, and an average of two per month that year already.[3] He was perplexed on seeing Andean features on a face with *payot,* the curled sidelocks worn by Haredim.

"I'm part of the Bnei Moshe community. We're Peruvian," Abraham Alon explained.

"How can I help you?" the chief rabbi asked.

"Help me bring my brothers and sisters from Peru. Why have they been forgotten?"

Moved, the chief rabbi promised he would help. He phoned the International Conversion Court, which reported to the Chief Rabbinate, to find out who these Peruanim were. His call was taken by the second-in-command, the French rabbi David Mamou, who didn't know who they were; Lau ordered him to look into it.

Mamou asked Rabbi Krauss, the Jewish Agency, and the Israeli embassy in Lima; finally, he flew to Peru and went to El Milagro himself. After meeting the Inca Jews, he concluded that they were simply trying to escape misery, like so many others in the world; each year, he analyzed some eight thousand conversion requests, and the experience had made him a skeptic. But Chief Rabbi Lau had promised Abraham Alon his help. What could he do?

Mamou diverted the case to Eliahu Birnbaum, another judge at the Conversion Court. A religious Zionist rabbi from Uruguay, who spoke Spanish and lived in a West Bank settlement in East Jerusalem, Birnbaum agreed to look into it.

The first step was to draw up a list, and Abraham Alon gave ninety-three names. Birnbaum passed the list on to Krauss, who was now back in Israel. Krauss agreed to travel to Peru to meet them, but upon his return he reported that he was opposed to converting them. They weren't serious, he said. As confirmation of this, some time later he received a letter from a rabbi at Elon Moreh, who declared himself opposed to more conversions. The first group of Peruanim had been genuinely observant, he wrote, but the new ones, those who had come on tourist visas and been converted in Israel, had different motives and did not lead religious lives.

But Birnbaum, in addition to serving on the Conversion Court, worked as educational director of an organization called Shavei Israel (Israel Returns), and he succeeded in getting Michael Freund, Shavei Israel's founder and director, to sign on to the Inca Jews' cause.

Born in New York to a millionaire father, Freund was a religious Zionist who had worked in Prime Minister Netanyahu's communications office in the late 1990s. There he'd heard about the Bnei Menashe and, intrigued, had done some investigating and ended up in contact with Avichail, who was old enough to be his grandfather. The young Freund became Avichail's disciple.

Avichail had never managed to turn his organization into a professional business, much less turn a profit. He lived off his yeshiva teacher's salary and used everything down to his last shekel traveling the world in search of his lost tribes, aided only by his wife, Rivka, and a handful of volunteers. Freund, on the other hand, came with a huge family fortune, as did his wife, Sarah Green, also the daughter of a millionaire.[4] Freund was pragmatic, and as shrewd as Avichail was romantic. He had direct contact with the new political generation that had brought Netanyahu to power and understood how to exert influence as a result of his contacts, his money, and that of others with similar agendas and interests. In the end their incompatible worldviews distanced teacher from pupil, and in an act Avichail viewed as a personal betrayal, Freund left Amishav to found Shavei Israel, a rival organization that put Amishav out of operation.

Avichail's mission, which Freund had usurped, became not just a hobby but a purpose in life. But Freund's quest was slightly different. Shavei Israel's objective was to populate Greater Israel with those who identified as Jewish, regardless of whether they were widely accepted as such or not, as a way to offset Palestinian population growth. It was now a matter of searching not for the descendants of the lost tribes, sixteenth-century Spanish and Portuguese conversos, and Jewish souls who were returning, as Avichail had done, but for any group who showed an interest in Judaism and was willing to convert. Freund believed that converts lent Israel the religious fervor that many traditional Jews had lost.

In addition to fervor, they served in what he considered the most urgent battle. The Arab-Israeli population growth rate was greater than that of the Jews. One day in the not-too-distant future, Arabs would outnumber Jews; an Arab could conceivably come to power in Israel.[5]

Shavei Israel didn't care if the Inca Jews' faith was shaky or lacked credibility; Israel would see to making them Jewish. Freund had no doubt. "We need them as much as they need us," he said. With his backing, Birnbaum could finally initiate the mass conversion.

Once more, the decision was repudiated by the colony's

leadership in Lima. Rabbi Ephraim Zik, the Israeli who had succeeded Krauss at the Israelite Union of Peru, agreed to receive the *beit din* and even allow them to use the mikveh for conversions performed in the city, on two conditions: that the aspirants not attend services at his synagogue, and that once their conversion was over, they be taken to Israel as quickly as possible.

Birnbaum readily agreed to both conditions; he was determined to accomplish his task. He told the skeptics that many of the Inca Jews had been practicing Judaism for more than ten years, but also attempted to ensure they were truly prepared. He visited El Milagro and La Esperanza several times, teaching the men to use tefillin and the women to make challah, light candles on Shabbat, and prepare a Pesach seder.

On one trip, he was alarmed to find the El Milagro synagogue full of new faces. How many more would there be to contend with? He notified them that only those who had been practicing for at least two years would be on the list of applicants to be examined by the *beit din*. And thus the list became a source of hopes, resentments, intrigues, and disputes. Some women alleged that others wore long skirts, as Rabbi Birnbaum had instructed them to do, only when he was around. Others were accused of drinking. Or eating forbidden foods. Or driving on the Sabbath.

After endless waiting and bickering, anxiety and sleepless nights, 160 Inca Jews—almost 70 more than those on Abraham Alon's list—managed to get a spot, and the day finally arrived. Rabbi Mamou accompanied the new *beit din,* which was this time presided over by Birnbaum and in addition to Uriah included one rabbi nobody had seen before. The interviews began, family after family was examined with no breaks in between; it was as if they wanted to race through them all that very day and were in a rush to get back to other obligations.

Julio Raza, now a widower, awaited his turn along with his single daughter, his stomach in a knot. What would become of him, and of her, if they did not pass the test? He'd studied the *Shulchan Aruch* intensely, but what if they failed? He'd come to the exam without eating; fasting would help.

"I'm nervous," his daughter said when they were called.

"There is a great God who is going to help us. Be calm," Julio said, feeling calmed by his own words.

Birnbaum asked the questions. Julio began to feel confident on seeing the rabbis smile, which he took as approval of his first replies.

"Do you wear your tefillin?"

"Yes."

"Do you know the *brachot*?"

"Yes."

He recited the blessings.

Things were going well.

"Why are your tefillin black?" the rabbi asked.

Why were they black? He grew tense. That wasn't in the *Shulchan Aruch;* no one had ever explained it to him. Why *were* they black? Was this a trick? He decided to improvise.

"They are black because the human mind is difficult. It is difficult to comprehend all that God wants to do for us, divine conception. And . . . I believe that's why they are black."

The rabbis smiled in seeming satisfaction.

They're pleased with me, Julio thought, congratulating himself.

Birnbaum asked how long one had to wait after eating meat to have milk.

"Six hours," Julio replied, certain.

"What if one is very hungry?"

That wasn't in the *Shulchan Aruch* either.

If one was very hungry . . .

Half that amount, Julio thought, and hazarded a guess.

"Three hours."

"Two, but that's okay," Birnbaum said, smiling.

Birnbaum asked to hear his story: how he'd begun to study the Torah, how he'd come to Judaism. Julio replied that he had begun twelve years earlier, after the first Bnei Moshe made aliyah.

"You've studied for twelve years," the rabbi observed. "How do you feel about twelve more?"

Julio felt himself growing hot under the collar; he lost his temper.

"Twelve more?" he cried. "No! No! I'm going to Israel today! This very day!"

He could have ruined his chances, lost it all. But he didn't: Julio and his daughter passed.

As did his two married daughters and their families, and eighty-four other candidates. They would all, Rabbi Mamou decided, live in a growing cluster of Jewish settlements in the Palestinian territories of East Jerusalem called Gush Etzion, close to where Mamou and Birnbaum lived.

Nearly half were rejected. Among them, Lucy Valderrama, who lost her opportunity yet again. She'd turned up with her children but not her husband, who wasn't sufficiently prepared. The *beit din* only accepted entire families. She then tried to claim that they were divorced, but one of the rabbis asked her young daughter where her father was, and the child replied, "At home."

Birnbaum counseled those rejected for insufficient knowledge, "Study hard, for I personally am going to see to it that you can get to Israel."

His promise, rather than calm people, worked them up further. No sooner had the rabbis left than fights to be on the new list intensified, and the list grew longer and longer. Preparations were a source of tension. Those with more experience instructed their fathers-in-law, nephews, brothers-in-law, and grandsons not to shake hands with women, not to leave their heads uncovered, not to drink too much in the presence of the rabbis or anyone who might tell the rabbis.

But what were all the preparations for? When would they actually be able to leave? Every once in a while, they heard that a new *beit din* was coming, only for the news to be proven false, exacerbating disputes. The community fractured. One group spent the Sabbath with Lucy in El Alambre. The Sánchez family spent them at home alone in El Milagro or at the synagogue, which few attended unless the rabbis or some envoy from Shavei Israel was visiting. The Yparraguirres, who had also failed to be converted, met at one of their homes in La Esperanza.

If the rabbis—or an envoy, or anyone possibly in communication with them—were visiting, everyone attempted to persuade them to visit *their* house, eat with *their* family, speak to *them* first.

And it was amid this war of influences, fears, and jealousies that Zerubbabel returned to El Milagro in 2003, thirteen years after he'd left. Wisely, he began by convening, one by one, those he knew from the past. But very few of them actually went to see him. He had no access to the conversion lists, they knew. So what was the point of meeting with him?

What's more, the few who did expressed alarm.

"Señor Segundo is acting a little strange," said José Urquiza, one of El Milagro's new Inca Jews.

"He doesn't believe in the sages," Agustín Araujo, leader of the Cajamarca Inca Jews, confirmed.

Lucy Valderrama confirmed that Segundo had stopped following Jewish law.

This was substantiated by a warning that arrived from Israel: The rabbis at Elon Moreh and Kfar Tapuach said that Zerubbabel rejected the sages, the Oral Torah. Anyone who spoke to him risked being censured by the new *beit din*.

More letters arrived, informing them that Zerubbabel had abandoned Judaism and joined the Karaites, and someone claimed to have seen him wearing the blue tzitzit of the Karaites. Someone else said that David Balban, the *talmid chacham* who'd lived in El Milagro, had sent word that meeting with Zerubbabel was forbidden because he was a "traitor" of the Torah.

Thus the isolation Zerubbabel had felt at Kfar Tapuach followed him to Trujillo. There, they had let him down; here, they wouldn't even hear him out. In order to tackle the situation head-on, one day he showed up at the El Milagro synagogue. During prayers, he told everyone that things in Israel were not what they thought; they were wrong.

This was not what anyone wanted to hear. Renounce Israel? No way. But Luis Raza, who still lived in El Milagro, took pity. He thought of all the things Segundo had done for him in the past; Luis Raza was one of the only people who hadn't forgotten the man Segundo had once been. Pained, he told Zerubbabel that they abided by the *Shulchan Aruch* and, with all due respect, would continue to do so.

On leaving the synagogue, Luis Raza walked him back to

Dominga's house. There, Zerubbabel began saying some of the strange things he was now known to say.

"The Messiah does not exist," Zerubbabel told him.

Luis Raza felt extremely sorry for his old teacher. What had happened to him?

Zerubbabel brought a few books out of the house and showed them to Luis Raza. They spoke of false messiahs, explained that messianism was but a lie. "It's all a fiction," he said. "People had a need for the Messiah, so the Messiah was invented."

Luis Raza didn't want to contradict him, but what on earth was the man talking about? What was wrong with him? Had he lost his faith . . . or his senses?

"Brother, I am very thankful for the first years I had with you," Luis Raza said, bidding Zerubbabel farewell. "I feel great appreciation for your person, for the things I learned from you . . . You always have a place in my heart."

"You are very great, brother," replied Zerubbabel, embracing him emotionally.

But Luis Raza did not come back and visit.

Embittered, Zerubbabel tried to demand the synagogue's property. It was his, he claimed, but he was willing to sell it. In truth, it was not his. His daughters had donated the land, the cost of construction had been borne by all, and no property deed existed. But he had been the pioneer, the teacher, the leader who had made it possible for them to dream of Israel, even if they refused to admit it. They owed him, and this was the only way of making them pay.

Nobody replied.

With no recognition, no followers, and no other choice, Zerubbabel was forced to return to Kfar Tapuach.

Many Inca Jews were converted in the years that followed—so many that there were more than five hundred Peruanim living in the settlements. The newer arrivals settled in Alon Shvut and Efrat, in Gush Etzion. Julio Raza ended up in Alon Shvut, where he grew old watching his grandchildren play in the trailer he was allocated. His brother Luis made the journey as well, moving to another small settlement near Ariel, in the north, not far from Kfar Tapuach. The Valderrama sisters, Gilberto Aquiles Luján, Arturo Vergara, the Urquizas, the Yparraguirres—all of them were eventually able to realize their dream of moving to Israel.

Yehoshua received his rabbinical degree. He married Ruti, the daughter of Czech and Hungarian Holocaust survivors, had two children, and moved to an apartment building in Petah Tikva, a city just outside Tel Aviv where Russian was the predominant language.

His uncle, Mordechai Meir, on the other hand, went back to Peru and to using the name Álvaro Villanueva for all intents and purposes. He still read the Torah, but now it was the Samaritan Torah.

Zerubbabel remained in Israel, forsaken by everyone and forsaking everything. Abraham Chicco visited him one day at his home in Tapuach and found him in decline. Was he ill? His family admitted that he was in a fragile state, lost in his own thoughts.

Very few people saw him or heard from him again. He was trapped between the four walls of his home, on a hilltop from which he could not escape.

One day, his daughter Naomi went in to bring him into the living room, where two blue parrots were making a racket in their cage. Naomi helped him get settled on a sofa. Zerubbabel had the same strong, sinewy body he always had, though he'd shrunk a bit. He wore black trousers and jacket and his wide-brimmed felt hat. He looked around with a lost expression. Naomi asked him something, but he didn't seem to notice. She got closer and repeated the question, louder. Zerubbabel listened and began to respond but then stopped in the middle of a sentence, fixed his gaze on a spot in the middle of the ceiling, and fell silent once more.

From then on, his speech became increasingly confused. He forgot words, then whole ideas. He spent his time sitting, staring off into space.

On January 3, 2008, four days before his eighty-first birthday, Zerubbabel retired to his bedroom after dinner. His wife, Miriam, and his daughter Rakhel heard him moan. They found him in bed, whimpering, waving his arms desperately, unable to speak.

By the time Oshea, who lived only a few houses away, arrived, Zerubbabel was unconscious. The women had called an ambulance, but the wait would be more than an hour. So they loaded him into Oshea's car and sped off to Jerusalem themselves.

He was still breathing, but his body was growing colder. It took an hour and twenty minutes to reach the Pisgat Ze'ev checkpoint.

The paramedics on duty couldn't find his pulse. They attempted to revive him via cardiac massage, but it was too late.

He'd died upon entering Jerusalem.

Epilogue

Rabbi Yehoshua Tzidkiya spends his days in his small living room in Petah Tikva surrounded by the many volumes of the Talmud, the books that his father, Zerubbabel, rejected, and a library's worth of research into the crypto-Jews' arrival in the Americas in the years after the Spanish conquest. Yehoshua writes and rewrites a manuscript in which he traces a straight line to link three distinct events: many Spanish and Portuguese Jews immigrated to the New World to escape anti-Semitism and the Inquisition; some old documents speak of a group of Portuguese arriving in Celendín in the sixteenth century; one of his father's ancestors, Dionisia Díaz, lived in Celendín in the seventeenth century. Yehoshua is convinced that Dionisia, Zerubbabel's great-great-great-great-grandmother, must have been a crypto-Jew, which amounts to asserting that his father's conversion to Judaism had *biological* grounds. Something that Zerubbabel never claimed.

During successive trips to Peru, Yehoshua scoured Celendín in search of concrete traces of objects that he couldn't find. He traveled to Sorochuco, carried on to Rodacocha, asked old people about any local customs that might seem vaguely Jewish. Some people still leave glasses of water beside coffins as a means of safeguarding the dead (sometimes they put flowers in the water); some wakes go on for seven days; sometimes people wash the bodies before burying them. He discovered that his maternal grandmother did not cook meat in the same pot she used for making jam because she didn't want the jam tasting of meat; this practice Yehoshua believes was an unconscious remnant of kashrut. Back in Petah Tikva, he ordered a DNA analysis, which placed him in a haplogroup (a group with specific chromosomal markings) common to Jewish populations.

For him, that was enough. It wasn't reading the Bible that led Segundo to make his way through so many churches before finding Judaism, he concluded, but the fact that *he was already Jewish* on a cellular level. His father's trajectory, he told me, was not a discovery but a *return.*

Yehoshua was not the only one. Rabbi Birnbaum was working on his own book. Titled *Do You Have Jewish Roots?,* it was intended as a "practical guide" to discovering those roots. "Thousands and thousands of people in the world—in Europe, Latin America, and the United States—are expressing their interest in Judaism and its values and declaring themselves descendants of Jews, attempting to return to the heart of the People of Israel," he wrote. "For many of these people, it's been more than five centuries since their Jewish families were separated from the People of Israel, but their souls seem to be awakening from a dream and claiming their missing identity."

The book asks readers to be on the lookout for traces of Judaism in things including family customs that might vary from those of their neighbors; certain surnames, some of which are common in Spain and Portugal, such as Villareal, Cardoso, and Molina; genealogical searches that might lead to some conceivably Jewish ancestor from as long as five centuries ago; the places their ancestors lived (Did many Jews live there?); family stories about unusual origins ("If your great-aunt says that her uncle Luis or Carlos had daughters named Mariana, or perhaps Mariela or María, but then says, 'There were always a lot of Marielas in our family,' that could be the most important piece of information discovered up to that moment! This is impor- tant because there is a lot of repetition of names in converso families"); spiritual signs ("Do you feel an attraction to Judaism that you cannot explain?").

Should a person stumble upon at least one of these signs, they can embark on the path to conversion. But Birnbaum advised converting only to Orthodox Judaism, "the style of community recognized by the Chief Rabbinate of Israel." And who might be there to help? "Shavei Israel has a conversion and return *ulpan* [institute] called Machon Miriam, which assists in the process of securing approval by the committee and offers conversion studies in a warm and personal atmosphere." The *ulpan* was run by Birnbaum's wife, Renana.

Birnbaum dreamed of his book becoming a regional best seller. His stated aim was to "awaken that type of historical or spiritual interest" in Judaism throughout Latin America. But he didn't truly believe that the majority of people who claim, or will claim, to have found Jewish roots actually have any. At most, he calculated, there might be 5 percent who truly have Jewish roots. The way Birnbaum saw it, the connection is merely "a psychological, ideological, personal need" rather than a historical reality. "There are people who despite being totally non-Jewish choose to turn to Judaism, arguing that they have certain Jewish roots," he explained to me. "I don't believe it's historically true, but it's a sort of need. It's easier to say, 'I was part of the family; my conversion is not simply a 180-degree turn.'"

He didn't care: he was searching not for authentic Jewish souls on the path of return but for any would-be recruit. This was Shavei Israel's new proselytism, which was unheard of in Orthodox Judaism but whose origins date back to the ancient history of the Jews, who only abandoned mass conversion, he maintained, due to persecution in the diaspora. The creation of the State of Israel, according to this thesis, put an end to those restrictions, and thus Judaism can and must return to proselytizing. To this historical argument he added another, moral justification. "If one considers Judaism to be the truth, why not transmit it to other people? If one has the cure for cancer, one should manufacture it for the masses," Birnbaum reasoned. And, of course, he relied on the Bible: God's promise, in the Torah, to make the Jews a "numerous people." Finally, and above all, he noted the Zionist impetus. "It's important to the Jewish people and to the State of Israel that we have an important, meaningful population; a critical mass" to maintain the ethnic identity of the state.

Yet his strategy was aimed not at sowing but at reaping. By converting the Inca Jews, Birnbaum discovered a budding phenomenon, an "effervescence" that had flourished since that time.

While more and more Peruvians in Cajamarca—those who didn't succeed in joining the Bnei Moshe, the Bnei Abraham, and the Inca Jews in Israel—were developing their new passion for Judaism, another community entirely unrelated to them was embarking on the same path in inland Colombia. Its members came from a Pentecostal church in Medellín, the Christian Church for the Family, where people spoke in tongues and fainted during services. This church had more than three thousand followers, among them young *sicarios* (hit men) or ex-*sicarios,* in the service of Pablo Escobar. The pastor, Juan Carlos Villegas, had discovered messianic Christianity in 1998 on a trip to Israel arranged by a world Pentecostal organization. Messianism was beginning to spread through Colombia as well as other Latin American countries. It was like Judaism with Christ at the center. Pastor Villegas was fascinated by the rituals, the music, and the objects used in the liturgy he knew so well.

On returning to Medellín, while still processing what he'd discovered on his journey, Pastor Villegas was kidnapped by a guerrilla group and held captive for a month, until his father handed over all the money he had to free him. Pastor Villegas returned to his congregation a changed man; the Pentecostalism he'd practiced and taught suddenly struck him as an exploitation of people's hopes, dreams, and emotions. What he'd seen in Israel was serious and true. He began wearing a kippa and tzitzit, asked his flock to call him rabbi, and emphasized Christ's Judaism in his sermons. As soon as he could, Pastor Villegas returned to Israel in search of answers he could no longer find in Medellín. He stood before the Western Wall to observe devout Jews at prayer, astonished at their seriousness and apparent erudition. He found Orthodox rabbis who spoke Spanish among them, and they agreed to answer his questions about the Messiah.

Villegas returned to Colombia convinced that messianic Christianity was an absurd hybrid, that Christ was a fallacy and the Messiah had yet to come. He was honest with his parishioners, most of whom were scandalized and left his church. Some six hundred, to his surprise, stayed with him, but after a year of what he described as his "rehabilitation" from Christianity, that number shrank to two hundred. The ex-pastor rented a place in Bello, the working-class neighborhood where he and his followers lived, nailed a mezuzah to the door, and began teaching Judaism at the same time he was learning it out of books sent from Miami, where he had an uncle.

Medellín's small, traditional Jewish community—no more than three hundred people who lived in El Poblado, a well-to-do neighborhood on the opposite side of the city—refused to let them enter their synagogue or provide any spiritual support whatsoever. Villegas and his followers took Judaism classes via the internet from a Cuban American rabbi in Miami, who put them in contact with another Orthodox rabbi in Florida, who traveled to Bello to convert them once they were sufficiently prepared. Villegas took the name Elad.

One day, two ultra-Orthodox Israeli rabbis, David and Isaac Goldstein, knocked on his door. They were traversing Colombia in search of students for their yeshiva in the Old City of Jerusalem and had heard about Elad. If he studied at their yeshiva full-time, they proposed, they'd make him a rabbi in two years. This was a good offer: the process normally required five years of study and a perfect grasp of Hebrew, which Elad did not possess. Two years, however, was too long to be away from his community and his family. He negotiated: one year. The Goldsteins agreed.

After ten months of studying night and day, sleeping in a small room with eight other students, and eating only two meals a day, Elad returned to Bello a rabbi. To the shock of Medellín's traditional Jews—a secular community with no permanent religious authority—Rabbi Elad began appearing in public, speaking about anti-Semitism, Israel, and kashrut.

The El Poblado Jews were the only ones to draw distinctions between the two communities; to the press and the general public, the only rabbi in Medellín was Elad.

A handful of his community succeeded in immigrating to Israel with the help of Shavei Israel, but Elad was determined to stay and grow the followers he'd amassed. Within a few years, he'd trained a second rabbi, also ordained by the Diaspora Yeshiva, who also acted as shochet. The Jewish Community of Antioquia synagogue occupied an entire two-story building and had its own mikveh, authentic Sefer Torah, study room, children's Hebrew school, bakery, and kosher butcher. Whereas the El Poblado synagogue required visitors to make appointments and bring their passports for admission, and often held no services for lack of followers or rabbi, the Bello synagogue was open to all, overflowing with people on Saturdays, and often frequented by Jewish tourists from all over the world during holidays or for Shabbat.[1]

Seven years after the death of Zerubbabel/Segundo, the Inca Jews were no longer an anomaly. In addition to the Jews of Bello, other groups and leaders were coming to similar conclusions on their own, leaving the Catholic Church or the evangelical or Pentecostal churches they'd grown up in, going through a transitional phase with messianism—or not—and finally coming to Judaism. In Colombia alone, there were more than thirty communities in Bogotá, Barranquilla, Cartagena, Santa Marta, Cúcuta, Villavicencio, Valledupar, Montería, Sincelejo, Corozal, Bucaramanga, Melgar, Ibagué, Neiva, Garzón, and Cali; in Medellín two other groups emerged, independent of Rabbi Villegas's.

In Peru, in addition to the Inca Jews of Cajamarca and

Trujillo, there were new communities in the Lima neighborhood of Los Olivos, and other independent communities had been established in Huánuco and Tarapoto. In Ecuador there were three thousand followers among seven groups: five in Guayaquil, one in Quito, and another in Zaruma. In Brazil, new groups were established in São Paulo, Ubatuba, Goiânia, Tatuapé, and Bahia, and every month another one seemed to spring up somewhere. Mexico had a dozen communities spread across Mexico City, Mexicali, San Miguel de Allende, Ciudad Juárez, Saltillo, Guadalajara, Xalapa, Morelia, and Tijuana; no one had counted their members. In Venezuela, there were four growing groups in Maracay, San Cristóbal, Maracaibo, and Cagua. In Guatemala City, eight families were awaiting conversion. In El Salvador there were a hundred people between the two communities found in San Salvador and Armenia. Nicaragua had one group in Managua and another in Granada. In Costa Rica, there was a group in Alajuela. And more in Puerto Rico, the Dominican Republic, Honduras, Bolivia, and Chile.

Traditional Jewish leaders in Latin America looked on in alarm as, generation after generation, their communities shrank through assimilation and interfaith marriage, but they refused to accept the newly emerging Judaism that eclipsed them in religious fervor and, in many places, in number. Rejected in their home countries, Latin America's new Jews committed themselves to anyone willing to help them, whether they be North American Orthodox and Reform rabbis who saw their emergence as a divine sign or an opportunity for personal enrichment; the handful of Latin American Conservative rabbis disgusted by the way traditional communities rejected them, which they saw as racism or classism; or Kulanu, the American proselytizing organization that had supported Rabbi

Zuber's trip to Peru and sent volunteers to offer spiritual support wherever they could.

None of these, however, could compete with Shavei Israel. Freund and Birnbaum scoured the entire region recruiting future converts whom two of their rabbis instructed in the Orthodox rites accepted by Israel's rabbinical authorities. They were preparing them, they clarified from the start, to take them to Israel.

By the early 2010s the Israeli religious establishment and the Chief Rabbinate had grown alarmed. "Israel may decide if it wishes to become the welfare state of the third world," warned Chief Rabbi David Lau, the son of Meir Lau, "but so long as it has not chosen to do so—it should stop the immigration of non-Jews."[2] New restrictions were created against conversions performed outside Israel; scores of Orthodox rabbis were deemed too progressive and blacklisted; the minister of the interior, who approves all immigration requests, added new layers of requirements. Aliyah became practically impossible to the Latin American converts. Then, in 2019, as Michael Freund was getting divorced, his wife, Sarah, sued Shavei Israel for allegedly stealing fourteen million dollars in funds that were her father's inheritance.[3] Birnbaum left Shavei Israel to create a new initiative through which he continues to offer support to the new aspiring Jews of Latin America until the doors of Israel open again.

Thus, a new Judaism was born in Latin America, inverting a movement two thousand years old. This was a Judaism with no past and no tradition, with no memory of persecution, the Holocaust, or the struggles for Zionism; a transformed religion that sought to resolve the age-old issues of poverty, politics, and war but that was also a new faith in the message of the same Book, a message that had made Segundo its unexpected, involuntary prophet.

The holiest cemetery for devout Jews is found on the Mount of Olives, in East Jerusalem. Zechariah himself is buried there, according to one medieval story; so are Eliezer Ben-Yehuda, the creator of modern Hebrew; the former prime minister Menachem Begin; the Nobel Prize winner Shmuel Yosef Agnon; and a dozen chief rabbis, including Abraham Kook and his son, Zvi Yehuda, Avichail's teacher.

At a tiny information booth at the entrance, a young man spreads a map out before me and, after consulting the computer, marks a small green dot at the far southeast: this is where Zerubbabel Tzidkiya's tomb lies.

Palestinian Arabs living nearby occasionally throw stones at visitors to the cemetery, but on the June day I came in search of Zerubbabel, there is not another living soul. Under the noonday sun, without a single tree to cast even the tiniest hint of merciful shade, the bright Jerusalem stone tombs are blinding. The area that looked on the map to be the size of a small parking lot turns out to be more like that of a stadium, and the tombs are so close together that without knowing the precise location in advance, the only way to find the correct one is to examine them one by one.

After an hour's sweltering search, I find Zerubbabel's. The inscription, on shimmering stone, claims the alleged converso origin that his family created for him, or for themselves, after his death:

Here is buried
My beloved husband, our father and elder

Zerubbabel Tzidkiya
Son of Avraham and Avigail, of blessed memory
Descendant of the conversos of Portugal
Who went back to his origins
Spread Torah to many
And returned many people to our Father in Heaven
Born in the town of Sorochuco[4]
In the district of Cajamarca, Peru
4th of Shevat 5687
Returned his spirit to its creator
In the Holy Land
25th of Tevet 5768
May his soul be bound in the bundle of life

I stay with him for a while, then place a stone on his tombstone.

I look around: an endless series of identical tombstones wend their way up the slopes in consecutive rows to the top of Har Ha-Zeitim, the Mount of Olives. This is where the Messiah's triumphal entry into Jerusalem will take place, according to Zechariah, when the Last Judgment comes. This is where the resurrection of the souls will begin.

More than 150,000 are buried here, awaiting that moment; some have already waited three thousand years. Others are more recent, though these days it's becoming harder and harder to find a plot.

Acknowledgments

Research for this book took a long time, in part because of the challenges of writing a global story as an independent journalist in Argentina, a country with an inflationary economy and a high exchange rate to the dollar, and in part due to the arrival of a son and the arduous experience of migration to New York City. I would never have pulled it off without the generous support of countless people: those who agreed to talk to me, who offered a room when I couldn't afford to pay for one, who helped me find and translate documents, who granted me fellowships and sponsored my visa, who suggested readings and sources, who read the manuscript and provided feedback. I will forever be in their debt.

First and foremost I am indebted to Segundo Villanueva's family, his son Josué (Yehoshua), his brother Álvaro (Mordechai), his late wife María Teresa (Miriam), his daughters Raquel (Rakhel), Noemí (Naomi), and Eva (Chava); his sister Rojana, his niece Marleni Pajares Villanueva, and Víctor Chico (Abraham Chicco). This book would not be possible without them, nor without the generosity of everyone else who spoke with me about their experiences, including (but not only) Víctor Castillo, Julio Raza, Luis Raza, César Rengifo, Manuel Guerra,

José Salirrosas, Gideon Tadmor, Jonathan Segal, David and Niela Kiperstock, Abraham Benhamú, Eliahu Avichail, Mordechai and Rivka Uriah, Eliahu Birnbaum, Michael Freund, Jacob Krauss, Ephraim Zik, David Mamou, Zvi Netzer, Déborah Frank, David Liss, Gamaliel Shilo, Alberto Chicco, Lucy Valderrama, Gilberto Aquiles Luján, Agustín Araujo, David and Lourdes Dayan, Pedro Urquiza Polo, Dominga Salazar Sánchez and her family, Cipriano and Manuel Yparraguirre and their families, Arturo Vergara, Wilfredo Ciudad, Rogelio Pumajulca, Dolores Bautista Reyes, Genoveva Linares Vázquez, Teresa Joya Calderón, Luis Bernabé Loyola Prado, Sara Elisa Villanueva, José Sánchez Eliaga, Román Moreno, Nelly Pérez, Perla López Cervantes, Isolina Sánchez de Berenstein, Luis Salazar Guerra, Manuel Camacho and his family, Dora Silva Salazar, Geiner Mendoza, Alón Rodríguez, Jorge González, and Esperanza Araujo.

I had the privilege to be awarded two fellowships to complete the research for this book. The first one, from the Dorothy and Lewis B. Cullman Center for Scholars and Writers at the New York Public Library, changed the course of my life and my career. Jean Strouse and Marie d'Origny, then director and deputy director, offered critical advice, contacts, encouragement, and, in time, their friendship. Paul Delaverdac and Julia Pagnamenta provided invaluable assistance. Denise Hibay, director for Collections and Research Services at the library, went out of her way to get me a copy of *El judaísmo y el cristianismo antiguo,* a fundamental book in Segundo's religious evolution that seemed impossible to find in its Spanish translation until she found it for me.

The second fellowship, a Prins Foundation for Writers-in-Residence at the Center for Jewish History, offered the additional luxury of two semesters spent reading from the center's fantastic collections. A big thank-you to Judith Siegel and Christopher Barthel for their enthusiastic support for this project and its author.

Karen Barkey took me in as a visiting scholar at the Institute for Religion, Culture and Public Life at Columbia University, and Brooke Kroeger had me as a visiting scholar at NYU's Arthur L. Carter Journalism Institute. Those appointments allowed me to complete the research on the emerging Jewish communities of Latin America and led to the publication of "The Faithful" in *The California Sunday Magazine,* my first feature story in English about the regional phenomenon I narrate in the epilogue. Thanks to Doug McGray, who accepted my pitch, and to Kit Rachlis for the care with which he edited the story.

I was also fortunate to receive a Tow professorship at the Craig Newmark Graduate School of Journalism at CUNY, where I work. My gratitude to dean Sarah Bartlett for her unwavering trust and mentorship.

I'm most grateful to the experts and scholars who helped shape my understanding of the contexts in which the events of this book took place, including Romina Yalonetzky, Juan Ossio, Fernando Armas Asín, León Trahtemberg, Elías Szcytnicki, Fernando Silva Santisteban, Sergio Dellapergola, Juan Mejía, Robbie Harris, Ed Allen, and Stefan Schorch. And to Ken Scott, who found a rare copy of Alfredo Loje's writings and took the trouble to mail it to me.

Special thanks for their hospitality to Laura Durán, Julio Villanueva Chang, Romina Mella, and Joseph Zárate (who helped me find some crucial documents and information) in Peru; to Rabbi Elad Villegas, Keren Villegas, Shlomo Cano,

David Behar, Rabbi Alfredo Goldschmidt, and Jack Goldstein in Colombia; to Gideon Lichfield, Noga Tarnopolsky, Ayelet Bechar, and David Ofek in Israel; and to Guillermo Bronstein, Rubén Saferstein, and Alex Felch on an unforgettable trip to Cajamarca and at many kosher *asados* in Buenos Aires. Thanks to Shakked Auerbach for her help with research in Israel and the West Bank.

Judith Thurman, Robbie Harris, Fernando Armas Asín, Daniel Alarcón, and Guillermo Bronstein read the manuscript and offered invaluable comments, corrections, and suggestions.

Lucky that I am, I found a perfect match in David Halpern, the most effective, supportive, and charming agent an author can wish for. He brought this book to Andrew Miller, a dream of an editor, who made it so much better with his wisdom and clinical eye. Thanks to everyone at Knopf who put their time and dedication into the process of making this book: Maris Dyer (assistant editor); Nicole Pedersen (production editor); Ingrid Sterner (copy editor); Maggie Hinders (book designer); Linda Huang (jacket designer); Jessica Purcell and Amy Hagedorn (publicity); and Emily Murphy (marketing).

The wonderful Lisa Dillman translated the manuscript from its original in Spanish with virtuosity and dedication; collaborating with her was a thoroughly delightful experience.

This book is dedicated to my husband, Gabriel Pasquini, who carried me on his shoulders through it all, making sure I kept going when I wanted to quit, always pushing me to do more and better. He has lovingly edited almost every page I've written in the past two decades, in Spanish and in English, including the many drafts of this book. The book is also dedicated to our extraordinary son, Ismael, whom I love all the way to *infinito punto rojo* and beyond.

Notes

A GENERAL NOTE ABOUT SOURCES

Research for this book began in September 2003 when I found Rabbi Zuber's letter on the internet and, on impulse, picked up the phone and called his number. My first personal source was his widow, Margalit, who provided me with the phone numbers of Segundo Villanueva's daughters in Kfar Tapuach. When I arrived in Kfar Tapuach a few weeks later, I found out that Segundo, then called Zerubbabel Tzidkiya, had gone back to Peru. I traveled to Peru almost a year later, in 2004, but he had returned to the West Bank. In 2005, I finally met him at his daughter Naomi's home in Kfar Tapuach. He had advanced Alzheimer's, and our awkward exchange could not be described as an interview.

So the facts of his life and his search for meaning in the Bible come from a multitude of other sources: his family, in particular his eldest son and his brother; his friends and followers; other Peruvian Bible readers of his generation; the many people involved in his conversion and aliyah; and others who knew him. Many important facts and details come from official and private documents, people's diaries and written accounts, and a few homemade films.

I am painfully aware of the preponderance of male voices in this book. The main reason for it is that the women did not actively participate in the discussions about biblical interpretation, nor in the decisions about religious doctrine, ritual, and institutional belonging that are the center of this narrative. The pastors, rabbis, and outsiders who helped them through the years in Peru and Israel were all men.

Almost every person directly involved in the story told in this book, including many women, agreed to speak to me and contributed valuable information. Particularly important were Álvaro Villanueva, Rojana Villanueva, Marleni Pajares Villanueva, Víctor Chico, Julio and Luis Raza, César Rengifo, Manuel Guerra, José Salirrosas; Rabbis Abraham Benhamú, Guillermo Bronstein, Eliyahu Avichail, Jacob Krauss, Mordechai Uriah, Ephraim Zik, and David Mamou; Gideon Tadmor, Jonathan Segal, David Kiperstock, and many members of the organizations called Bnei Abraham and Inca Jews.

A note about the use of biblical translations: in the original manuscript in Spanish, I quoted from the Bible editions that Segundo/Zerubbabel and the other protagonists of this story had read from whenever I could, starting with the Reina Valera 1909 that Segundo found in his father's trunk. For the period after their conversion to Judaism and their migration to Israel and the West Bank, I tried to quote from the Hebrew Bible in Spanish. When I didn't know which specific Bible they were reading from, I quoted from contemporary translations (particularly the Nueva Versión Internacional). To respect these choices, translator Lisa Dillman quoted from the King James Version for the Peruvian period and from the Jewish Publication Society Bible 1917 for the Israeli/West Bank period, except when those versions didn't include terms that were key to the readings in Spanish. Because this is a story about self-guided Bible readers who liked to consult all Spanish-language translations they could get their hands on, it felt appropriate to include quotations from a variety of versions.

PART ONE

1. I visited Rodacocha in April 2016 with Marleni Pajares Villanueva, Segundo's niece, as my guide. She took me to see the ruins of Segundo's childhood home and introduced me to Segundo's cousin Tadeo Correa, the man in this opening scene. Correa and his fellow Rodacochans Termópilo Arévalo, Crisencio Marín, and Félix Valera Zelada, who joined us later that day, recalled many details about Segundo's childhood and his family history.

2. For the description of the arrival of Pizarro in Cajamarca and the fall of Atahualpa, I relied on Sabine G. MacCormack, "Atahualpa y el Libro," *Revista de Indias* 48, no. 184 (1988); John Hemming, *The Conquest of the Incas* (London: Macmillan, 1970); Iván R. Reyna, "La Chicha y Atahualpa: El encuentro de Cajamarca en la *Suma y narración de los Incas* de Juan Diez de Betanzos," *Perífrasis: Revista de Literatura, Teoría y Crítica* 1, no. 2 (2010); and José Dammert Bellido, *Cajamarca en el siglo XVI* (Lima: Pontificia Universidad Católica del Perú, 1997).

3. The full text can be found here: www.cervantesvirtual.com/bib/historia/CarlosV/9_9.shtml.

4. The following books were particularly important in shaping my understanding of the evangelization of Peru: Fernando Armas Asín, comp., *La construcción de la iglesia en los Andes (siglos XVI–XX)* (Lima: Pontificia Universidad Católica del Perú, 1999); Fernando Armas Asín, ed., *La invención del catolicismo en América: Los procesos de evangelización, siglos XVI–XVII* (Lima: Universidad Nacional Mayor de San Marcos, Fondo Editorial de la Facultad de Ciencias Sociales, 2009); Bellido, *Cajamarca en el siglo XVI;* and Carlos Contreras and Marina Zuloaga, *Historia mínima del Perú* (Mexico: El Colegio de México, 2014). The scholars Armas Asín and Fernando Silva Santisteban (a historian of Cajamarca) generously guided me through facts and interpretation.

5. The information about the first Villanueva to arrive in the Andes comes from a series of documents obtained by Josué, Segundo's son, including Cristóbal Fernández Nieto's will from 1668. One such document states that Cristóbal was accused of exploiting Indigenous people in Celendín, near Cajamarca.

6. The Villanueva family tree, tracking thirteen generations of Villanuevas, was shared with me by Segundo's son Josué.

7. The details of Álvaro's last days and murder, and the events that followed, are contained in the 155-page murder case file, a copy of which I obtained in Cajamarca's Regional Archive in May 2018 (Corte Superior de Justicia de Cajamarca, Causas Criminales, Año 1944, Legajo 998, expediente 15). Additional details about these events came from Segundo's youngest sister, Rojana

Villanueva Correa, whom I interviewed in Lima in April 2016. Segundo's cousins Marleni Pajares Villanueva and Tadeo Correa and the Rodacocha neighbors Termópilo Arévalo, Crisencio Marín, and Féliz Valera Zelada also shared their memories about the murder and its aftermath.

8. Rojana Villanueva Correa told me about the impact her father's murder had on the family.

9. I obtained a copy of the notebook's page.

10. Segundo's children Noemí, Eva, and Josué told me about Segundo's account of their grandfather's murder and the discovery of the hidden Bible.

11. I used a pocket edition of the Santa Biblia Reina Valera 1909, identical to the one Segundo inherited from his father, for reference and quotations in the Spanish-language version of this book.

12. The account of this first reading of the Bible, and the impact it had on him, comes from multiple sources: Segundo's children Josué, Noemí, Eva, and Raquel; his sister Rojana; his brother Álvaro; and the many people Segundo would tell this story to through the years, including some of his followers, and, later, the Israeli rabbis who converted him.

13. Segundo's sister Rojana, a direct witness, told me about the impact that this first reading of the Bible had on Segundo's feelings of vengeance. His son Josué told me about the lasting impact of the passage in Zechariah and what the figure of Zerubbabel meant to his father from early on.

14. These books were especially useful for background on the Protestant Reformation: Kenneth G. Appold, *The Reformation: A Brief History* (Oxford: Wiley-Blackwell, 2011); and Diarmaid Macculloch, *The Reformation: A History* (New York: Viking, 2004).

15. A critical source for my understanding of the arrival and expansion of Protestant movements in Peru was Juan B. A. Kessler, *Historia de la evangelización en el Perú* (Lima: Puma, 1993). Also insightful was Jean-Pierre Bastian, *La mutación de los protestantismos en América Latina: Una perspectiva sociohistórica* (Mexico: Instituto Mexicano de Doctrina Social Cristiana, 1992). I interviewed both Kessler and Bastian to update and expand on some points.

16. For details about the 1910 World Missionary Conference in Edinburgh, I consulted the History and Records of the Conference. They can be found here: http://www.edinburgh2010.org/en/resources/1910-conference.html.

17. A critical source for the history of the Adventist mission in Peru is Floyd Greenleaf, *The Seventh-Day Adventist Church in Latin America and the Caribbean,* 2 vols. (Berrien Springs, Mich.: Andrews University Press, 1992).

18. See M. Michelet, ed., *The Life of Luther Written by Himself,* trans. William Hazlitt (London: George Bell and Sons, 1904), 85–95.

19. See Kessler, *Historia de la evangelización en el Perú.*

20. My conversations with Professor Edward Allen, dean and chair of the Division of Religion at Union College in Nebraska, were critical to shape my understanding of Adventist beliefs. For general background on the Seventh-Day Adventist movement I relied mainly on Richard W. Schwarz, *Light Bearers to the Remnant: Denominational History Textbook for Seventh-Day Adventist College Classes* (Ontario: Pacific Press Publishing Association, 1979); and Greenleaf, *Seventh-Day Adventist Church in Latin America and the Caribbean.* I also consulted the online archive of *The Advent Review and Sabbath Herald.*

21. Her maiden name was Ellen Gould Harmon, but she would be known in the Adventist church by her married name.

22. White's books were translated into Spanish by Eduardo Forga, Manuel Zuñiga's mentor. Forga had married Marguerite Lacey, whose sister was married to W. C. White, son of Ellen White.

23. An important source to further understand the history of the Seventh-Day Adventist movement in Peru is Merling Alomía Bartra, *Breve historia de la educación Adventista en el Perú, 1898–1996* (Lima: Universidad Peruana Unión, 1996).

24. I found some interesting anecdotes about the history of the Adventists in Cajamarca in Eduar Clemente Zavaleta García, "Historia de la Iglesia Adventista del Séptimo Día en la ciudad de Cajamarca, años 1930–2017" (master's thesis, Universidad Peruana Unión, 2018).

25. For the story of the Reform Adventist movement, the following sources were especially useful: Alfons Balbach, *The History of the Seventh Day Adventist Reform Movement* (Roanoke, Va.: Reformation Herald Publishing Association, 1999) (this is the church's official account); Vance Ferrell's critical *The Truth About the Adventist Reform Church* (Beersheba Springs, Tenn.: Pilgrims Books, 1998); the official website of the Seventh-Day Adventist Movement (sdarm.org), which includes the full archive of the church's magazines, periodicals, and Sabbath Bible lessons; and the article "The Seventh Day Adventist Reform Movement: Have You Heard of It?," *Messenger,* April 12, 2013.

26. Balbach, *History of the Seventh-Day Adventist Reform Movement.*

27. A collection of these periodicals can be found online here: sdarm.org /publications/periodicals.

28. I visited the house in April 2016. The family who bought it from Segundo in the 1970s still lives there, and they kindly showed me in. They had made a few structural changes, but, they told me, it was still pretty much as it was then.

29. A comprehensive account of this schism can be found in Balbach, *History of*

the *Seventh-Day Adventist Reform Movement,* and in Ferrell, *Truth About the Adventist Reform Church.*

30. Ignacio Vergara, *El protestantismo en Chile* (Santiago de Chile: Pacífico, 1962).

31. Not much has been written about José Alfredo Loje, but I found valuable references to his life and religious ideas in books and articles about Ezequiel Ataucusi Gamonal and his church. Particularly helpful to understand Loje's Adventist origins and his role in importing the ideas of the Chilean *cabañistas* to Peru were Juan Ossio, *El Tahuantinsuyo bíblico: Ezequiel Ataucusi Gamonal y el mesianismo de los Israelitas del Nuevo Pacto Universal* (Lima: Biblioteca Nacional del Perú, 2014); Arturo Enrique de la Torre y López, *Movimientos milenaristas y cultos de crisis en el Perú: Análisis histórico y etnológico* (Lima: Fondo Editorial PUCP, 2004); and Kenneth D. Scott Eunson, *Nuevos movimientos religiosos andinos: Un acercamiento interdisciplinario,* vol. 1 (Lima: Puma, 2016).

32. Valuable sources to understand the figure of Ezequiel Ataucusi Gamonal were the Peruvian anthropologist Juan Ossio (whom I interviewed in Lima in 2004) and his book *El Tahuantinsuyo bíblico;* Torre y López, *Movimientos milenaristas y cultos de crisis en el Perú;* and Abel B. Paucar Ambrosio, "Asociación evangélica de la Misión Israelita del Nuevo Pacto Universal" (master's thesis, Seminario Adventista Latinoamericano de Teología, Perú, 1985).

33. Peter Lloyd, *The "Young Towns" of Lima: Aspects of Urbanization in Peru* (Cambridge, U.K.: Cambridge University Press, 1980).

34. See Carlos E. Aramburú, "Las migraciones a las zonas de colonización en la selva peruana: Perspectivas y avances," *Debates en Sociología* 4 (1979): 81–94.

35. "Ten Rules Concerning Prohibited Books," Council of Trent.

36. See Arthur Gordon Kinder, *Casiodoro de Reina: Spanish Reformer of the Sixteenth Century* (London: Tamesis Books, 1975). The Spanish-language entry for Bible translations in Wikipedia is quite thorough and includes a list of all available translations in Spanish.

37. Bowman Foster Stockwell, ed., *Prefacios a las Biblias castellanas del siglo XVI* (Buenos Aires: Aurora, 1951).

38. Erna C. Schlesinger, *Tradiciones y costumbres judías: Un viaje alrededor del año hebreo* (Buenos Aires: Editorial Israel, 1942).

PART TWO

1. Descriptions of the Jewish community in Peru are based on several bibliographical sources and on my own conversations with members of the com-

munity, some of them my friends, over several years. Romina Yalonetzky's excellent doctoral thesis, "Diferenciación social e integración en Lima: El caso de la población judía de la ciudad (1944–2014)" (Pontificia Universidad Católica del Perú, 2014), is essential to understand the history of Lima's Jews and their successful integration into the city's upper classes. For the history of Jewish migration to Peru, I consulted León Trahtemberg's classic books *Los judíos de Lima y las provincias del Perú* (Lima: Unión Israelita del Perú, 1989) and *Inmigración judía al Perú, 1848–1948* (Lima: Asociación Judía de Beneficencia y Culto de 1870, 1987). Also useful was Gunter Böhm, *Judíos en el Perú durante el siglo XIX* (Santiago: Universidad de Chile, 1985).

2. Yalonetzky, "Diferenciación social e integración en Lima," 182.

3. Marcel Simon and André Benoît, *El judaísmo y el cristianismo antiguo: De Antíoco Epífanes a Constantino* (Barcelona: Labor, 1972).

4. I spent a week in El Milagro in June 2004.

5. The jurors were Zeev Goldik, Jewish; Héctor Vega Centeno, Catholic; Marco Ochoa, Methodist; Pedro Merino, Presbyterian; and David Evans, Anglican.

6. I obtained a copy of Víctor Chico's exam questions.

7. A little over 18 percent of the Peruvian adult population was then illiterate, according to the 1981 census.

8. *Discurso del presidente de la república, arquitecto Fernando Belaúnde Terry, en la ceremonia de entrega de premios y clausura del concurso bíblico realizado en el auditorium del Colegio Santa Úrsula en San Isidro,* Lima, Empresa Servicio de Informaciones Perú, May 14, 1981.

9. Yalonetzky, "Diferenciación social e integración en Lima," 202–5.

10. The details about the reaction of Lima's Jewish leadership to Chico's victory come from my interviews with several sources in the Jewish community, mainly Rabbi Guillermo Bronstein and the former community leaders Nissim Mayo and Zurik Radzinky.

11. Víctor Chico kept a brief diary of his trip, which he kindly shared with me.

12. Eliezer Ben Rafael, *Jewish Identities: Fifty Intellectuals Answer Ben-Gurion* (Leiden: Brill, 2002). For a brief explanation, see "Reform Judaism" in the JewishEncyclopedia.com.

13. For the history of conversion to Judaism, I consulted Joseph R. Rosenbloom, *Conversion to Judaism: From the Biblical Period to the Present* (Cincinnati: Hebrew Union College Press, 1978); Emil Schürer, *A History of the Jewish People in the Times of Jesus Christ,* vol. 1 (Edinburgh: T. & T. Clark, 1908); and David Max Eichhorn, ed., *Conversion to Judaism: A History and Analysis* (New York: Ktav, 1965). Also valuable were Joseph Goldschmidt, *The New Dimen-*

sions of Who Is a Jew? (Jerusalem: Mercaz Olami Press, 1972); and Shaye J. D. Cohen, "Was Judaism in Antiquity a Missionary Religion?," in *Jewish Assimilation, Acculturation, and Accommodation: Past Traditions, Current Issues, and Future Prospects,* ed. Menachem Mor (Lanham, Md.: University Press of America, 1992), 14–23.

14. See Louis Ginzberg, "Caro, Joseph B. Ephraim," in JewishEncyclopedia.com.

15. Joseph Karo, *Síntesis del Shuljan Aruj: Código de prácticas, rituales y leyes judías,* trans. Natan Lerner (Buenos Aires: Sigal, 1978).

16. I obtained a copy of the Bnei Moshe's detailed meeting minutes for the years from its founding in 1986 until its last meeting in 1989.

17. I interviewed Rabbi Avichail at length during my first visit to Jerusalem for this book, in September 2003. We watched homemade VHS films of his trips around the world, including the one to convert the Bnei Moshe in Peru. I found a good description of him in Hillel Halkin, *Across the Sabbath River: In Search of a Lost Tribe of Israel* (New York: Houghton Mifflin, 2002). To better understand his religious ideas and ideology, I consulted his book *The Tribes of Israel: The Lost and the Dispersed* (Jerusalem: self-published, n.d.) and scholarly work on his mentor, Zvi Yehuda Kook, and the Gush Emunim movement. Rabbi Avichail died in September 2015 at the age of eighty-three.

18. I found the following works especially useful to understand Kook father and son's ideas: Yehuda Mirsky, *Rav Kook: Mystic in a Time of Revolution* (New Haven, Conn.: Yale University Press, 2014); Aviezer Ravitzky, *Messianism, Zionism, and Jewish Religious Radicalism* (Chicago: University of Chicago Press, 1996); Michael L. Morgan and Steven Weitzman, *Rethinking the Messianic Idea in Judaism* (Bloomington: Indiana University Press, 2014); and Shlomo Fisher, "Fundamentalist or Romantic Nationalist? Israeli Modern Orthodoxy," in *Dynamic Belonging: Contemporary Jewish Collective Identities,* ed. Harvey Goldberg, Steven M. Cohen, and Ezra Kopelowitz (New York: Berghahn Books, 2012), 92–111.

19. Ravitzky, *Messianism, Zionism, and Jewish Religious Radicalism.*

20. See Eliyahu Avichail's self-published book *Tribes of Israel.*

21. Central sources for this narrative are Tudor Parfitt and Emanuela Trevisan Serri, *Judaising Movements: Studies in the Margins of Judaism* (London: RoutledgeCurzon, 2002); Velvl Chernin, *The Subbotniks* (Ramat Gan: Rappaport Center for Assimilation Research and Strengthening Jewish Vitality, Bar Ilan University, 2007); and Schifra Strizower, *Exotic Jewish Communities* (London: Yoseloff, 1962).

22. There are at least three books on the San Nicandro Jews, but the most accu-

rate and complete, in my opinion, is John Davis's *Jews of San Nicandro* (New Haven, Conn.: Yale University Press, 2010).

23. Details about this trip and the Bnei Moshe's conversion come from interviews with Avichail, Rivka and Mordechai Uriah, Jacob Krauss, and several of the Bnei Moshe who were converted. I watched Avichail's VHS tape of the events, in which he interviewed Segundo, his son Josué, and other members of the community.

24. See Idith Zertal and Akiva Eldar, *Lords of the Land: The War over Israel's Settlements in the Occupied Territories, 1967–2007* (New York: Nation Books, 2009).

25. Ibid., 104–10.

26. Ohad Gozani, "Israel Welcomes the Jungle Jews," *Sunday Telegraph,* March 25, 1990.

27. Herb Keinon, "Extraordinary New Jews," *Jerusalem Post International Edition,* March 24, 1990, 11.

28. Harry J. Lipkin, "Not Jewish Enough to Be Saved?," *Jerusalem Post,* March 25, 1990.

29. My main sources for this were D. Aptekman, "Jewish Emigration from the USSR, 1980–1992: Trends and Motivations," *Jews and Jewish Topics in the Soviet Union and Eastern Europe* 1, no. 20 (1993): 19–33; and Larissa I. Remennick, *Russian Jews on Three Continents* (New Brunswick, N.J.: Transaction, 2007).

30. See Remennick, *Russian Jews on Three Continents.*

31. Keinon, "Extraordinary New Jews."

32. Steve Lipman, "Olim from Peru Prove Direct Absorption Works," *Jewish Week,* Oct. 4–10, 1991.

33. Gozani, "Israel Welcomes the Jungle Jews."

34. See Y. Yaron et al., *An Introduction to Karaite Judaism: History, Theology, Practice, and Culture* (New York: Qirqisani Center, 2003).

35. I am indebted to Professor Stefan Schorch, an expert on the Samaritans and chair of Bible Studies in the Faculty of Theology at the Martin-Luther-Universität Halle-Wittenberg, for his guidance on Samaritan history and beliefs.

36. This description and what follows are from my trips to Tapuach in 2003 and 2005.

37. Zertal and Eldar, *Lords of the Land.* See "Kahane, Meir," at *Encyclopaedia Britannica,* and *The New York Times* obituary of Kahane, Nov. 6, 1990.

38. Marjorie Miller, "Peres Appeals for Unity as a Shocked Israel Mourns Rabin," *Los Angeles Times,* Nov. 6, 1995.

PART THREE

1. Gilberto read the letter out loud to me during a visit to his home in Lima in 2004.
2. Avichail and Krauss both told me about their mistrust of Zuber. By the time I began the research for this book, Zuber had already died.
3. Suicide and Other Bombing Attacks in Israel Since the Declaration of Principles, Israel Ministry of Foreign Affairs web page.
4. I interviewed Freund in Israel in 2003 and 2015. The reporter Judy Katz published a detailed exposé on Freund and his organization: "How a Former Netanyahu Aide Is Boosting Israel's Jewish Majority, One 'Lost Tribe' at a Time," *Haaretz*, Feb. 19, 2015. For a more sympathetic profile, see Matthew Fishbane, "Becoming Moses," *Tablet*, Feb. 19, 2015.
5. In September 2001, Freund wrote in *The Jerusalem Post*, where he was a columnist, "It seems fair to say that, aside from the danger posed by nonconventional weapons in the hands of Israel's neighbors, the issue of demography might very well be the greatest threat to the future of Israel as a Jewish state. As the percentage of Jews continues to decline, it will grow increasingly difficult for Israel, as a democracy, to ignore mounting calls by its Arab minority for cultural autonomy and perhaps even self-rule. And if the day were to come when Arab Israelis could elect more representatives to the Knesset than Jewish Israelis, the Jewish identity of the State would be in grave doubt."

EPILOGUE

1. For a complete story about this community, see my article "The Faithful," *California Sunday Magazine*, April 28, 2016 (online), and June 2016 issue (print).
2. Kobi Nahshoni, "Nine Million People Are Not Recognized as Jewish," *Ynet*, Nov. 1, 2014, quoted in Renen Yezersky, "Israeli Immigration Policy at Odds: Emerging Jewish Communities and the 'Return' of the Converts from Latin America," *Nationalism and Ethnic Politics* 25, no. 3 (2019): 292.
3. Judy Maltz, "Millions in Stolen Money Behind Return of 'Lost Tribes' to Israel, Lawsuit Alleges," *Haaretz*, Sept. 26, 2019.
4. Sorochuco, thirty-seven miles northeast of Cajamarca and the closest town to Rodacocha, is where Abigail gave birth to Segundo.

Bibliography

BOOKS, THESES, AND DISSERTATIONS

Alomía Bartra, Merling. *Breve historia de la educación Adventista en el Perú, 1898–1996.* Lima: Universidad Peruana Unión, 1996.

Appold, Kenneth G. *The Reformation: A Brief History.* Oxford: Wiley-Blackwell, 2011.

Armas Asín, Fernando, comp. *La construcción de la iglesia en los Andes (siglos XVI–XX).* Lima: Pontificia Universidad Católica del Perú, 1999.

———, ed. *La invención del catolicismo en América: Los procesos de evangelización, siglos XVI–XVII.* Lima: Universidad Nacional Mayor de San Marcos, Fondo Editorial de la Facultad de Ciencias Sociales, 2009.

Armstrong, Karen. *A History of God: From Abraham to the Present: The 4,000-Year Quest for God.* London: Vintage, 1999.

Asociación de Amistad Israel-Perú. *Bajo la estrella de David y el sol del Perú: 50 años de aliá del Perú.* Tel Aviv: Aurora, 1998.

Avichail, Eliyahu. *The Tribes of Israel: The Lost and the Dispersed.* Jerusalem: self-published, n.d.

Balbach, Alfons. *The History of the Seventh Day Adventist Reform Movement.* Roanoke, Va.: Reformation Herald Publishing Association, 1999.

Bastian, Jean-Pierre. *Breve historia del protestantismo en América Latina.* Mexico: CUPSA, 1986.

———. *La mutación de los protestantismos en América Latina: Una perspectiva socio-histórica.* Mexico: Instituto Mexicano de Doctrina Social Cristiana, 1992.

Ben Rafael, Eliezer. *Jewish Identities: Fifty Intellectuals Answer Ben Gurion.* Leiden: Brill, 2002.

Ben Rafael, Eliezer, and Stephen Sharot. *Ethnicity, Religion, and Class in Israeli Society.* Cambridge, U.K.: Cambridge University Press, 1990.

Böhm, Gunter. *Judíos en el Perú durante el siglo XIX.* Santiago: Universidad de Chile, 1985.

Brettler, Marc Zvi. *How to Read the Jewish Bible.* Oxford: Oxford University Press, 2007.

Burnett, Stephen G. *Christian Hebraism in the Reformation Era (1500–1650).* Leiden: Brill, 2012.

———. *From Christian Hebraism to Jewish Studies: Johannes Buxford (1564–1625) and Hebrew Learning in the Seventeenth Century.* Leiden: Brill, 1996.

Cassin, Elena. *San Nicandro: The Story of a Religious Phenomenon.* Translated by Douglas West. London: Cohen & West, 1959.

Chernin, Velvl. *The Subbotniks.* Ramat Gan: Rappaport Center for Assimilation Research and Strengthening Jewish Vitality, Bar Ilan University, 2007.

Chesnut, Andrew. *Competitive Spirits: Latin America's New Religious Economy.* Oxford: Oxford University Press, 2003.

Contreras, Carlos, and Marina Zuloaga. *Historia mínima del Perú.* Mexico: El Colegio de México, 2014.

Dammert Bellido, José. *Cajamarca en el siglo XVI.* Lima: Pontificia Universidad Católica del Perú, 1997.

Davis, John. *The Jews of San Nicandro.* New Haven, Conn.: Yale University Press, 2010.

Deere, Carmen Diana. *Household and Class Relations: Peasants and Landlords in Northern Peru.* Berkeley: University of California Press, 1990.

Eichhorn, David Max, ed. *Conversion to Judaism: A History and Analysis.* New York: Ktav, 1965.

Ferrell, Vance. *The Truth About the Adventist Reform Church.* Beersheba Springs, Tenn.: Pilgrims Books, 1998.

Freund, Michael, and Eliahu Birnbaum. *¿Tiene usted raíces judías? Guía práctica para descubrir sus raíces.* Jerusalem: Shavei Israel, 2015.

Ginzburg, Carlo. *The Cheese and the Worms: The Cosmos of a Sixteenth-Century Miller.* Translated by John Tedeschi and Anne Tedeschi. Baltimore: Johns Hopkins University Press, 1980.

Goldschmidt, Joseph. *The New Dimensions of Who Is a Jew?* Jerusalem: Mercaz Olami Press, 1972.

Greenleaf, Floyd. *The Seventh-Day Adventist Church in Latin America and the Caribbean.* 2 vols. Berrien Springs, Mich.: Andrews University Press, 1992.

Halkin, Hillel. *Across the Sabbath River: In Search of a Lost Tribe of Israel.* New York: Houghton Mifflin, 2002.

Hemming, John. *The Conquest of the Incas.* London: Macmillan, 1970.

Johnson, Paul. *A History of the Jews.* New York: Harper & Row, 1987.

Karo, Joseph. *Síntesis del Shuljan Aruj: Código de prácticas rituales y leyes judías.* Translated by Natan Lerner. Buenos Aires: Sigal, 1978.

Kessler, Juan B. A. *Historia de la evangelización en el Perú.* Lima: Puma, 1993.

Kinder, Arthur Gordon. *Casiodoro de Reina: Spanish Reformer of the Sixteenth Century.* London: Tamesis Books, 1975.

Lafaye, Jacques. *Mesías, cruzadas y utopías: El judeocristianismo en las sociedades ibéricas.* Translated by Juan José Utrilla. Mexico: Fondo de Cultura Económica, 1997.

Lapide, Pinchas. *De San Nicandro a Galilea: Una aventura moderna en el descubrimiento de la fe.* Buenos Aires: Candelabro, 1954.

Lewis, Donald M. *The Origins of Christian Zionism: Lord Shaftesbury and Evangelical Support for a Jewish Homeland.* Cambridge, U.K.: Cambridge University Press, 2009.

Lichaa, Shawn, Nehemia Gordon, and Meir Rekhavi. *As It Is Written: A Brief Case for Karaism.* Atascosa, Tex.: Hilkiah Press, 2006.

Lloyd, Peter. *The "Young Towns" of Lima: Aspects of Urbanization in Peru.* Cambridge, U.K.: Cambridge University Press, 1980.

Loje, José Alfredo. *Manual de creyentes—principios y prácticas de fe.* Lima: Asociación Israelita Evangélica del Nuevo Pacto, n.d.

———. *Tratado de las siete palabras de la sabiduría,* Lima: Asociación Israelita Evangélica del Nuevo Pacto, n.d. *Tratado de las siete palabras de la sabiduría,* Lima: Asociación Israelita Evangélica del Nuevo Pacto, n.d.

MacCulloch, Diarmaid. *The Reformation: A History.* New York: Viking, 2004.

Marzal, Manuel M. *La transformación religiosa peruana.* Lima: Pontificia Universidad Católica del Perú, Fondo Editorial, 1983.

Marzal, Manuel M., Catalina Romero, and José Sánchez, eds. *Para entender la religión en el Perú.* Lima: Pontificia Universidad Católica del Perú, Fondo Editorial, 2004.

Matos Mar, José. *Desborde popular y crisis del estado.* Lima: Instituto de Estudios Peruanos, 1984.

Mirsky, Yehuda. *Rav Kook: Mystic in a Time of Revolution.* New Haven, Conn.: Yale University Press, 2014.

Morgan, Michael L., and Steven Weitzman, eds. *Rethinking the Messianic Idea in Judaism*. Bloomington: Indiana University Press, 2014.

Nirenberg, David. *Anti-Judaism: The Western Tradition*. New York: W. W. Norton, 2013.

Ossio, Juan. *El Tahuantinsuyo bíblico: Ezequiel Ataucusi Gamonal y el mesianismo de los Israelitas del Nuevo Pacto Universal*. Lima: Biblioteca Nacional del Perú, 2014.

Parfitt, Tudor, and Emanuela Trevisan Serri. *Judaising Movements: Studies in the Margins of Judaism*. London: RoutledgeCurzon, 2002.

Paucar Ambrosio, Abel B. "Asociación evangélica de la Misión Israelita del Nuevo Pacto Universal." Master's thesis, Seminario Adventista Latinoamericano de Teología, Perú, 1985.

Pease G.-Y., Franklin. *Breve historia contemporánea del Perú*. Mexico: Fondo de Cultura Económica, 1995.

Ravitzky, Aviezer. *Messianism, Zionism, and Jewish Religious Radicalism*. Chicago: University of Chicago Press, 1996.

Remennick, Larissa I. *Russian Jews on Three Continents*. New Brunswick, N.J.: Transaction, 2007.

Romero, Catalina, ed. *Diversidad religiosa en el Perú: Miradas múltiples*. Lima: Centro de Estudios y Publicaciones, 2016.

Rosenbloom, Joseph R. *Conversion to Judaism: From the Biblical Period to the Present*. Cincinnati: Hebrew Union College Press, 1978.

Schlesinger, Erna C. *Tradiciones y costumbres judías: Un viaje alrededor del año hebreo*. Buenos Aires: Editorial Israel, 1942.

Scholem, Gershon. *The Messianic Idea in Judaism and Other Essays in Jewish Spirituality*. New York: Schocken Books, 1971.

Schorch, Stefan. *The Value of the Samaritan Versions for the Textual History of the Samaritan Pentateuch*. Leiden: Brill, 2021.

Schürer, Emil. *A History of the Jewish People in the Times of Jesus Christ*. Vol. 1. Edinburgh: T. & T. Clark, 1908.

Schwartz, Bryan. *Scattered Among the Nations: Photographs and Stories of the World's Most Isolated Jewish Communities*. New York: Simon & Schuster, 2015.

Schwarz, Richard W. *Light Bearers to the Remnant: Denominational History Textbook for Seventh-Day Adventist College Classes*. Ontario: Pacific Press Publishing Association, 1979.

Scott Eunson, Kenneth D. *Nuevos movimientos religiosos andinos: Un acercamiento interdisciplinario*. Vol. 1. Lima: Puma, 2016.

Simon, Marcel, and André Benoît. *El judaísmo y el cristianismo antiguo: De Antíoco Epífanes a Constantino*. Barcelona: Labor, 1972.

Stahl, Ferdinand. *En el país de los Incas*. Lima: Editorial Imprenta Unión, 2006.

Stockwell, Bowman Foster, ed. *Prefacios a las Biblias castellanas del siglo XVI.* Buenos Aires: Aurora, 1951.

Strizower, Schifra. *Exotic Jewish Communities*. London: Yoseloff, 1962.

Torre y López, Arturo Enrique de la. *Movimientos milenaristas y cultos de crisis en el Perú: Análisis histórico y etnológico.* Lima: Fondo Editorial PUCP, 2004.

Trahtemberg, León. *Inmigración judía al Perú, 1848–1948.* Lima: Asociación Judía de Beneficencia y Culto de 1870, 1987.

————. *Los judíos de Lima y las provincias del Perú.* Lima: Unión Israelita del Perú, 1989.

Vergara, Ignacio. *El protestantismo en Chile*. Santiago de Chile: Pacífico, 1962.

Yalonetzky, Romina. "Diferenciación social e integración en Lima: El caso de la población judía de la ciudad (1944–2014)." PhD diss., Pontificia Universidad Católica del Perú, 2014.

Yaron, Y., Joe Pessah, Avraham Qanaï, and Yosef El-Gamil. *An Introduction to Karaite Judaism: History, Theology, Practice, and Culture.* New York: Qirqisani Center, 2003.

Zavaleta García, Eduar Clemente. "Historia de la Iglesia Adventista del Séptimo Día en la ciudad de Cajamarca, años 1930–2017." Master's thesis, Universidad Peruana Unión, 2018.

Zertal, Idith, and Akiva Eldar. *Lords of the Land: The War over Israel's Settlements in the Occupied Territories, 1967–2007.* New York: Nation Books, 2009.

Zetterholm, Karin Hedner. *Jewish Interpretation of the Bible: Ancient and Contemporary.* Minneapolis: Fortress Press, 2012.

ACADEMIC ARTICLES

Aptekman, D. "Jewish Emigration from the USSR, 1980–1992: Trends and Motivations." *Jews and Jewish Topics in the Soviet Union and Eastern Europe* 1, no. 20 (1993): 19–33.

Aramburú, Carlos E. "Las migraciones a las zonas de colonización en la selva peruana: Perspectivas y avances." *Debates en Sociología* 4 (1979): 81–94.

Cohen, Shaye J. D. "Was Judaism in Antiquity a Missionary Religion?" In *Jewish Assimilation, Acculturation, and Accommodation: Past Traditions, Current Issues, and Future Prospects,* ed. Menachem Mor, 14–23. Lanham, Md.: University Press of America, 1992.

Duthurbburu Busto, José Antonio del. "Tres conversos en la captura de Atahualpa." *Revista de Indias, Madrid* 27 (1967): 109.

Fisher, Shlomo. "Fundamentalist or Romantic Nationalist? Israeli Modern Orthodoxy." In *Dynamic Belonging: Contemporary Jewish Collective Identities,* ed. Harvey Goldberg, Steven M. Cohen, and Ezra Kopelowitz, 92–111. New York: Berghahn Books, 2012.

Ginzberg, Louis. "Caro, Joseph B. Ephraim." JewishEncyclopedia.com.

Held, Shai. "What Zvi Yehudah Kook Wrought: The Theopolitical Radicalization of Religious Zionism." In *Rethinking the Messianic Idea in Judaism,* ed. Michael L. Morgan and Steven Weitzman, 229–55. Bloomington: Indiana University Press, 2015.

Kohler, Kaufmann, Emil G. Hirsch, and David Philipson. "Reform Judaism from the Point of View of the Reform Jew." JewishEncyclopedia.com.

Leonardini, Nanda. "Los funerales de Atahualpa y el imaginario histórico peruano." *Illapa Mana Tukukuq* 9 (2019): 22–37.

MacCormack, Sabine G. "Atahualpa y el Libro." *Revista de Indias* 48, no. 184 (1988).

Meneses Lucumí, Lucía Eufemia. "Tras la tierra prometida en la Amazonia: La Asociación Evangélica Israelita del Nuevo Pacto Universal." *Boletín Cultural y Bibliográfico* 49, no. 89 (2015): 87–101.

Reyna, Iván R. "La Chicha y Atahualpa: El encuentro de Cajamarca en la *Suma y narración de los Incas* de Juan Diez de Betanzos." *Perífrasis: Revista de Literatura, Teoría y Crítica* 1, no. 2 (2010).

Sutcliffe, Adam. "Hebrew Texts and Protestant Readers: Christian Hebraism and Denominational Self-Definition." *Jewish Studies Quarterly* 7 (2000): 319–37.

"Ten Rules Concerning Prohibited Books." Council of Trent, Cf. Sess. 25, decree concerning the index of books.

Yezersky, Renen. "Israeli Immigration Policy at Odds: Emerging Jewish Communities and the 'Return' of the Converts from Latin America." *Nationalism and Ethnic Politics* 25, no. 3 (2019): 291–310.

NEWSPAPER AND MAGAZINE ARTICLES

Advent Review and Sabbath Herald, July 21, 1910, and Aug. 11, 1910.

Amitai, Laví. "Buscando un futuro en Israel." *Aurora,* Nov. 19, 1988, 9.

———. "Un viejo sueño hecho realidad." *Aurora,* March 8, 1990, 9.

Fishbane, Matthew. "Becoming Moses: Michael Freund Is on a Mission to Lead Millions of Self-Declared Jews Home to Israel. What Happens if He Succeeds?" *Tablet,* Feb. 19, 2015.

Gozani, Ohad. "Israel Welcomes the Jungle Jews." *Sunday Telegraph*, March 25, 1990.

Hayes, Monte. "King Solomon's Mines in Peru?" *Winnipeg Sun*, Dec. 7, 1989, 2.

Hobsbawm, Eric. "A Niche for a Prophet." *London Review of Books*, Feb. 3, 2011.

Jewish Voice. "In the Peruvian Andes, the B'nai Moshe Wait for the Chance to Convert and Make Aliyah." March 1991.

Keinon, Herb. "Extraordinary New Jews." *Jerusalem Post International Edition*, March 24, 1990, 11.

Kiperstock, David. "A Longing to Be Jews." *WIZO* 54 (1989): 1–3.

Lande, Robert H. "The Peruvians Who Yearn to Join the Jewish People." *Kulanu* 3, no. 4 (Winter 1996–1997): 7–8.

Liebb, Julius. "Marrano Descendants Return to Their Roots." *Jerusalem Post*, Feb. 17, 1989, 28.

Lipkin, Harry J. "Not Jewish Enough to Be Saved?" *Jerusalem Post*, March 25, 1990.

Lipman, Steve. "Olim from Peru Prove Direct Absorption Works." *Jewish Week*, Oct. 4–10, 1991, 2.

Livne, Neri. "With the Help of the Shaman." *Haaretz*, July 17, 2002.

Maltz, Judy. "How a Former Netanyahu Aide Is Boosting Israel's Jewish Majority, One 'Lost Tribe' at a Time." *Haaretz*, Feb. 19, 2015.

———. "Millions in Stolen Money Behind Return of 'Lost Tribes' to Israel, Lawsuit Alleges." *Haaretz*, Sept. 26, 2019.

Maltz, Judy, and Etinger, Yair. "The Jewish Agency Is Establishing Independent Court for Conversions." *Haaretz*, June 25, 2015.

Messenger. "The Seventh Day Adventist Reform Movement: Have You Heard of It?" April 12, 2013, 4.

Miller, Marjorie. "Peres Appeals for Unity as a Shocked Israel Mourns Rabin." *Los Angeles Times*, Nov. 6, 1995.

Mochkofsky, Graciela. "The Faithful: René and Juan Carlos Set Out to Convert Their Colombian Megachurch to Orthodox Judaism. This Is What Happened." *California Sunday Magazine*, April 28, 2016.

Perednik, Gustavo D. "The Incas and the Jews." *Jerusalem Post*, July 20, 1991.

Sexton, Joe. "Assassination of Rabin Raises Alarm over Role of Kahane's Violent Followers in U.S." *New York Times*, Nov. 13, 1995, 10.

A Note About the Author

Graciela Mochkofsky, a native of Patagonia, is the author of six books of nonfiction in Spanish. *The Prophet of the Andes* is her first book in English. She is a contributing writer for *The New Yorker*. Her work has appeared in *The California Sunday Magazine, The Paris Review, The Atlantic* online, *The Jewish Forward,* and numerous publications in Latin America and Spain. A winner of the 2018 Maria Moors Cabot Prize for outstanding reporting across Latin America and the Caribbean, she has served as a Nieman fellow at Harvard University, a Cullman fellow at the New York Public Library, a Prins Foundation fellow at the Center for Jewish History, a visiting scholar at the Arthur L. Carter Journalism Institute at New York University, and a visiting scholar at the Institute for Religion, Culture and Public Life at Columbia University. She is the founding director of the Bilingual Journalism Program and the executive director of the Center for Community Media at the Craig Newmark Graduate School of Journalism at CUNY.

A Note on the Type

This book was set in Adobe Garamond. Designed for the Adobe Corporation by Robert Slimbach, the fonts are based on types first cut by Claude Garamond (c. 1480–1561). Garamond was a pupil of Geoffroy Tory and is believed to have followed the Venetian models, although he introduced a number of important differences, and it is to him that we owe the letter we now know as "old style." He gave to his letters a certain elegance and feeling of movement that won their creator an immediate reputation and the patronage of Francis I of France.

Composed by North Market Street Graphics, Lancaster, Pennsylvania

Printed and bound by Berryville Graphics, Berryville, Virginia

Designed by Maggie Hinders